# SURVIVING THE STORMS OF LIFE

## HOW TO TRIUMPH IN TRAGEDY

DAVID B. WHITLOCK

Parson's Porch Books
Cleveland, TN

# SURVIVING THE STORMS OF LIFE

## HOW TO TRIUMPH IN TRAGEDY

DAVID B. WHITLOCK

# Parson's Porch Books
www.parsonsporchbooks.com

Copyright (C) 2011 by David B. Whitlock

ISBN: 978-1-936912-33-9            Perfect Bound

Unless otherwise noted, all Scripture quotations are taken from the *Holy Bible*, New Living Translation, copyright © 1996, 2004. Used by permission of Tyndale House Publishers, Inc. Carol Stream, Illinois 60188.

Scripture quotations "NASB" are taken from the New American Standard Bible©, 1960, 1962, 1963, 1968, 1971, 1972, 1973, 1975, 1977, by the Lockman Foundation. Used by permission.

Scripture quotations marked "NKJV' are taken from The New King James Version© / Thomas Nelson Publishers, Nashville: Thomas Nelson Publishers 1982. Used by permission. All rights reserved.

Scripture quotations marked "NIV' are taken from the HOLY BIBLE, NEW INTERNATIONAL VERSION©, copyright© 1973, 1978, 1984 by International Bible Society. Used by permission of Zondervan Publishing House. All right reserved. The "NIV©" and "New International Version©" trademarks are registered in the United States Patent and trademark Office by International Bible Society. Use of either trademark requires permission of International Bible Society.

Scripture quotations marked "KJV" are taken from the Holy Bible, King James Version©, Cambridge, 1769. Contents

All rights reserved. No part of this book may be reproduced or transmitted in any form or by any means, electronic or mechanical, including photocopying, recording, or by any information storage and retrieval system, without permission in writing from the publisher.

Cover Art: Rembrandt's 1633 Christ in the Storm on the Sea of Galilee

This book is dedicated

To my mother who first taught me to pray

To my wife, with whom I pray daily

And to my children, Mary-Elizabeth, Dave, Harrison, and Madison, who hopefully will carry on the tradition

# Contents

Chapter One:     9
An Introduction to Surviving the Storms of Life

## Section One: When Storms Come

Chapter Two:     33
Be Prepared

Chapter Three:     59
Find a Safe Place

Chapter Four:     91
Know When to Call for Help

Chapter Five:     133
Staying Tuned to a Reliable Source

## Section Two: Jesus is Praying for You

Chapter Six:     139
Faith: It Comes by Hearing the Message

Chapter Seven:     163
Joy: It's More than a Feeling

Chapter Eight:     185
Holiness: A Faintly Familiar Fragrance

Chapter Nine:  213
Mission-Mindedness: Set Apart to be Sent Out

Chapter Ten:  239
Unity: The Power of Many in One

Chapter Eleven:  273
Security: A Place with Him Forever

Chapter Twelve:  301
Love: Passing it On

Chapter 13:  327
Conclusion: Crossing Your Kidron Valley

# Foreword

*Surviving the Storms of Life* is a timely book, and it offers timely help to any who are experiencing such storms. In the past few years we have witnessed hurricane Katrina, which laid waste the gulf coast of America and came near to wiping out New Orleans; the tsunami in the Indian Ocean basin that claimed nearly 200,000 lives; the earthquake and tsunami off the coast of Japan that threatened to and did partly melt down a nuclear reactor; a level 5 tornado that wiped out much of Joplin, Missouri, snuffing out 122 lives; and Hurricane Irene, which, even downgraded to a tropical storm, wreaked havoc with flooding on the northeastern United States, especially Vermont.

David Whitlock has such intimate acquaintance with these and other events and skillfully crafts so many stories about them that you might suspect that he is a storm tracker for the Weather Channel. But he isn't. He's pastor of a Baptist church and sometimes a professor at Campbellsville University in Kentucky. And his reason for writing a book about coping with the storms of life, I suspect, stems from something much more personal and inescapable than witnessing storms in macrocosm could have caused, the valiant but losing battle of his first wife, Katri, with cancer. When any of us endure such grievous experiences that wound us and sap the life out of us, we join a vast company of fellow sufferers, for, like it or not, suffering occupies a place at the very center of the human story and also the Christian story.

What can we do to survive not only such terrifying events as these but to get our shattered lives together again and live anew? When you read *Surviving the Storms of Life*, you will recognize immediately that David Whitlock has been through some storms and knows what he is talking about. In opening chapters he offers down-to-earth counsel. I can imagine my family going through these steps during a tornado alert when sirens at local fire stations blare a warning. We survived a devastating tornado ripping through the campus and area around Southern Seminary on April 4, 1974, so we don't hesitate to take this advice. (1) *Be prepared*. For us that usually has meant flashlights, candles, battery radio, cell phone, and first aid kit. For more personal storms it would be wise the follow the rest of this book's directions. (2) *Find a safe place*. We go to the basement, and we worry above people who don't have basements. (3) *Know when* [and I would add *where*] *to call for help*.

All of these practical counsels fit almost any storm situation we may confront, but David Whitlock moves beyond this to what will be critical for our survival in the long run in circumstances beyond our human control. He points us to God, God as we have come to know God in and through Jesus Christ. Several years ago, just after the tsunami hit Indonesia, when I was teaching at Baptist Seminary of Kentucky in Lexington, one of our brightest students, Brandy Albritton (now Mullins), e-mailed me around 11:30 p.m. with an anguished plaint. She was doing a CPE internship at Central Baptist Hospital. A thirty-year old mother, desperately ill, had rushed into the hospital an hour or so before. Two small children trailed behind her. Hospital staff immediately rushed her to surgery. A half hour later she was dead. Brandy wrote, "Dr. Hinson, how can I believe in God in a world where tsunamis wipe out 178,000 lives and thirty-year old mothers suddenly die, orphaning two small children?" I took some time to reply because answers to such questions do not come easily, but I said, "Brandy, I can't answer all the questions you can raise about God in a world where tsunamis take the lives of tens of thousands and where thirty-year old mothers die unexplainably leaving behind two small children. But I would ask a counter-question: 'Can you face a world in which tsunamis wipe out all those lives and thirty-year old mothers die leaving behind two small children **without God?' I can't!**"

The impressive thing about *Surviving the Storms of Life* is that David Whitlock directs us to a God of infinite, unconditional love and compassion who shares our human lot, even death, to the full. He directs us to the God John 3:16 describes: "For God loved the world so much that God gave us the only Son God has ever had so that everyone who commits him/herself to him may not perish but may have eternal life" (my paraphrase). No one knows better than this husband who has walked with his beloved wife through the valley of the shadow of death how much we must attune ourselves to hear the voice of the Shepherd, saying, "I am with you. Do not be afraid." That's what he means when he advises us to *"stay tuned to a reliable source."*

God is our ultimate 911, a source we can dial in emergency, but, please, not only then. The challenge put to us by the Apostle Paul and sought by Christians through the centuries is to "pray without ceasing" (1 Thess 5:17). I have a feeling that that explains why I have met David Whitlock so often when I have taken students or gone alone to the Abbey of

Gethsemani, where monks strive to live a life of attentiveness to God. We who live active lives must draw back from our busyness in order to reinvigorate our attentiveness to God. We need to spend time in solitude, away from the distractions that blunt our sensitivities. We need to be still and know that God is.

All preparation for surviving the storms of life, David Whitlock tells us, must start with faith, not faith as subscription to a set of propositions but faith as response to the besieging love of God, what Abraham Heschel called "a blush in the presence of God." God loves us. As we open minds and hearts to the love of God, God pours into us God's love energies that can "cast out fear" (1 John 4:18) and replace anxiety with *shalom* (Phil 4:6-7). Not only so, perhaps to our surprise, the indwelling of God can generate joy in the midst of suffering. We don't rejoice and give thanks *for* the pain and suffering. We are not masochists. Rather, as the Apostle Paul made clear to the Philippians, he rejoiced (Phil 1:18) and called on them to rejoice in the Lord *in all circumstances* (4:4) despite the raging storms.

Living through storms with God's love attending, Dr. Whitlock aptly points out, may result in changed lives in the way the Apostle Paul envisioned. "Affliction produces stick-to-itiveness, and stick-to-itiveness integrity, and integrity hope" (Rom 5:3-4; my paraphrase). Very clearly, infilling with the love of God during life's most trying times ought to result in lives set apart and dedicated to God in new ways and charged with an urgency to share what we have experienced with others. Thomas R. Kelly labels holiness one of the fruits of such an experience wherein "God inflames the soul with a burning craving for absolute purity."[1] A wonderful discovery like this, however, as David Whitlock argues, should also create within us a desire to publish the good news of God beyond in our midst.

I'm happy to find in this fine book a strong plea for Christian unity. Baptists all too often gloss over the first part of Jesus' "high priestly prayer" in John 17:21 "that all may be one, just as you, Father, are in me and I am in you, that they too may be in us, so that the world may believe that you have sent me." Whitlock underscores "*the power of many in one.*" He recognizes rightly that, as in Jesus' prayer, oneness need not mean organizational or structural unity. As Thomas Merton observed in *Conjectures of a Guilty Bystander*, such unions may only lead to further conflict. "We must contain all divided worlds in ourselves and transcend them in Christ."[2]

Facing realities that threaten our lives ultimately forces us to ask what comes after this life. Dr. Whitlock interprets somewhat more literally than I can Jesus' promise to his disciples of a "place" he was going to prepare for them. Although I can't conceive of heaven as a place, I feel confident that the God who has been present to me as infinite suffering love during the storms of life will be even more intimately present to me as I step off into the sea of love that God is. And like David Whitlock, I want to pass on the love that has infused my life as I have opened like a flower to the morning sun. All of us might emulate him in writing love notes to his children, who have learned to reciprocate. One thing I covet mightily is to be a

---

[1] Thomas R. Kelly, *A Testament of Devotion* (New York: Harper & Row, Publishers, 1941), 65.
[2] Thomas Merton, *Conjectures of a Guilty Bystander* (Garden City, NY: Doubleday Image Books, 1966), 21.

conduit of the love of God to others. You will learn a lot about becoming one in this book.

*E. Glenn Hinson*
*2011*

*"Then they were eager to let him in the boat, and immediately they arrived at their destination!"*

—John 6:21

*"God left the world unfinished for man to work his skill upon. He left the electricity still in the cloud, the oil still in the earth. How often we look upon God as our last and feeblest resource! We go to Him because we have nowhere else to go. And then we learn that the storms of life have driven us, not upon the rocks, but into the desired haven."*

George MacDonald, *Annals of a Quiet Neighborhood*

Chapter One

# AN INTRODUCTION TO SURVIVING THE STORMS OF LIFE

THIS BOOK IS ABOUT COPING WITH THE STORMS all of us inevitably face. Even as you are reading this page, you are either in the midst of a storm, just coming out of one, or about to enter another. Just as there are different kinds of atmospheric storms, there are also a variety of life storms. From the storm that destroys an office building to the one that takes your job, from the storm that floods a house to one that drowns a family in debt, from the storm that devastates a farm to the one that ruins a reputation, from the storm that comes in the loss of a job to the one that comes in the loss of a life, from the storm that destroys a house to the one that destroys a family—storms come in different sizes, shapes, and forms—and how we deal with those storms determines the kind of life we live. Storms have a way of finding us, no matter how hard we may try avoiding them.

Some people actually search for storms. To them, storms have a certain mystique, mystery—even magnetism that these folks find irresistible. When it comes to storms of nature, these folks are called, "storm chasers."

No one knows who the first storm chaser was. Maybe some prehistoric caveman out for a midnight hunt got caught in a lightning storm, experienced the power of electricity flying through the air, and was thereafter hooked on the adrenaline rush that comes with being so close to danger. We'll never know.

We do know that chasing storms as a hobby began in the 1950s. One of the pioneers in that field was a man named Roger Jensen. As far back as he could remember, Roger was fascinated with storms. Roger lived near Fargo, North Dakota. The rumbling of distant thunder, the crack of lightning announcing the approaching storm, the swirl of wind in his ears—all this Roger loved, and he became virtually addicted to the thrill of the storm. He photographed hundreds of storms. Roger said he was "born loving storms."[3]

Some people, like Roger Jensen, are "born loving storms." But storm chasing can be dangerous. The 1996 film Twister and the television series, Storm Chasers, which premiered on the Discovery channel in 2007, both depict the risks involved in chasing storms. Indeed, much of the attraction of storm chasing is based on the threat of danger. At one point in Twister, Dusty (played by Philip Seymour Hoffman) spots a tornado and yells to his fellow storm chaser, Bill (actor Bill Paxton), "It's coming! It's headed right for us!"

And Bill screams back, "It's already here!"

---

[3] http://www.weathergraphics.com/chasing/0970684088_ebook_sample_body.pdf

Storms are like that. All at once, they are "here." Flirting with storms can be perilous; the fact that we seek them doesn't diminish their power to harm us.

Then, there are others who chase storms of another kind. Not always intending harm, these people walk a moral tightrope just for the thrill, the excitement of it. They are somewhat like Emma Bovary, the central character in Gustave Flaubert's nineteenth century novel, Madam Bovary. Emma's marriage was dull and boring, and she fell, naively enough, into several affairs, only to hurt and be hurt. To her the storm represented something scintillating, sensuous, even sacrilegious—shining new life on the dull canvass backdrop of her barren and empty marriage. Flaubert describes not only Emma but others like her: "She loved the sea for its storms alone, cared for vegetation only when it grew here and there among ruins. She had to extract a kind of personal advantage from things; and she rejected as useless everything that promised no immediate gratification..."[4]

But the storm shipwrecks her, leaving her alone, rejected by her lovers, marooned by the vengeance of the storm. Like Icarus, she flew too close to the sun, (thinking that's where the fun was), and when her wings were singed, she fell to her death. Actually, Flaubert has her swallow arsenic, portraying her dying a dreadfully painful death.

Flirting with life storms can be as dangerous as it is thrilling.

Whether the word "storm" is used metaphorically or literally, some people love to chase them. But storms can chase

---

[4] Gustave Flaubert, *Madame Bovary*, translation by Francis Steegmuller (New York: Random House, 1957), p.41.

us. And they can appear suddenly and unexpectedly, wreaking havoc in their path of destruction. In one case, so the story goes, a tornado completely whisked a farm house away, leaving only the foundation and first floor. A silver-haired farm lady was seen sitting dazed in a bathtub---the only remaining part of the house left above the floor. The rescue squad rushed to her aid and found her unhurt, sitting there in the tub, talking to herself.

"It was the most amazing thing. . . it was the most amazing thing," she kept repeating, trance-like.

"What was the most amazing thing, Ma'am?" asked one of the rescuers.

"I was visiting my daughter here, taking a bath, and all I did was pull the plug and dog-gone-it if the whole house didn't suddenly drain away."

Storms crash into our lives without considering the damage they do. And suddenly, like water draining down the bathtub, we watch as a house, a job, a marriage, a family, a reputation, or a life is whisked away in a whirlwind of chaos. And many times regaining what was lost is impossible.

But often the storms are not the result of a natural disaster, our own foolish actions, or poor decisions. Sometimes we are the victim. We are not looking for a storm of any kind. We are at home, playing it safe, living right. Other people's choices can hurt us; they bring the storm into our lives; we are innocent bystanders.

A patient in New York underwent a successful kidney transplant from a live donor in 2009. The male donor tested negative for HIV ten weeks before the operation. But sometime in that ten week period, he had unprotected sex. Neither he nor the recipient of his kidney knew they had been infected until about a year after the transplant.[5] And then it was too late.

It can happen to anyone: a faithful wife discovers her husband has another lover; a police officer visits the parents of a teenager in the middle of the night, informing them that their daughter has been hit by a drunk driver; a child carries the mental and emotional damage from sexual abuse. The list of possibilities for being hurt by others is endless.

Regardless of the kind of storm you are facing, no matter where it originated, if you will let Jesus on board, he will, by his grace, bring you through your storm. In fact he is praying for you.

That's why I wrote this book: I want to assure you that Jesus is praying for you during your storm. And as you look to him, it's as if you have invited him on board your ship. He will bring you safely to shore, and you will be stronger as a result. Getting to shore may take some time, usually longer than we like, and even once we've made it through the storm, others can still strike. As you read this book, you'll discover the trials and tragedies, triumphs and defeats of other people who have struggled through the storms of life.

You will also learn some coping skills that will help as you travel your journey through this life of storms. And hopefully, you will experience Jesus as you learn how he is praying you through your storm. The very thought of Jesus praying for me in the midst of my trial gives me confidence to face the storm.

---

[5] "HIV infection linked to organ donation," *The Washington Post*, March 18, 2011, A3.

Through most of my Christian life, it never really occurred to me that Jesus was actually praying for me. I appealed to Jesus; I prayed to Jesus; but I didn't realize that he was already praying for me. What does he say? What kind of prayer does he offer on my behalf?

In John 17 we get a glimpse of what he is praying. This prayer is called the "High Priestly Prayer," because Jesus prays to God the Father as our "high priest." He intercedes for us as none other can. The heart of this book is about Jesus' prayer in John 17 and how that prayer can make a difference in your life, especially as you face your own trials and tribulations. After praying for himself (John 17:1-5), Jesus prayed for his disciples (John 17:6-19), and then he prayed for all future believers (John 17:20-26). You will be encouraged as you take in his prayer for you.

As the disciples listened to Jesus praying for them that night before he went to the cross, they didn't quite understand the enormity of the storm they would face; neither did they realize how imminent it was, just a few hours away. They didn't comprehend that Jesus would be crucified and that they would be left alone. Later, after the resurrection, something they learned earlier in their life with Jesus would come back to them. It was a lesson they would not forget again. Here it is: no matter how difficult, or how violent, or how destructive the storm, Jesus will see his followers through the storm.

That's it. That thought would guide them through the trials they would face in the days following Jesus' resurrection. As they ministered—as they shared in his sufferings even to the point of death, that truth would strengthen them.

*Surviving the Storms of Life*

They first learned this lesson in a real life storm. They weren't storm chasers, at least not in this instance; this storm found them. It happened late one night while they were on the Sea of Galilee. Jesus appeared to them, walking on water, and he brought the disciples safely through the storm. They must have sighed with relief, having safely reached the shore.

But as quickly as their robes dried, the lesson evaporated. When they faced a much more devastating storm---the crucifixion and death of their Master, they lost hope and jumped ship. And it wasn't until Jesus was victorious over his storm—the storm of all storms—that their hope was renewed, their faith restored, and their purpose reborn. It was possible because God the Father proved himself faithful to his Son, Jesus. He defeated death. Perhaps it was then---after they had seen the resurrected Lord---that the disciples remembered the time Jesus had overtaken them on a boat in the midst of a storm. And looking back on it, they realized the meaning they had almost forgotten: Jesus will see us safely through the storms of life because he has already overcome the world. And today, some 2,000 years later, the truth still holds: when we let him onboard , He will guide us home.

How does that happen? How do you let Jesus guide you through the storm? How can you survive the storms of life?

## Accept the fact that storms happen

The opening sentence to M. Scott Peck's classic book, The Road Less Traveled, is, "Life is difficult." [6]Once you accept

---

[6] M. Scott Peck, M.D. *The Road Less Traveled, A New Psychology of Love, Traditional Values and Spiritual Growth* (New York: Walker and

that fact, you can direct your energy toward successful solutions rather than wasting energy finding someone or something to blame.

It seems so obvious, but I'm amazed at the people who don't seem to get it, and they fight it all their life. What I'm referring to is the fact that storms happen. Once we've accepted that, we can deal with it in constructive ways. When, however, we deny it, we inevitably end up blaming someone or something, and the result is often a life of anger, resentment and bitterness. It's a waste of time, and let's face it, our life is made of a string of days that turns into years. Those years become a life. Why spend time brooding about what you can't change?

Once we've acknowledged that storms are a part of life, we can move forward, anticipating them along life's way. Storms are a part of the world we live in. It's inevitable. If you live long enough, you will encounter storms.

We've all had to suffer consequences from our own bad choices. And none of us can totally isolate ourselves from others' mistakes. Furthermore, the physical world we live in is often unpredictable and dangerous.

It's the world we live in. But Jesus doesn't leave us alone in the storm, although it often appears that way to us.

This is clear from the story I was referring to, the one where the disciples found themselves caught in a bad storm. John tells the story in chapter 6 of his gospel. Quite suddenly the disciples found themselves in the midst of a storm. It happened late one night, in the early morning hours. Earlier that day, Jesus

---

Company, 1978), p. 1.

had fed 5,000 people on a hill near the Sea of Galilee at Bethsaida. The people were ready to make Jesus their king. But Jesus would have none of that; the king they envisioned was not the king he was to be. So, Jesus rejected the crown, and escaped to a mountain. And there he prayed.

Meanwhile the disciples, under the instruction of Jesus, left the crowd and went down to the shore to wait for him before getting in the boat.[7] They waited and waited until, late into the night, they started across the lake toward Capernaum. Actually, they were following Jesus' instructions when they started across the lake. What's interesting is that, according to Matthew and Mark, Jesus had given them instructions to go home (Matthew 14:22; Mark 6:45). Following Jesus' orders surely means a journey with no trouble, right?

---

[7] Matthew and Mark's account has Jesus, "making," or "compelling," his disciples to get in the boat, while John only says the disciples waited on Jesus into the night. Mark has Jesus instructing the disciples to go to Bethsaida, (Mark 6:45), which happens to be on the same side of the shore where Jesus performed the miracle of feeding the five thousand and not on "the other side of the lake," as Matthew informs us. (Matthew 14:22). Some commentators have attempted to resolve these discrepancies by surmising that Jesus commanded the disciples to go to Bethsaida and wait there for a period of time before crossing the lake. See Frank E. Gaebelein, gen.ed., *The Expositor's Bible Commentary*, 12 vols: (Grand Rapids: Zondervan Publishing House, 1984), vol. 8: *Matthew, Mark,* Luke by D.A. Carson, p. 343, for an analysis of the problem. Whether they waited at Bethsaida or closer to the location where Jesus had fed the 5,000, the fact that they waited explains why the disciples didn't encounter the storm until the fourth watch, about 3 a.m., after rowing three or four miles.

Well, not exactly. Following Jesus doesn't mean we are exempted from storms. But the disciples discover that Jesus is there when the torrent overcomes them. They were so preoccupied with the storm's intensity they almost didn't notice he was there.

Storms are a common occurrence on the Sea of Galilee. That's because it's 600 feet below sea level. It's nestled at the bottom of some hills and when the sun sets, the cooler westerly air rushes down over the hillside onto the water, churning the lake into something of a whirlpool. John tells us, "a gale swept down upon them, and the sea grew very rough" (John 6:18). This made rowing very difficult, very fatiguing. But worse than their fatigue was the danger of the storm itself: they surely feared for their lives.

Now, let me back-up a moment. Mark's Gospel account notes in Mark 6:45 that, "Immediately after this, (feeding the 5,000), Jesus insisted that his disciples get back into the boat and head across the lake to Bethsaida, while he sent the people home." After telling everyone goodbye, he went up into the hills by himself to pray. (Mark 6:45). As I mentioned, if Jesus gave them instructions to leave, he knew they would encounter that storm.

So, the question becomes: Does Jesus permit storms into our lives? Does obeying Jesus, at least sometimes, place us in situations where we encounter storms?

The answer would appear to be, "Yes, he does."

Do you have trouble with that? The fact is that being a follower of Christ, being obedient to him, does not assure us that we will never face a storm; it only assures us that we will ultimately make it through the storm. The world we live in is a stormy one, fraught with storms; it's the world we live in, the world God created. And sometimes in the process of following Jesus, we encounter storms, problems, trouble. We are no different than those disciples who were subject to the forces of nature on the Sea of Galilee.

Storms happen.

On another occasion, Jesus was on board the boat when, as Matthew put it, "a fierce storm struck" (Matthew 8:23.) Jesus was sleeping soundly while the disciples were panicking. Frantic with fear, they woke Jesus who simply said, "Why are you so afraid? You have so little faith" (Matthew 8:26). And then he calmed the storm. The disciples were amazed: "Even the winds and waves obey him!" (Matthew 8:27)

Then why didn't he prevent the storm in the first place? We'll get to that in just a bit.

For now, notice that Jesus allows the disciples to live in a situation where the laws of nature were not suspended simply because they chose to obey him. Whether we are following Jesus or not, storms are a part of life. They are unavoidable.

This means that accusing your wife or your ex-husband, or your boss, or the government, or the weather won't make the storm go away, although that may give you some temporary satisfaction.

A pastor placed this sign on his door: "If you have problems, come in and tell me all about them. If you don't have any problems, come in and tell me how you avoid them."

So, when a storm disrupts your calm life, know that you are not alone. Storms are a part of everyone's life, to a greater or lesser degree. And just as Jesus was praying, fully aware that his disciples would encounter that storm, so he knows all about your storm, and he is praying you through it. He is watching you. Remember, he was praying up there on the hillside while the disciples were down below in the storm. And moments later he would suddenly step on board with them. In both places, whether he was on the hillside praying or in the boat with them, Jesus was thinking of his disciples. And he is thinking of you as you encounter your storm.

He is praying for his disciples today. From the right hand of the throne of God, Hebrews 7:24 tells us, Jesus is praying for his followers. That particular Scripture reminds us that Jesus "lives forever to intercede on their (referring to believers) behalf." So take heart: Jesus is praying for you.

### Look for Jesus in the midst of the storm

Jesus left the hillside and went to the lake to be with his disciples, who were by that time, tired and afraid. But when Jesus showed up, they didn't recognize him. "They had rowed three or four miles when suddenly they saw Jesus walking on the water toward the boat. They were terrified..." (John 6:19). Matthew tells us why they were so terrified: they thought Jesus was a ghost.

We have a tendency to miss Jesus when he shows up. We don't recognize him. In our despair we overlook the one who can always without fail help us. With our eyes on the storm, all we can think of is the danger of the storm. We lose hope. It's no wonder, we've missed Jesus.

Think of the people who missed Jesus: when Jesus was born, the innkeeper missed him; Herod missed Jesus; the religious leaders missed Jesus; the crowds, looking for a political savior missed Jesus; Pilate missed Jesus.

Even Jesus followers could miss him. Thomas almost missed him; and Mary Magdalene, blurred by her own tears, didn't recognize him. It wasn't until Jesus called her by name that she saw him for who he was and not a gardener.

Gardeners aren't normally as frightening as ghosts, but that's what the disciples on the boat in the storm thought they were seeing. Then Jesus called out to them. Like Mary Magdalene, it's as if in hearing his voice their eyes were opened and they saw him. In all three accounts of this story---in Matthew, Mark and in John, it's when Jesus speaks that they recognize him. And in that moment, fear vanishes. "Don't be afraid. I am here!" Jesus commanded.

When we are in the storm, our tendency is to run scared, seeking some kind of help from this person or that one, from that author's piece of advice to another's suggestion, from horoscopes to fortune tellers, as we desperately search everywhere for what we already have in Jesus: the assurance that we will make it safely home, and with it a peace, confidence, and security that the one who allowed us to come to it will bring us through it.

Listening to godly voices can be good; God can speak words of wisdom through his servants. But don't forget to listen for that still, small, yet all powerful voice of God. And remember, if you want to hear the voice of the Lord, you have to take time; you have to listen, really listen.

Do you remember the story of Elijah? He was in an emotional fire storm, under attack from Queen Jezebel, who had vowed to take his life. Elijah, who had in dramatic fashion defeated 850 prophets of Baal, was now afraid and running for his life. After a long journey, he was hiding in a cave. Then the Lord told him to step outside the cave. Elijah did, and a mighty windstorm hit the mountain so fiercely that rocks were torn loose. But the Lord was not in the powerful wind. Then an earthquake shook the ground where Elijah was standing. But the Lord was not in the earthquake. Then there was a fire, but the Lord was not in the fire. And after the fire there was a gentle whisper. And that's when Elijah heard the voice of the Lord. And the Lord comforted him and gave him instructions about what he was to do.

It is most often in the silence that God speaks the loudest; it is frequently in the chaos that God speaks most clearly; it's usually in our pain that we feel his soothing voice. But we have to get our souls still enough to hear him. In the stillness of the night, or perhaps in the quiet of the morning, we sit with God's Word before us and listen. We open the darkness of our heart to him, and he shines his heavenly light.

Donald Grey Barnhouse tells the story of a man who owned an icehouse. This man lost an expensive watch in the sawdust of that icehouse. He had several employers scour the place in a futile effort to find the watch. Soon, it was lunch time, and they all left the building, except for a young boy who had been hanging around the ice house. When they returned, the young boy was holding the watch. He'd found it. When they asked him how, he replied, "I just lay down in the sawdust and listened. Finally, I heard the watch ticking."

Like that boy, we have to get low, down in the sawdust, and humble ourselves before God. We listen to his still, small, but oh so powerful voice. And having heard his voice, we arise with our confidence in him renewed, our faith revitalized, and our hope restored.

### Allow the storm to make you more like Jesus

We live in the world we live in. It's not perfect; it's not heaven. It's a world where hurricanes strike, planes crash, people lose jobs, and loving mammas and daddies die. It's a world where sooner or later, death comes. We all die. Within this world, God uses trouble to increase our faith. He is teaching us to trust him through the storms of life. God uses storms, troubles and trials---to stretch our faith.

That's why he doesn't always prevent storms from intruding into our life.

The Apostle Paul, a man who was quite familiar with trials and tribulations, put it like this in Romans 5:3-4: "We can rejoice, too, when we run into problems and trials, for we know that they help us develop endurance. And endurance develops strength of character, and character strengthens our confident hope of salvation. And this hope will not lead to disappointment. For we know how dearly God loves us, because he has given us the Holy Spirit to fill our hearts with his love."

One day we will be in a world where there are no problems, no trials, and no storms. That place is heaven. This is not heaven. This is the place for character development. Mark this, write it down, etch these words in your mind: Every storm that enters my life can make me more like Jesus. This is our life purpose: we are to become more and more like Jesus.

Accepting that thought doesn't mean we like the storm. It doesn't mean the storm in itself is a good thing. It doesn't mean we say, "Bring on the storm!" It's okay to ask Jesus to take the storm away. After all, that's what he asked the Father to do. Listen to Jesus in the Garden of Gethsemane as he prayed to God the Father: "My soul is crushed with grief to the point of death" (Mark 14:34). And a short time later Jesus made this request, "Please take this cup of suffering away from me. Yet I want your will to be done, not mine" (Mark 14:36). Jesus was pleading that the storm be avoided; but overriding that desire was his greater passion that God's will be accomplished.

It's easy to trust God when we are sailing smoothly on the calm waters. It's when the lightning strikes and the storm crashes into our lives, when everything goes awry, when we are grieving, when we are crushed, when our faith is in the crucible---that's when Satan's deceptive words become most believable, "You are alone, no one cares, you are hopelessly adrift on turbulent waters," and feeling confused, clouded, and chided, we, entertaining the allure of his deceit, hear something strangely enticing in his words, something intriguingly attractive, charmingly assuasive, captivatingly appealing to us with our damaged emotions, despotic fears, and dashed hopes. And as quickly as the serene waters of the Sea of Galilee can turn into a nightmare of turbulence, so can Satan take us down in an instant, grasping us tightly in his powerful jaws like a crocodile its victim, dragging us into the water, drowning us in an abyss of despair. He has a way of doing that to the best of seafarers.

But when we shut our ears to the Enemy's enchanting voice, along with the melodious, bewitching song of his sirens---his minions, which tempt us with acedia, isolation, and self deprecation, we will escape shipwreck. How? By looking for Jesus. The more we look to him, the more we look like him. In the instant we trust him, he is there. Seeking him, we find him. Anticipating him, we fellowship with him. Searching for him, we find ourselves surrounded by him. The more room we give him aboard our ship, the larger he grows in our lives, and the more confident we become in the midst of the storm.

So the next time a storm comes, maybe you are in the midst of one now, and you find yourself asking "Why?" as we frequently do, remember this: we triumph over trials as we lean into him, learning to trust him in the storm. Our faith grows stronger, and we can experience the joy of victory. Ironically, we often don't recognize we have grown until after the storm has passed.

How do you know your faith is growing? You will find yourself less stressed about your storm because you have a confident hope that Jesus will bring you through it. In your weakness, you will experience his strength, a power that enables you to look beyond the fears that paralyze you to a love that liberates you; you will find yourself encouraging others who are struggling even though you are still in your own storm.

A lady who was going through a difficult time sent this to me:

"I asked God to grant me patience.

God said, 'No. Patience is a byproduct of tribulation; it isn't granted.'

I asked God to give me happiness.

God said, 'No. I give you blessings. Happiness is up to you.'

I asked God to spare me pain.

God said, 'No. Suffering draws you apart from worldly cares and brings you closer to me.'

I asked God to make my spirit grow.

God said, 'No. You must grow on your own, but I will prune you to make you fruitful.'

I asked God for all things that I might enjoy life.
God said, 'No. I will give you life so that in my will you might enjoy all things.'

I asked God to help me love others, as much as God loves me.

God said, 'Ahhh, finally you have the idea.'

Stop telling God how big your storm is. Instead tell your storm how big your God is."

It's true. But it takes courage to do that.

## Invite Jesus on board

Once Jesus was on board the boat with the disciples, the remaining few miles seemed like nothing to them. It was as if they were immediately on the shore. This is the way John put it: "Immediately they arrived at their destination!" (John 6:21). I don't think the boat suddenly became a speed boat that broke a modern day speed racing record. With Jesus on board, time no longer mattered, the storm was over, they had arrived.

Isn't that the way it is? We struggle, we strain, we strive, and the moment we let Jesus on board, it's as if we are suddenly standing on shore, basking in the sunshine. Perhaps everything doesn't fall into place at once, but you have the assurance that Jesus will get you through it. And we, looking back, perhaps years later, recall that although passing through that storm seemed turbulent and frightening at the time, it was but brief in its duration---almost like swishing and spinning through an elevated chute at a water park that promptly deposits us in shallow water where we suddenly find ourselves standing there, wiping the water from our eyes, squinting to the top of the chute, wondering how it happened so fast.

Then later, maybe at lunch or while enjoying a soft drink, we have to catch our breath and look back on what happened. We have time to reflect, "Now, if Jesus has authority over nature, why doesn't he stop storms earlier? Why did I have to endure that rough ride through the storm, anyway? Why doesn't he do away with storms completely, since he has the power to do so?" The answer is, for the same reason he allows the storms in the first place. Without storms we wouldn't know his faithfulness. God proves himself in the storm by bringing us safely home. And as we remain faithful during the storm, God uses the very thing we dread and despise to strengthen our faith. And when we do arrive, we arrive stronger and more like Jesus wants us to be.

Christian author Joanie Yoder experienced agony in her own garden of Gethsemane. She was diagnosed with cancer, and then her husband died. That was in 1982. As she grieved his death, she had to fight cancer alone. In a letter she wrote, "I have relinquished my destiny to God's will. Nothing praise God, not even cancer, can thwart His will. I may have cancer, but cancer doesn't have me---God alone has me. So in this light, I would value your prayers that Christ be magnified in my body, whether by life or by death." Joanie's storm lasted until 2004, when the Lord brought her safely home to heaven. But in the storm, she had magnified the Lord.[8]

I don't know why sometime bad things happen to good people or why good things happen to bad people. Jesus said God gives sunlight to both the evil and the good, and he sends rain on the just and the unjust alike" (Matthew 5:45).Sometimes that may mean too much sunlight to some or too little rain for others. There is a tension in the fact that God is sovereign and in control, and yet he is not the author of evil. Our world is fallen, imperfect. People do evil things. And it's the world we live in.

I do know this: being victorious, arriving at shore doesn't mean the absence of more storms; it does mean the presence of the Lord. And truly, home is where he is.

I like the way author and preacher Chuck Swindoll put it: "It may be the most difficult time in your life. You may be enduring your own whirlwind...or you may be the innocent bystander caught in the consequential backwash of another's sin. You may feel desperately alone, and it may seem that it will never, ever end. But believe me, the whirlwind is a temporary experience. Your faithful, caring Lord will see you through it."[9]

Life is comprised of one storm after another; we arrive on shore with a sigh of relief and then, sometimes sooner,

---

[8] Joanie Yoder, quoted in *Our Daily Bread*, 7/29/2005
[9] Charles R. Swindoll, *Bedside Blessings* (Nashville: J Countryman, 2002), p.226

sometimes later, we find ourselves in another storm, and in each instance, as we trust God, we emerge stronger and stronger until finally one day, as with Joanie Yoder, we are there on the eternal shore, in our forever home, where there are no more storms, the place where, as John expressed it in his revelation: "God will wipe every tear from their eyes" (Revelation 7:17) It's the place where the sun will never set. And in the meantime, the Lord has promised us he will never leave us or forsake us.[10]

A minister was on a long flight between church conferences. The first warning of approaching weather problems was that the sign on the airplane flashed on: "Fasten Your Seat Belts." Then the voice over the intercom said, "We shall not be serving the beverages at this time as we are expecting a little turbulence. Please make sure your seat belt is fastened."

Some passengers paid little attention, others looked a bit anxious.

Then the storm hit.

Ominous cracks of thunder could be heard. Lightning lit up the darkened skies, and within moments the plane was being tossed around like a cork on the ocean. One moment the plane would be lifted up on a terrible current of air; the next it dropped as if it were about to crash.

Like the other passengers, the pastor was nervous. He looked around the cabin and noticed that some passengers were praying, others were darting their eyes toward the cockpit as if they were hoping the pilot would appear and calm them. Then other passengers would glance outside their window, trying to see what the weather would do.

---

[10] Hebrews 13:5

The pastor then noticed a little girl. Apparently the storm meant nothing to her. She sat there calmly, as if everything was just fine. Her feet were tucked beneath her seat, and she was reading a book. Sometimes she closed her eyes, and then she would start reading again. But worry and fear did not seem to be part of her world.

The situation got even worse as the terrible storm seemed to increase in its intensity. Then as suddenly as the storm had grabbed the plane, it released it. All was smooth as the passengers welcomed the sunlight through the plane's windows.

After the plane landed, the pastor lingered a bit so he could speak to the little girl. After commenting about the plane and the severity of the storm, the pastor asked the child if she had been afraid or worried about the situation.

"No sir," the little girl politely answered.

The pastor asked her why.

"Because," she replied, "my daddy is the pilot, and he's taking me home."

Remember, as you face the storms of life, the Lord is the pilot. He is in control. And he will take you safely home.

In the next chapter, we'll take a look at what Jesus did when he encountered his fiercest storm: the cross. With the cross looming over him, Jesus was mainly concerned about his disciples and how they would respond to what was about to happen. He wanted them to be prepared. What Jesus did to get his disciples ready can be applied to us as we face our storms. So, find out in the next chapter what Jesus did to prepare his disciples for their storm and how what he said to them can make the difference in whether you survive your own storm.

# Section One: When Storms Come

"After saying all these things. . ."
—John 17:1


"If there is a hurricane you always see the signs of it in the sky for days ahead, if you are at sea. They do not see it ashore because they do not know what to look for..."
— Ernest Hemingway, The Old Man and the Sea [11]

---

[11] Ernest Hemingway, *The Old Man and the Sea* (New York: Scribner, 1952, First Scribner trade paperback edition, 2003), p. 61.

## Chapter Two
## Be Prepared

SHE WAS BORN INCONSPICUOUSLY ENOUGH, far from the Caribbean, in the warm waters off the west coast of Africa. At first she was just another nameless tropical depression. But like a newborn struggling to survive, she stretched, and having yawned for air, began moving, searching for energy in the spiraling winds fueled by the water vapors of the sea, until, gaining strength and generating gale force winds on her journey to the Bahamas, she earned herself the classification of a tropical storm on August 23, 2005. The next day she received her name, Katrina, Tropical Storm Katrina. Katrina landed on the southeastern coast of Florida with 80 m.p.h. winds, briefly reached hurricane status before she weakened over land and was downgraded to a tropical storm. But then she entered the Gulf of Mexico, and finding nourishment in the warm waters of the Gulf Loop Current, she regained her momentum, quickly mushrooming into a category five hurricane with frightening and ferocious winds, and having reached full maturity, she made her second landfall on August 29, this time near Buras-Triumph, Louisiana. Before it was over, 1,836 people had lost their lives, and property damage was estimated at $81 billion. Katrina was not only one of the costliest natural disasters but also among the five deadliest hurricanes in U.S. history.

And Louisiana didn't see it---at least, not in time. Those who should have known better weren't prepared.

Even with computer projections, the exact path of a hurricane is an inexact science. By August 26, Katrina was projected for a possible hit on New Orleans. This prompted then Mayor Ray Nagin to declare a state of emergency and issue a call for a voluntary evacuation on August 27. The next day, as the chances of the storm hitting New Orleans increased, he issued the first ever mandatory evacuation of the entire city. The evacuation plans met with good success and over 80% of the city made a safe exit from New Orleans as thousands of lives were saved. But this would prove to be one of the few bright spots in the government's response to Katrina's fury.

The evacuation plan had a glaring flaw; no provision had been made for those unable to provide their own transportation: the elderly, the disabled and those without cars. And it would only get worse: utilizing the New Orleans Superdome as a "shelter of last resort," presented its own set of problems. And oh yes, I forgot to mention one other little problem: because of the inadequate levee structure, the levees broke and consequently, 80% of the city was flooded.

In the aftermath of the storm's devastation, the lack of preparation would become more and more problematic and blame would be spread to people in various positions of authority. Mayor Nagin was criticized for not having a plan for the evacuation of the elderly and disadvantaged; Louisiana Governor Kathleen Blanco was questioned for not deploying the Louisiana National Guard sooner; and President George W. Bush and Homeland Security Secretary Michael Chertoff were criticized for the federal government's inadequate response. FEMA chief, Michael D. Brown, took the fall for much of the federal government's failure and resigned. One year after Katrina he admitted, "There was no plan."[12]

There was no plan? Those experienced in leading relief efforts for dozens of other killer hurricanes, tornadoes and earthquakes over the years were left scratching their heads, wondering why there was no plan in place for this killer hurricane. They chastised leaders for forgetting the simple Boy Scout motto: Be Prepared.[13]

When a storm is on the way, it's essential that proper preparations be made. The people charged with preparing for Hurricane Katrina apparently failed to do that. Jesus knew a storm was brewing out there on the horizon. It had been gaining momentum for quite some time. And he knew his disciples weren't prepared for it. How would the gospel survive if these men weren't prepared to face the approaching storm? The story of Jesus, as it's told in the Gospel of John, gives considerable attention in explaining how Jesus got the disciples ready. By looking at what Jesus did to prepare the disciples, we can learn what we can do to be better prepared for our storms in life.

## The Approaching Storm

The storm approaching Jesus and the disciples intensified in the last year of his earthly ministry. Early in that last year,

---

[12] www.wikipedia.org/wiki/Hurricane_preparedness_for_New_Orleans
[13] Seth Borenstein, "Federal Government Wasn't Ready for Katrina, Disaster Experts Say," *Knight-Ridder News*, Thursday, September 1, 2005.

Jesus chose to stay in Galilee to avoid the religious leaders who, John tells us in John 7:1, were plotting Jesus' death. When Jesus returned to Jerusalem for the Jewish Festival of Shelters and began teaching in the Temple, the Pharisees sent the Temple guards to arrest Jesus, but after listening to him, the guards could find no grounds for an arrest and returned without Jesus. When asked why they had returned empty handed, the guards could only exclaim, "We have never heard anyone speak like this!" (John 7:46).

Despite another close call with the Pharisees, Jesus continued to teach in the Temple area. After making the declaration that "before Abraham was even born, I Am!" (John 8:58), some of the people took up rocks to stone Jesus. Then he was somehow hidden from them as Jesus left the temple area. But he was back in Jerusalem for Hanukkah, and the Pharisees attempted to have him arrested again, and once more, Jesus managed to elude them. He then retreated to a safer place beyond the Jordan River.

He stayed there for a brief period of time, but upon hearing of Lazarus's sickness, Jesus decided to return to Judea. The disciples, sensing that the storm clouds of opposition were threatening, questioned Jesus' decision: "Only a few days ago the people in Judea were trying to stone you. Are you going there again?" (John 11:8). Then, when Jesus brought Lazarus back to life, opposition from the Pharisees crescendoed, and Caiaphas, the high priest, made his decision about the fate of Jesus: "It's better that one man should die for the people than for the whole nation to be destroyed" (John 11:50). The storm was moving ever more close.

After the high moment when Jesus rode triumphantly into Jerusalem on a donkey amidst the waving of palm branches and shouts of joy, he warned the crowds of the approaching storm, "The time for judging this world has come when Satan, the ruler of this world will be cast out. And when I am lifted up from the earth, I will draw everyone to myself" (John 12:31-32).

But the people didn't comprehend what Jesus was saying. They understood from Scripture that the Messiah would live forever: "How can you say the Son of Man will die? Just who is this Son of Man, anyway?" (John 12:34). In one of the saddest sentences in Scripture, John notes that despite all his miraculous signs, "most of the people still did not believe in him" (John 12:37).

The storm was gathering strength, and in a matter of hours Jesus would be taken into custody, scourged, mocked, ridiculed, beaten, and crucified. And he knew his disciples weren't ready. John devoted five chapters, 13-17, in recounting what happened on the last night the disciples were together with Jesus. Jesus wanted his disciples to be prepared, and he knew if they were going to be ready, he would have to do the preparing.

Do you ever get the feeling, as you read the gospels, that the disciples were more often than not, clueless? As I read this portion of Scripture, I want to shout, "Don't you get it?" It's the night of Jesus' departure, and the disciples are still struggling to understand. Jesus was preparing them for his death, reminding them that he would be gone but would be back: "In a little while you won't see me anymore. But a little while after that, you will see me again" (John 16:16). But some of the disciples look incredulously at each other, "What does he mean? We don't understand."

Jesus is less than 24 hours from Golgotha, and the disciples don't understand.

And yet, even if the disciples didn't recognize it at the time, Jesus had given them several resources that would enable them to overcome the approaching storm, even though they would experience a momentary collapse between his death and resurrection.

The great thing is that these resources are available for us today, even when we too fail to get it and falter and fail. It's easy for us, looking back at the disciples, to conclude they had some sort of spiritual learning disability. But how often are we just as slow as the disciples were in comprehending Jesus? More often than we would like to admit, I would guess. Rather than obeying Jesus, we want to take the easy route during a crisis, and that so-called safer road turns out to be fraught with danger. We, just like the disciples, collapse under pressure. Just like them, we are unprepared.

But, the good news is, we too can pick ourselves back up and move forward. We can prepare for the next storm. Most often, our experience is mixed: tragedy and triumph, success and failure are often intertwined. Success is never permanent because the storms keep coming. Triumph is frequently followed by tragedy which often prepares the way for a blessing that's followed by a setback that leads to a victory. That's the way it is when we live in a storm infested world. It's the world we know; we will always be a part of storms this side of eternity.

John introduces Jesus' prayer in John 17 with the words, "After saying all these things." "All these things," could include all that Jesus said in the upper room that night. Jesus was telling the disciples what was going to happen. The storm of all storms would temporarily black out all communication between Jesus and the disciples. Then, three days later the fog would lift, and Jesus' words of preparation would come back to them in the clear light of the resurrection. They would see that he had prepared them even though they didn't realize it at the time.

Perhaps if the disciples had asked the right questions before the storm hit, they would have weathered the storm better. Jesus had given them the answers. But they weren't asking the right questions, so they missed it; they weren't ready to receive it. They simply were unable to comprehend that there was an intense storm on the horizon, a storm that would destroy their Lord, at least temporarily. The disciples might have gotten it earlier had they only asked the right questions. Had the people in New Orleans had the answers to some basic questions, they might have been better prepared as well. When a storm approaches, it's important to ask the right questions.

The answer to the questions that would prepare the disciples was in the spoken words of Jesus. And they are there for us as well.

## Asking the Right Questions: The Key to Preparation

### How Severe is the Storm?

One essential storm preparation question is: How Severe is the Storm? How can any realistic preparation be made if the strength of the storm is unknown? Failure to properly answer this question can be disastrous.

Days after a snow storm hit New York City in late December, 2010, many streets were still impassable, senior citizens were stranded at home with little or no food, and emergency vehicles were unable to respond to 911 calls because roads had yet to be cleared. "Like many New Yorkers, I woke up two days straight to an unplowed street outside my front door," said city Public Advocate Bill de Blasio. "This is not business as usual, and frustration is mounting." Part of the problem was misreading the severity of the storm. Early forecasts called for a much milder storm, and by the time the unexpected blizzard warning was announced on Christmas day, city workers were home unwrapping gifts instead of treating the streets. That didn't change the fact that the problem was still there in the streets, and city officials, especially New York City Mayor Michael Bloomberg, were criticized: "There's no way you can have a failure of this magnitude and someone doesn't give a letter of resignation," said state Senator Eric Adams.[14] What you don't know can hurt you. In this case not knowing the severity of the storm proved disastrous.

Jesus knew the severity of the approaching storm. Bible commentator William Barclay observed: "One thing is certain---no Christian who was involved in persecution could say that he had not been warned. On this matter Jesus was quite explicit. He

---

[14] Erin Einhorn and Helen Kennedy, "Chastened Bloomberg fights to save reputation after string of snow-removal snafus," http://articles.nydailynews.com/2010-12-28/local/27085742_1_plow-side-street-snow-choked

had told his people beforehand what they might expect."[15] The values of Christ and the values of the world would inevitably collide. Jesus made that much clear to his disciples: "If the world hates you, remember that it hated me first" (John 15:18).

How severe would the storm be? It would involve hatred. There is no limit to what people filled with hatred can do to other people. Innuendo leads to slander, slander to shunning, shunning to bullying, and bullying to violence and violence to murder. People react against those who go against the stream, and if Jesus' disciples lived by his values, the world would punish them just as they had Jesus. As Raymond Brown notes, Jesus mainly wanted to explain that conflict would occur with the world and that the conflict stems from the world's attitude of rebellion toward God.[16]

By the time John wrote his gospel, Christians were beginning to experience hatred from the world. As Barclay points out, the Roman government would persecute Christians because they had a higher loyalty than Rome; they had no king but Christ. Rome had a fairly tolerant approach to the religious practices of the people under its supervision. Essentially, all a person had to do was burn a pinch of incense, say aloud, "Caesar is Lord," and go away to worship any god he or she chose. But of course, this is one thing Christians would not do: confess anyone other than Jesus as Lord.[17]

---

[15] William Barclay, *The Daily Bible Series, The Gospel of John, v.2*, (Philadelphia: Westminster Press, Revised Edition, 1975), p. 181.

[16] Raymond E .Brown, *The Gospel According to John (xiii-xxi)* (Garden City: Doubleday, 1970), p.701

[17] Barclay, p.183.

But Christians would not only experience persecution from pagans, that is, those who make no claim to knowing God, but from the religious as well. "For you will be expelled from the synagogues, and the time is coming when those who kill you will think they are doing a holy service for God" (John 16:2).

As Christians live their lives for Christ, clashes with other belief systems are inevitable. Naturally, the intensity of conflict will depend on where one lives. The persecution of Christians in countries dominated by Islam is astonishing. For example, up to 1.4 million Christians in Iraq have fled. No Christian population is expected to survive in the Islamic countries of the Middle East by 2050. Muslim majority nations seem increasingly incapable of tolerating non-Muslim minorities.[18] And, an even cursory glance at history reveals that Christians themselves, not just other religions, have been the persecutors, mistakenly believing they were performing a holy work for God.

While violence in the name of God is disturbing, Christians face a challenge from another unexpected source. The world can be an inviting place. Christians can unwittingly blend in with the world until they lose their distinctiveness and are "neutralized" in another way.

Christians can be like the frog in the kettle. Remember that story? If you put a frog in boiling water, he will jump out immediately. But, if you put a frog in a kettle of cool or lukewarm water and very slowly raise the temperature to boiling, the frog will not become aware of the threat until it's

---

[18] Joseph Bottum, "A Mideast target: Christians," *USA Today*, February 7, 2011, 9A.

too late. The frog's instincts have been dulled; he is programmed to react against sudden changes.

Virgil's mythological Trojan Horse appeared to the citizens of Troy as a wooden trophy of their victory over the Greeks. By the time the Trojans figured it out, it was much too late. They didn't see the Greek soldiers hidden in the horse; the citizens of Troy were fast asleep when, late in the night, the Greeks crept out and opened the city gates for the rest of the Greek soldiers to enter.

Has it happened to us? We have supposed that by identifying with the world, by accepting the world's gifts, its ways, its Trojan Horses, we could win the world to our side. But in doing so we've grown accustomed to the world. We nodded off and when we awoke, the world had invaded the church, overtaking it with its values and outlook. And one wonders if we have been mastered by the world not in a flash flood of persecution but by the slow fade of a thousand compromises---like a steady, constant rain that over time almost imperceptibly weakens the ground beneath a building's foundation until it crumbles---saturating the bedrock of Christian values with the world's perspective so that the church suddenly collapses into a sink hole of insignificance.

## What are our resources?

Do we have an adequate water and food supply? What about a generator in case electricity is lost? Are the laptop and cell phones fully charged? When a storm approaches, it is good to know what resources are at your disposal.

Jesus not only warned the disciples of the severity of the

approaching storm, but he also clearly told them what their resources would be. Having told the disciples the world would hate them just as it hated him, Jesus encouraged them, "But I will send you the Advocate---the Spirit of truth. He will come to you from the Father and will testify all about me" (John 15:26).

Jesus calls the Holy Spirit the *parakletos* or "the one called alongside" us to guide and help us. The Holy Spirit will keep us from abandoning our faith during the storms of life. "It is the Holy Spirit who gives us our sea legs during the storms of persecution. He's the one who keeps us from falling on our faces or getting washed overboard altogether," notes Bible teacher Charles Swindoll.[19]

Part of the work of the Holy Spirit would be to remind the disciples what Jesus had said; the Holy Spirit would guide the disciples into "all truth" (John 16:13). During these final moments Jesus had with his disciples, he comforted them by telling them the Holy Spirit would teach them everything, bringing back to their minds what Jesus had taught them. (John 14:26) The disciples would forget many of the events related to Jesus' life, death, and resurrection, but the Holy Spirit would remind them, and in time they would put the stories and teachings into written form which we now know as the gospels---Matthew, Mark, Luke, and John, as well as the book of Acts.

As we face our storms of life, we have an amazing resource---the Holy Spirit, who not only comforts and guides us in the midst of the storm, but points us to Jesus Christ as well. We find his story---his words, his life, his death, his resurrection

---

[19] Charles R. Swindoll, *Beholding Christ...The Lamb of God, A Study of John 15-21* (Fullerton, Ca.: Insight for Living, 1987), p.19.

and ascension, in the words of Scripture, a written guidebook for the storms of life.

We have more than just a historical document. The German pastor/theologian of the nineteenth century, Friedrich Blumhardt, described Scripture like this: "The point is always that it says something meaningful about God. In the case of Lazarus, for example, the central point is, 'I am the resurrection and the life.' This momentous truth is the focus of Jesus' message, framed by the events surrounding Lazarus. Whatever happened afterwards is not told. The truth that Jesus has risen and is alive is the heart of what has to be said."[20]

Scripture points to Christ, our ultimate Resource in the storm.

## How long will the storm last?

Storms often arrive with suddenness and fury. We may not have the luxury of questioning how long. But the National Weather Service usually gives us warnings such as storm alerts, weather advisories, storm warnings and watches that help us at least know a time frame in which a storm is likely to hit and when it will pass from our area.

Although Jesus gave no hourly forecast, he did help the fearful disciples by telling them the storm would pass. Just before he began his prayer, he did warn them that as long they were on "this earth," they would have tribulation (John 16:33). Storms are built into the system we live in. It is part of being in this world. But even this would pass. Not only had Jesus already

---

[20] http://www.blumhardts.com/bl/Subscribe.htm

overcome the world prior to the cross, he would, as he had said a few moments earlier (John 14:1-5), come again.

As for the immediate situation, the disciples would experience grief and agony. But, like a woman who has given birth to a baby, the joy of the child overshadows the pain of the birth. (John 16:21-22) This storm---the crucifixion and death of Jesus, would bring darkness and despair to the followers of Christ, but the joy of the resurrection would overshadow those feelings of grief. The disciples would face many intermittent storms before the Lord would finally bring them safely home, but each sorrowful storm would pass; no storm would be permanent; ultimately they would rejoice in heaven.

George Foreman has a section in his book, *God in My Corner, A Spiritual Memoir,* entitled, "Storms Don't Last." He tells the story about an elderly lady who was asked what her favorite Scripture was. She replied, "And it came to pass." The questioner objected that this particular Scripture didn't mean anything. And the dear lady insisted, "Yes, it does... I know that whenever a trial comes, it doesn't come to stay; it comes---to pass. It's not going to be around forever."[21]

She may not be a biblical scholar, but her interpretation was spot on: storms surely come and just as surely as they come, they go. They pass. We can rest assured that Jesus will see us through the storm. Our faith grows because we don't know *exactly* how long the storm will last. Knowing the precise time and the exact results leaves no room for faith. With each passing storm our faith grows a little stronger.

---

[21] George Foreman, with Ken Abraham, *God in My Corner* (Nashville: Thomas Nelson, Inc., 2007), pp.132-133

## Should I evacuate?

One of the few successful aspects of the response to Hurricane Katrina was the evacuation. Hundreds of lives were saved because 80% of the population got out in time. Of course, the evacuation was not enough---those without transportation were left behind. But, emergency teams led in a huge evacuation effort. When a potentially life threatening storm is approaching, it is important to know if it is necessary to evacuate.

As Hurricane Irene approached New York City in August of 2011, Mayor Michael Bloomberg issued an unprecedented mandatory evacuation of certain low-lying areas in the city. Then, as the storm drew closer, he warned residents of certain areas that "the time to leave is now."[22] New Jersey Governor Chris Christie was more forthright: when people were trying to get in a little more beach time before the hurricane hit, he said, "Get the hell off the beach in Asbury Park."[23]

Earlier in John's story about Jesus' last day, many of his disciples did leave him. Maybe it was because his teaching was difficult for his followers to understand; perhaps it was because he was not the kind of Messiah-King they had hoped for; it could have been a fear of being associated with such a radical leader. Probably for a variety of reasons many left him; they evacuated.

Now, so close to the hour of his arrest, the remaining eleven were confused. But they would not evacuate, at least not

---

[22] "Irene Storms Ashore," *The Courier-Journal,* Sunday, August 28, 2011, A12.
[23] http://www.washingtonpost.com/national/nj-gov-chris-christie-get-the-hell-off-the-beach-with-hurricane-irene-inching-toward-state/2011/08/26/gIQAMxXuJ_story.html

yet. They chose to stay for the storm. Once they had a taste of the storm's devastating effects, they would be scattered, each retreating to the safety of his own home. But they would regroup. They would come back. They would return. And in doing so, they would find peace in Jesus.

And, having come back, they would be stronger, more equipped to face the next storm, and then the next, and next. Jesus warned them that as long as they were on this earth, they would have one storm after another. The word he used to describe what they would face is *thlipsis*. Jesus used the same word earlier. It's how he described the anguish of a woman in labor. But because Jesus would die the next day and rise on the third, and at Pentecost send the Holy Spirit, the disciples would no longer need to evacuate, if that means leaving the cause of Christ. The only kind of evacuation followers of Christ need to make is to the Holy Spirit. In him, we find safety and courage to face the storm.

In the midst of the storm we have peace as long as we abide in Jesus. Whenever we take our eyes off him, fear overwhelms us, our courage vanishes, and we run and hide. But it doesn't need to be that way because in him we have peace and from that peace comes the courage to face the onslaught of the storm. By enduring it, we conquer it.

M. R. Dehaan tells about two artists who were both commissioned to portray an image of peace. One painted a picture of a boy relaxing on a boat in a calm, serene lake. It was a picture of serenity. But the other artist painted a thunderous waterfall with raging winds spraying the water into a mist. On a limb that stretched near the waterfall a bird had built a nest, and in this painting, the bird was peacefully brooding her eggs, protecting them from the roaring water so close by.

Real peace, Dehaan reminds us, is remaining calm in the midst of the storm.[24] Courage is the natural overflow from the gift of peace. We find that peace in Christ.

But I must tell you, it's a process. We never fully, completely arrive. My life of storm fighting has been one of victory followed by defeat, then victory and defeat again, and sometimes the defeat has been profound. At times, in the midst of the storm, I've wondered if God is there and if he has abandoned me. It's like running the rapids, swooshing through them, hanging on for life, sometimes bruised and hurt as a result of my own poor judgment or outright stupidity. Then God brings me to a calm place, and in that placidness, I am able to thank God for his provision, but before I have time to stretch out and relax, suddenly my boat's rocking through turbulent waters again.

It's not easy or painless or ever done.

### Horatio Spafford's Struggle in the Storm

Horatio G. Spafford learned this truth in the most difficult way. Spafford, a successful attorney living in Chicago in the middle of the nineteenth century, is remembered today for writing the words to the hymn, "It is Well with My Soul." In 1860 he was a 32 year old bachelor and had good reason to be optimistic and hopeful. Spafford was part of a thriving law firm: Spafford, McDaid, and Wilson. He was investing wisely in real

---

[24] Paul Lee Tan, *Encyclopedia of 15,000 Illustrations* (Dallas, Texas: Bible Communications, Inc., 1998), p.2062.

estate. And he was a leader and Bible teacher at Fullerton Presbyterian Church. Moreover, Anna Larssen, who had emigrated at the age of four with her parents from Norway, would soon be of marriageable age. Anna, thirteen years younger than Horatio, had attended his Sunday School class. They were immediately attracted to each other, but when Horatio discovered she was only fifteen years old, he would not talk about marriage. He paid for her tuition at a boarding school near Chicago and three years later in 1861, they were married.[25]

By 1870, they were a family with four children. Their oldest daughter, Annie, was seven, Maggie, five, Horatio Jr., four, and Bessie was two. And the next year Anna would give birth to another baby girl, Tanetta. Horatio's real estate investments continued to grow, his law practice was thriving with Horatio now a senior member of the firm, and Anna had a French governess to help her with the five children. It was a good life.

The Spaffords were active in the evangelical reform movement. Frances E. Willard, a leader in the women's temperance movement and D. L. Moody, who was becoming a world renowned evangelist, were frequent guests in the Spafford home.[26]

Then, in 1871, things went terribly wrong for the Spaffords. Like Job of old, the Spaffords encountered one tragedy after another, trial after trial, storm upon storm. First in 1870 the Spafford's only son, Horatio, Jr., died of scarlet fever at the age of four. While still grieving the death of Horotio, Jr., the

---

[25] www.loc.gov/exhibits/americancolony/amcolony-family.html
[26] www.rootsweb.ancestry.com/~nyrensse/bio220.htm

Spaffords suffered considerable financial loss when the Great Chicago Fire destroyed much of Horatio's real estate investments. The Spaffords responded to their personal tragedies by throwing themselves into the relief effort to the victims of the fire. They worked in a soup kitchen, helped the homeless, and cared for the sick. And it took its toll on Anna. By 1873 her health was virtually broken.

Horatio decided the family needed a break and planned a trip to Europe. They would relax, and along the way, attend the revival being held in England by their friends, D.L. Moody and Ira Sankey.

But it didn't quite work that way. On the very day they were to board the British liner, Ville du Havre, Horatio was detained by urgent business. He would have to join his wife and four daughters a few days later.

It never happened. On the second day of the voyage the Ville du Havre was struck by a British iron sailing ship, the Lochearn. The luxury liner sank within twelve minutes in the middle of the Atlantic Ocean. Of the 307 passengers and crew members, only 81 survived.

As the ship was going down, Anna held baby Tanetta tightly to her chest. Then she was struck by debris with such force that the baby was thrown from her arms. Anna reached for the baby's gown, momentarily grasping it before the force of the water sucked Tanetta from Anna's arms again. Maggie and Annie survived for a while by holding to the pockets of a man's pants. Losing consciousness, they slipped forever into the frigid waters. No one reported the whereabouts of Bessie. Anna lost consciousness but miraculously clung to plank of wood until she was rescued by the Lochearn. After arriving nine days later in Cardiff, Wales, she cabled Horatio: "Saved alone. What shall I do...?"[27]

What indeed? What do you do when the storm takes all of your children and you are "saved alone"? I wonder what she did in those days when she waited alone for Horatio to join her on what was supposed to be a European vacation.

Meanwhile, Horatio boarded the first available passenger ship to Wales. When it approached the location where the Ville du Havre was struck, the Captain sent word to Horatio to come to the bridge. There the Captain informed the distraught father: "A careful reckoning has been made and I believe we are now passing the place where the Ville du Havre was wrecked. The water is three miles deep." Horatio returned to his cabin and penned the now famous words that became the hymn, "It Is Well with My Soul."

> *When peace, like a river, attendeth my way,*
> *When sorrows like sea billows roll;*
> *Whatever my lot, Thou has taught me to say,*
> *It is well, it is well, with my soul.*[28]

Spafford would write Anna's half-sister, Rachel: "On Thursday last we passed over the spot where she went down, in

---

[27] www.loc.gov/exhibits/americancolony/amcolony-family.html
[28] Robert J. Morgan, *Then Sings My Soul, 150 of the World's Greatest Hymn Stories* (Nashville: Thomas Nelson Publishers, 2003), p.184.

*Surviving the Storms of Life*

mid-ocean, the waters three miles deep. But I do not think of our dear ones there. They are safe, folded, the dear lambs."[29]

And that is where most people leave the story, with Horatio Spafford's faith intact, unblemished by doubt, triumphant in tragedy, a candidate for sainthood. After such tragedy, it surely was smooth sailing for the rest of his life.

Unfortunately, it didn't happen that way.

The truth of Jesus warning, "Here on this earth you will have many trials and sorrows," became even more real for the Spaffords. They returned to Chicago to start afresh. And the Lord blessed them with another child, a son, whom they again named, Horatio. He was born in 1876, and then in 1878 Anna gave birth to a daughter, Bertha. But tragedy struck again when two years later Horatio died at the age of 4, just like his brother of the same name, and just like his brother, he died of scarlet fever. The loss of Horatio was devastating and left some in their church, Fullerton Presbyterian Church, wondering why the Spaffords experienced so much tragedy. The usual questions surfaced, "Had they done something to deserve God's judgment? Had God turned away from them in disfavor?"[30]

And the man who wrote, "It Is Well with My Soul," was now crying out, "How Long, Lord?!" That's the title of a poem he wrote during this period. It's one of 20 poems he printed in a little booklet, *Waiting for Morning*. Can you sense his grief and agony in his words? "How long shall heart-strings break and bleed? /How long, O Lord---my God, how long, how long?"[31]

---

[29] www.loc.gov/exhibits/americancolony/amcolony-family.html
[30] ibid
[31] www.local.gov/exhibits/americancolony/amcolony-jerusalem.html

On the title page of this volume, Horatio is identified as the author of "Twenty Reasons for Believing the Coming of the Lord is Nigh," a topic that would dominate his thinking in the remaining years of his life as he became more and more obsessed with end-time prophesies. Like many other Christians, he believed the Jews' return to Jerusalem would be a sign that the second coming was imminent.[32]

Soon the Spaffords, along with 13 adults and three children from their church, decided to leave Chicago and start a mission in Jerusalem. It became known as "The American Colony." They arrived in August 1881, just few months after Anna had given birth to another daughter, Grace. Their small group was soon helped by a contingent from Sweden, and together they focused on ministering to the poor and needy regardless of what religion or race they were. Because they did not try to proselytize, they gained the trust of both Jewish and Muslim people, as well Christians in various denominations. Many of these people had experienced loss; they knew suffering. Their mission was to help the hurting, and that they did. They set up soup kitchens, established a hospital, bought and worked a small farm, and built a carpentry shop.

Spafford had given much, but was convinced he should give more to his Lord. A year after arriving in Jerusalem he wrote in his diary, "Lord, I have always up to this day been holding on to something of the flesh. I crucify the flesh with its affections and lusts. Henceforward I live as a eunuch for the

---

[32] Jane Fletcher Geniesse, *American Priestess, The Extraordinary Story of Anna Spafford and the American Colony in Jerusalem* (published by Nan A. Talese, an imprint of Doubleday, 2008), pp.22-23.

Kingdom of Heaven's sake. I rely exclusively, exclusively on the power and grace of God in [Christ]. I am a miracle of grace! Blessed God how patient thou hast been with me!"[33]

The American Colony took on a utopian flavor as the members attempted to live a communal life patterned after the early Christian community in Acts 2:42-47. And Horatio searched the Bible for signs of the end time when Jesus would return to Jerusalem. He even corresponded with Charles Piazza Smyth, the astronomer who had popularized the theory that the Great Pyramid in Giza, Egypt, was a repository of mysteries revealing the fulfillment of Biblical prophesies. As he peered into the heavens, looking for the second coming of Christ, he grieved the loss in his life, became more and more despondent, refused to work, and was immersed in debt.[34]

Sometime during the 1880s Spafford began to suffer some form of mental illness. As it progressed he became delusional and was rumored to have believed himself to be the Messiah. On October 16, 1888, he died of malaria and was buried in Mount Zion Cemetery in Jerusalem.[35]

## Hardly a happy-ever-after ending.

Is the story of Horatio Spafford and his family one of triumph or tragedy, victory or defeat, loss or gain? It is all of that. His story reminds us that regardless of how well we are prepared for a storm, we still get rocked by its waves, rolled by its winds, and ripped by its wreckage. And even when the storm

---

[33] ibid
[34] Geniese, *American Priestess*, p. 312.
[35] www.rootsweb.ancestry.com/~nyrensse/bio220.htm

has passed over us, leaving us stripped of all that is dear to our soul, even then---with peace flowing like a river in spite of the pain---our grief and agony is no guarantee that we have suffered enough and are therefore insulated from more storms that can bring us to our knees again, causing us to cry out, "How long, O Lord,---my God, how long, how long?"

It's a chilling reality. Just because we have survived one terrible storm doesn't mean the storms decrease in the intensity of their strength, the frequency of their occurrence, or the immensity of their scope. There is tragedy in triumph and triumph in tragedy because the saga continues as long as we are on earth. It's the world we live in. We deceive ourselves if we pretend otherwise.

We should not expect otherwise. As Teddy Roosevelt said, "The virtue that is worth having is the virtue that can sustain the rough shock of actual living." That's the only place we can live, "actual living." Paul, the apostle recognized it: "We are pressed on every side by troubles," he wrote to the church in Corinth, "but we are not crushed. We are perplexed, but not driven to despair. We are hunted down, but never abandoned by God. We get knocked down, but we are not destroyed. Through suffering, our bodies continue to share in the death of Jesus so that the life of Jesus may also be seen in our bodies"(II Corinthians 4:8-10).

But it's not always difficult. Remember, Jesus assured us that we receive comfort from the Holy Spirit during the trying times. We are warmed, strengthened, and nourished by the Spirit of God. The Holy Spirit refreshes us in between storms, just as he strengthens us during the storm. And there are those times when it is smooth sailing on calm waters, those days, thank God for them, when the children are fine, the work rewarding, and the relationships smooth.

But the storms will come. That's why it's important that we are not only prepared for the storms of life, but that we know what to do when they strike. What do you do when you are faced with what seems like an impossible situation? Turn to the next chapter and find out.

*"Jesus looked up to heaven…"*
—John 17:1

"Everything was being torn apart around us. It was terrifying. We were sure we were going to die."

—Brenna Burzinski, survivor of the Joplin, Missouri tornado, May 22, 2011

# Chapter Three
# Find a Safe Place

I WRITE THIS CHAPTER ABOUT FINDING a safe place in the storms of life barely a week after the deadliest tornado in modern weather recordkeeping history devastated Joplin, Missouri on May 22, 2011. So sudden was the descent of the tornado on the city, that thousands of people didn't have time to find a safe place. The death toll was 141. Many barely escaped with their life.

Floyd and Donna Rockwell were attending Harmony Heights Baptist Church the evening the storm struck, and the two almost didn't make it out of the church building alive. The people inside the church rushed to the safest place they could find, the children's Sunday School room. Floyd, 74, lay across his 71 year-old wife, trying to shield her from the cinder blocks that were flying through the air after the twister tore the roof off the church building.

The Rockwell's survived, but when they went home, they discovered it was no longer there. It was completely destroyed, leveled, gone; nothing but rubble was left where their home had been. Floyd is convinced that if they had stayed home rather than going to church, they would have been killed by the tornado.

But, not everyone who found shelter in that Sunday School room survived. Three people didn't live to walk out of the church building that night.[36]

Finding a safe place in a storm is not always easy and sometimes impossible.

But, while there may not always be a safe place, we can say that some places are safer than others. Lying in a ditch may not be the ideal shelter but it beats being in your car. A closet under the stairwell on the first floor is usually better than the den on the second floor.

The challenge is finding a safe place and getting to it in time. Interestingly enough, sirens sounded for about 20 minutes in Joplin, Missouri the day the tornado hit. That's better than the 13-14 minute average warning time. Some people may not have heard the sirens because of the noise from the strong winds and heavy rains. But there may have been another reason why some did not immediately seek shelter when the sirens were activated. Meteorologist Greg Carbin observed that many people have become increasingly complacent about warnings. "That is something we grapple with all the time," said Carbin. "If we want to push the envelope with respect to predictions are we also going to overwarn or cry wolf too often? I would argue that there may be some signs we are already doing that."[37]

Jesus warned the disciples of the oncoming storm: "The time is coming---indeed it's here now---when you will be

---

[36] http://www.huffingtonpost.com/2011/05/23/joplin-tornado-survivors-death n 865847.html

[37] www.guardian.co.uk/world/2011/may/24/tornado-missouri-improved-warning-systems.

scattered, each one going his own way, leaving me alone" (John 16:32). His words were like a siren, warning a city of imminent danger.

But apparently the disciples didn't get it. They were either still trying to process what Jesus had been saying about leaving them and returning---"In a little while you won't see me, but in a little while after that you will see me again" (John 16:19)---or they were simply complacent. After all, Jesus was going to set up his kingdom, and all problems would dissolve, right?

The disciples weren't ready for the impending storm; they were scattered, scared, and scorned. They had failed to secure a safe place in the midst of the storm, and their safe place was always right there in their midst, in the person of Jesus: "Don't let your hearts be troubled. Trust in God, and trust also in me" (John 14:1). They missed it because they weren't aware they needed a safe place.

Some new homes are being built with "safe rooms," which are structured to withstand the high winds of a storm. The people who have these rooms installed have obviously made a decision to have a safe place before any storm approaches; they've taken the time to make sure it's properly structured to withstand the storm. Because it's right there in their home, they know how to get to it. All that's left for them to do is make sure the room is equipped with a supply kit.

When it comes to the storms of life, it is essential that we recognize the necessity of a safe place, a "safe room," a room to shield us from danger. But for it to be effective in protecting us from the storm, we have to make a decision to find such a place and then practice going to it so that when the storm strikes, we don't panic. And it's helpful to have that supply kit already in the room.

The night before he faced his worst possible storm, Jesus already knew his safe place. He had been there many, many times. It was natural for him to "look up to heaven" (John 17:1), because prayer was Jesus' safe place.

And it can be yours and mine as well.

Church buildings can be destroyed like any other, but our Lord has never lost one of his own. The safest place we can be in the midst of our life storms is in the arms of the Father. Our access to his arms is prayer. Prayer is the key that unlocks the door of our "safe room."

Do you remember what it was like when you were a kid, and you played "tag, you're it"? Do you recall having a place where no one could get you called "base"? "Base" was the place of security; it was the safe place where you could go if you got tired or afraid or bored with the game. Being the youngest and smallest of four brothers, "base" was an important place for me. It could be a refuge when my brothers and their friends liked to beat up on "little Whitlock."

We all need a "base" in life, don't we? Maybe you need several: one at work, one at home, and maybe one when you travel. It is important to have those bases in life. It is a place of refuge, of security, of comfort. When the "heat is on" and stays on longer than you would like, when you know you are about to enter a time of trial, having that "base" can be a source of peace that gives you confidence for the daily battles of life.

*Surviving the Storms of Life*

### When you want to cry, "Sanctuary"

In the 1996 Disney movie, *The Hunchback of Notre Dame*, there is a scene where Esmeralda, the heroine, helps Quasimodo, the hunchback, when he is under attack. Quasimodo has been crowned the king of fools. The crowd of people is making fun of him. He has been tied to a wooden wheel, and the mob is throwing tomatoes, eggs, cabbages and other food at him. It's a horrible, embarrassing situation. Esmeralda helps Quasimodo escape. They are in the Cathedral, and there she is trapped. From the Cathedral she cries out the word, "sanctuary." By claiming "sanctuary," the law couldn't touch her as long as she was in the Cathedral. The archdeacon commands Frollo, the bad guy, to leave, and he reluctantly does. But as he exits, he warns Esmeralda that if she leaves, she will be arrested.

Actually "sanctuary" was a concept that developed in medieval law. A person could, under certain circumstances, be safe in the sanctuary of a church. In fact, a King Ethelbert made the first laws regulating sanctuary in about 600 A.D.

There are times in my life when I've wanted to yell, "Sanctuary." It's kind of like running to "base" when you're a kid.

God instructed the Israelites to build a tent-like structure at Mount Sinai. It followed a specific pattern given by God. This structure was known as the Tabernacle or Tent of Meeting. As you might guess from that name, Tent of Meeting, this was the place where God dwelt in the midst of the people. In Exodus 25:8, we read that God instructed Moses to have "the people of Israel build me a holy sanctuary so I can live among them." The Hebrew word, "sanctuary," is the translation of the Hebrew word, *miqdash*. The root form of that word means "to set apart" or "consecrate." The Tabernacle conveyed to the people that God's presence was truly there with them as they traveled on their journey in the wilderness.[38]

It's interesting that the first thing the people saw when they entered the Temple area was something called the "Altar of burnt offering." The altar is described as having an ornate projection on each corner called a horn. These had a purpose beyond mere decoration. They were the called "horns of refuge." When Israelites were in danger for their life because of some serious offense, they could run to the tabernacle and lay hold to the horns of the alter. As long as they stayed there, no one dare touch them. (I Kings 1:50-51; I Kings 2:28-34). What's fascinating is that the blood of a sacrificial animal was sprinkled on these horns during worship to symbolize that the sin of the person offering the sacrifice had been placed on the altar. Sin had been atoned for; fellowship with God was restored.[39] Not only could someone find security by grasping those horns of refuge, but they also symbolized, after a sacrifice had been made, that the sinner was safe, secure, cleansed before God.

For the Christian, Christ is our sacrificial lamb come to redeem the sinner. We all have committed serious offenses; we have sinned against a holy God. But we can lay hold of Jesus Christ, whose blood atoned for our sin, and in him we find sanctuary or refuge. We have the assurance of knowing him as our "base," our "safe room." Because of what he did on Calvary,

---

[38] Alex Varughese, ed., *Discovering the Old Testament, Story and Faith* (Kansas City: Beacon Hill Press, 2003), 106-107
[39] www.storylight.org/dic/hbd/view.cgi?number=T261

God the Father embraces us as the Holy Spirit draws us into his presence. In times of trouble, we enter his presence, lift our eyes to heaven, and cry, "Sanctuary! Sanctuary!"

In his hour of tribulation, Jesus looked to heaven and found sanctuary in the arms of his heavenly Father. That didn't make the storm go away. Jesus tasted death for us. He was crucified, he died, he was buried. But he had the assurance in that moment, when he looked to heaven, that ultimately, he would be safe with the Father. And Jesus was resurrected; he did ascend to heaven; and today, he sits at the right hand of God where he intercedes for us. So, as we look to heaven, we find the sweet embrace of our Lord.

But Jesus didn't just happen to look to heaven. He was intentional about seeking sanctuary in the arms of the Father. And so must we. We have to be intentional about finding our safe place in the presence of the Father. We make a decision to pray and in so doing find ourselves in a safe place, or we choose not to pray and fight the storm alone; we practice the presence of God in prayer and experience peace in the midst of the storm, or we look to our own selves and the storm, and we experience frustration in life's trials and troubles.

## Make a Decision to Find a Safe Place Before the Storm Arrives

I don't like being forced to make a quick decision. But sometimes I have to, and when that happens, it's often my own fault. I've procrastinated until a decision has to be made NOW. Let's say my air conditioner at home is making a strange noise, and furthermore, my car has a tire that looks like it needs more air. "I need to get that fixed," I might say to myself. Then suddenly, the air through the vents at home feels warm, and it's 100 degrees outside. I call the first air conditioner expert who is willing to come. Then, in a hurry to get to work, I rush to my car, only to find it has a flat tire. If that were to occur, there would be no casual leaving the car at the garage for that repair; I would have to attend to it myself because I would have allowed an emergency situation to develop.

It's best to make a decision before you have to. Then you can be prepared for the inevitable storm.

The day the tornado struck Tuscaloosa, Alabama on April 27, 2011, Stuart Mitchell, 23, a junior, at the University of Alabama was lying in bed, watching the news on TV and taking a break from studying for his statistics class. Hearing the report of a tornado south of Tuscaloosa, but not thinking much about it, Stuart jokingly shouted to his two roommates as he called dibs on the closet in the middle of the house, the one without windows. They all laughed with him.

Then, Mitchell heard "this weird, strange roaring sound."

That's when one of his roommates went outside and saw the huge tornado barreling towards their house. Quickly, the three of them followed Mitchell's plan and dove into the closet, barricading the doors with a sofa.

They could hear the sound of shattering glass, and after one of the double closet doors was torn away, they saw debris flying through the air like thousands of tiny darts being sucked down the hallway. When they stepped out of the closet, they discovered that the bed Mitchell had been lying on had been crushed beneath the gigantic brick fireplace and chimney which the tornado had blown down.

"If we didn't jokingly discuss this beforehand, we probably wouldn't have made it," Mitchell said.[40]

Any plan is better than no plan, even if it's made at last moment, just before the storm.

But how much better to have scouted out the best and safest place when there is no pressure to find it.

Long before he came to his last night with the disciples, Jesus had made a decision to commune with his father in prayer. It was only natural that he "lift his eyes to heaven," when the storm was about to strike.

Early in his ministry, as recorded in Mark 1:35, we find Jesus up before daybreak, finding an isolated place to pray. Apparently, this was his habit throughout his ministry. In what is almost merely a footnote contrasting Jesus' lifestyle to that of the growing crowds attracted to his miraculous works, Luke says, "But Jesus often withdrew to the wilderness to pray" (Luke 5:16). And on the day he was baptized, Jesus was praying (Luke 3:21). He prayed for forty days during his fast in the wilderness (Luke 4:1-2). And before he chose the twelve disciples, he went up on a mountain and prayed all night (Luke 6:12).

We can follow Jesus' example by making a decision to pray. Jesus chose to arise before the disciples were awake and go to a solitary place. He chose to pray before important decisions

---

[40] Richard Fausset and David Succhino, "Survivors tell tales of horror," http://articles.latimes.com/2011/apr/30/nation/la-na-tuscaloosa-tornado-20110430

like choosing the twelve. And when his ministry was growing, he chose to sneak away from the hustle and bustle and pray. These times of prayer were preceded by deliberate decisions to pray.

If you don't have a place already, find someplace where you will be less distracted by others. Schedule a time when you will be less apt to be interrupted by family and friends. As you train yourself in those quiet moments to focus on God, you will learn the art of praying at other times, like when you are at work or at home, or even driving down the road. The idea is to practice the presence of Christ.

When I say, "Make a decision to pray," that doesn't mean prayer always and only takes place at a certain prescribed time and place. It can happen, as Joyce Rupp observes, when we are "going for a walk or a run, stopping at night to bless sleeping children, driving past a homeless person, looking up to see a bright star in the heavens, receiving a note from a cherished friend, turning toward a spouse in pleasurable love, reading a story in the newspaper, hearing the pain in a colleague's anguish, waiting in a check-out line---an any time and place we can be surprised and drawn into communion by the unanticipated sense of God's nearness."[41]

A monk of the 17th century known today simply as Brother Lawrence did just that. *Practicing the Presence of God*, is the title posthumously given to the *Conversations* and *Letters* of this Christian mystic, Nicholas Herman of Lorraine. When he was over 50 years old, he entered the Carmelite Order in Paris as

---

[41] Joyce Rupp, *Prayer* (Maryknoll, New York: Orbis Books, 2007), p. 13.

a lay brother and served humbly as a kitchen aide. What we know of Brother Lawrence comes to us because Cardinal de Noailles sent his envoy, Abbe de Beaufort, to investigate the reports of this wise man of God. Brother Lawrence granted four interviews, or "conversations," in which he described his way of life and how he came to it.

As a young man, he had been forced to join the army because of his poverty. The military promised him meals and a small stipend. It was while serving that Nicholas had a deep experience with God that transformed his life. He was 18 at the time, and while gazing at a barren tree in the dead of winter, he was encouraged by the simple realization that the leaves would reappear. It wasn't so much a supernatural vision as a deep insight into the grace of God. Nicholas felt his life was barren and in many ways lifeless, just like that tree. But like the tree, God would in due time, in the turn of a season, bring new life and fruit into his life. The sense of God's providence and unfailing grace gleaned from this experience never left him. It turned him from the world and ignited a deep love for God. From that moment his passion for God never waned.

Several years later, after an injury forced his retirement from the military, Nicholas Herman entered the Discalced Carmelite monastery in Paris as Brother Lawrence. It was while working in the monastery kitchen that he developed his practice of the presence of Christ. Brother Lawrence's goal was to think of nothing but God.

How does one practice the presence of God? According to Brother Lawrence, practicing the presence begins when we first receive the new life received by the gift of salvation through the blood of Jesus Christ. Then, we must make a decision to practice the presence of God, "gently, humbly, and lovingly, without giving way to anxiety or problems." After that, "the soul's eyes must be kept on God, particularly when something is being done in the outside world." When our attention drifts away from God, as it inevitably does, a conscious decision must be made to refocus on God. Short phrases like, "Lord, I am all yours," or "God of love, I love you with all my heart," or "Lord, use me according to your will," can be repeated to train the heart to come back to practicing the presence of God.

Although practicing the presence of God may not be easy, it has tremendous rewards when faithfully pursued. "It shows the soul how to see God's presence everywhere with a pure and loving vision, which is the holiest, firmest, easiest, and the most effective attitude of prayer."[42] According the Brother Lawrence, blessings of practicing the presence of God include a livelier faith and stronger hope in God, a consuming desire to live in the presence of God, and spontaneity in the worship of God.[43] "By practicing God's presence and continuously looking at Him, the soul familiarizes itself with Him to the extent that it passes almost its whole life in continual acts of love, praise, confidence."[44]

Whether he was washing pots, cooking meals, or running errands, Brother Lawrence lived with an awareness of God's presence. Notice that he had to be intentional about that. Like

---

[42] Brother Lawrence, *The Practice of the Presence of God* (New Kensington, PA.,: Whitaker House, 1982), pp., 69-70.
[43] Ibid., p. 71-72
[44] Ibid., p. 72.

him, if we want to abide in the shadow of the Almighty, we must move in his direction. The continual practice of the presence of God, as Brother Lawrence knew it, sprang from a deliberate, daily walk with the God he had learned to trust and love in a relationship of intimate friendship. God is always there, and the more we experience him, the less we know of the world. When storms come, we are already secure in our "safe room."

### Don't just find any place, find the safest place

Before a storm hits, I want to know where the safest place is. Is it the southwest corner of the house or the northeast? Rooms on the north and east are supposed to be better. But interior rooms are supposed to be safer than rooms on the exterior. And a basement is best of all, usually.

When the storms of life strike, I want the safest of all places. I know where that is: in the arms of God. But what does that mean? Just how do we rest in the arms of God? Once a decision has been made to practice the presence of God, just what do you do? How does prayer work? Does it work?

There are so many different ways to pray; we can utilize a vast variety of prayers. One of the first prayer techniques I learned was the ACTS acrostic. It stands for Adoration, Confession, Thanksgiving, and Supplication. Then, I learned more about practicing intercessory prayer through Peter Lord's *29/59 Plan, A Guide to Communion with God*.[45] The title stood for 29 minutes and 59 seconds of prayer time. That little

---

[45] Peter Lord, *The 2959 Plan, A Guide to communion with God* (Grand Rapids, MI, Baker Book House, revised edition, 1989).

workbook was a nice introduction in directed prayers of praise, thanksgiving, confession, intercession, petition, and in listening. The notebook had a place to note answered prayer, so it was my first introduction to journaling as well.

Later in life, I was introduced to other forms of prayer. My friends at the Abby of Gethsemani in Trappist, Kentucky, introduced me to the Jesus Prayer, Centering Prayer, and *Lectio Divina*. All are forms of contemplative prayer. I've incorporated all these forms of prayer into my daily routine of life. I usually start my day with the Jesus Prayer and quiet mediation. (I'll discuss these prayers in a later chapter.) As I meditate, I peacefully rest in the arms of the Lord and later move to Bible readings and intercession. Intercession lasts, sprinkled in bits and pieces, through my entire day. My prayer life is a compilation of the different forms of prayer I've learned along life's way. I agree with J.I. Packer that "most Christians pray differently during different life stages."[46]

But, let me emphasize that the technique or form of prayer is *not* the important thing. Prayer is the means to an end, the end being the experience of God. The Trappist monk, Thomas Merton, admonished us not to seek a "method," or a "system," but rather to cultivate what he called an "attitude" for the "outlook of prayer," which to Merton is characterized by "faith, openness, attention, reverence, expectation, supplication, trust, and joy." The goal is not the mastering of a method but the

---

[46] J.I. Packer, and Carolyn Nystrom, *Praying, Finding our Way Through Duty to Delight* (Downers Grove, Illinois: IVP Books, 2006), p.,12

awareness by faith that we are "in the presence of God," and "that we live in Christ..."[47]

So, it shouldn't be that we get more excited about the *method* of prayer than we do about the *object* of prayer. Such a fixation on the technique naturally leads to the dullness of routine. Again, I agree with Packer, that a danger of routine prayer is that it can reduce prayer "to an item to be ticked off in the checklist of things to do---preferably with as little mental and emotional engagement as possible."[48]

Prayer won't become drudgery when we remember our goal is to experience God and not to become experts in the techniques of prayer. God is very much alive, and in prayer, we experience his power. But when prayer is reduced to something we do in order to get something we want, it loses its significance in our lives.

And that brings up an important question: What is prayer, really? If it's not just a technique of putting certain memorized words together or asking for something we want, what exactly is it?

According to one ancient definition, it's simply, "keeping company with God." Philip Yancey likes that definition because it encompasses the variety of experiences we have in the daily routine of life. "By incorporating those experiences into my prayers, I prolong and savor them so that

---

[47] Thomas Merton, *Contemplative Prayer* (New York, New York: Doubleday, 1996), 34.
[48] Packer, 14

they do not fall too quickly into my memory bank, or out of it," he writes.[49]

Of course, part of that day by day experience of life includes life's trials and tribulations---storms. "About the time we settle in and feel satisfied with our prayer, life upends us with some unexpected event or internal rumbling, and we find ourselves wondering how best to pray amid the circumstances," notes Joyce Rupp. [50]

That's why prayer has to be more than a means to get what we want. And that forces another question: How does prayer work? Or maybe we should say, *does* prayer work?

If we mean by "working" that prayer is getting what we want from God, then, no, prayer doesn't work, at least not like that. If you've prayed very much at all, you've experienced times when your prayers weren't answered in the way you wanted. We mistakenly believe God didn't answer our prayer because he didn't answer it like we wanted.

I remember praying as a sixteen year-old that I would grow to be at least six-feet tall. I didn't tell God but I would have been elated with 5'11 and would have taken 5'10 with gratitude. I had a good reason for making such a request: My height was essentially the only thing I could think of that would keep me from a scholarship to a Division 1-AA football program, particularly the one at Oklahoma University. I recall trying to convince God that playing for a "big-time" football program would increase my opportunities to witness for him. Somehow I

---

[49] Philip Yancey, *Prayer, Does It Make Any Difference?* (Grand Rapids, Michigan: Zondervan, 2006), pp., 62-63
[50] Joyce Rupp, *Prayer*, p.10.

thought God would be impressed enough to increase my height, despite the genetics evident in a 4'11 mom and a 5'10 dad.

I remember the preacher saying we should put prayer to action. For me that meant grasping a bar that I had put across my bedroom doorway and hanging on for as long as I could. Hopefully I thought, that would stretch my height to a more gridiron acceptable stature. I also read where a Russian athlete had gained height, he believed, by a diet heavily laden with liver and onions. It took one meal for me to decide I would be better off to double up on my prayers than partake of that delicacy. After the hanging bar, the liver and onions, and all the prayers, here I am today, 5'6, essentially the same height I was when I prayed that prayer the first time.

Later in life there would be unanswered requests of a more serious nature: like praying that my wife be healed of cancer. Katri battled breast cancer for six years before succumbing to it. I prayed every day for her healing.

What about you? Have you had unanswered prayer? I asked a few people. When I asked my wife, Lori, she immediately answered that her prayer for her infant, Jordan, wasn't answered. She desperately cried out to God for her son to live. He didn't.

Another person I talked to prayed that God would give her sole custody of her child. It didn't work out that way. I asked our Wednesday night prayer group if they had unanswered prayers. Unanswered prayers ranged from one who prayed for a negative report from a biopsy to another who prayed that her mother wouldn't have Alzheimer's to another who prayed that a friend would accept Jesus. These Christians were being obedient to God. They were asking God to work in these situations. Some claimed Jesus' words as they prayed: "If you remain in me and my words remain in you, you may ask for anything you want, and it will be granted!" (John 15:7).

Do you ever wonder if prayer makes any difference? So, why do you pray, anyway?

Maybe you are like the little girl who was aggravated with God. She knelt down to pray and said, "Now, God, Aunt Nell still has the sciatica, sissy still doesn't have a date to the prom, and Uncle Leo can't get the mule to plow. I am tired of praying for this family without getting results!"

It reminds me of the preacher's five-year old daughter who noticed that her daddy-preacher always bowed his head for a moment before starting his sermon. She asked him why. "Well, honey," he said, "I'm asking the good Lord to help me preach a good sermon."

"How come he doesn't?" she asked.

Indeed, how come he doesn't? How come God doesn't always seem to show up on time? How come he seems absent, just when he is needed the most? How come he didn't come through? Where was God when you prayed for an answer, and it didn't come? Where was God in the midst of that painful experience? And where was God, after all, when you promised your life away, if only he would get you out of that tight spot?

I like the story of Pedro, who was driving in downtown Mexico City. He was in a sweat because he had an important meeting and couldn't find a parking place. Pedro looked toward heaven and said "Lord, take pity on me. If you find me a parking place I will go to Mass every Sunday for the rest of my life and give up tequila."

Miraculously, a parking place suddenly appeared.

Pedro looked up again and said, "Never mind. I found one."

Haven't you been like Pedro? This is the trouble with prayer as the celestial code for a divine ATM machine: We want what we want more than we want God. And when we get what we want, it's another, "Never mind, God." We seek the blessing, not the blesser. If we are going to learn anything about the process of prayer and how it works, we have to understand that prayer is not essentially a means for getting what we want.

I trust God for his plan, even though at times I can't see the end of a particular road he seems to be taking me on. At times I am not sure where God is going with my life. But I trust him. And as I pray I am participating in the plan he has for me as well as in the community of faith.

In the midst of all the mess of life, there is one who is praying for us and that is Jesus himself. Here in John 17 we get a glimpse of what is on his heart for us. Even though we will have trouble, Christ has triumphed already.

Jesus prays for us. With the shadow of the cross looming over him, he prayed for you and me. And he still prays for us today. Romans 8:34 tells us that he is sitting at God the Father's right hand, "pleading for us." The word "plead" can also be translated "intercede." Think of it: Jesus is interceding for you and me, even right now. As we examine his prayer in John 17 we will see what Jesus wants for us, but for now, remember that most of all he wants us to love and know him and his ways. So, prayer is not lobbying God with prayer requests to get what we want as opposed to what God wants. Prayer is finding out what our Lord wants and receiving that.

Prayer is not about getting our way or convincing God to change his will and give us what we want. Pray is simply talking to and listening to God. "Prayer is first and foremost," one person has written, "about relationship, relationship with God and our relationship with one another in the body of Christ."[51] Prayer is, as John Killinger put it, "communion with God. It is a matter of making connections with the One who stands at the center of all life and joy, and of learning to live with those connections all the time. That's all it is. Nothing more, nothing less."[52]

And this relationship with God is expressed in love. Prayer is then an expression of my love for God. When I pray, I am loving God, "making connections" with him.

Jesus talked about the importance of our love for God. He said, "The most important commandment is this: 'Listen, O Israel! The Lord our God is the one and only Lord'" (Mark 12:29). That statement in and of itself should get our attention. In answer to a teacher in one of the local "schools of religion" about what is the most important of all the commandments, Jesus lays down for this man and for us what is most important. If we want to be followers of Jesus here is the most important thing we can do. You can, I believe, go so far as to say here is a

---

[51] *The Little Book of Hours, Praying with the Community of Jesus*, Revised ed. (Brewster, MA: Paraclete Press, 2007), vii.
[52] John Killinger, cited by Brian Harbour, "Does Prayer Really Work?" *Brian's Lines*, May/June, 2008, p.2.

statement of the believer's life purpose. Do you want to know what that is? Listen to Jesus words: "You must love the Lord your God with all your heart, all your soul, all your mind, and all your strength" (Mark 12:30) But Jesus doesn't stop there, for if we truly love God, that love for him will be expressed to others. His very next words are "The second is equally important: 'Love your neighbor as yourself'" (Mark 12:31).This commandment encapsulates not only our life purpose, but our "first and foremost" prayer as well.[53]

God has a purpose for us. He wants to have a relationship with us. He loves us and desires that we love him back. "'I know the plans I for you,' says the Lord. 'They are plans for good and not for disaster, to give you a future and a hope'" (Jeremiah 29:11). That's good news. God has a plan for me, and it's a good plan. As we find and participate in that plan, we pray. In the very next verse in that text from Jeremiah, God says, "In those days when you pray, I will listen." We have the assurance that God will listen to the prayers of his people. What a comfort: God has a good plan. As we I fulfill that plan, living out his life purpose for us, we pray. He can, as we pray, be found. "If you look for me wholeheartedly, you will find me" (Jeremiah 29:13). God loves us so much that he created me to have an everlasting love relationship with him.

Prayer, then, is about relationship, and the most important relationship is the one with God. In prayer we praise God for the wonderful, awesome God he is. We thank him for

---

[53] For a detailed explanation of how this passage is incorporated into the life of the believer see Scot McKnight *The Jesus Creed, Loving God, Loving Others* ( Brewster, MA: Paraclete Press, 2004).

what he has done, is doing, and will do. We confess our shortcomings, our waywardness, and our shame. We can talk to him about our failures, and he listens and forgives. We make requests to him as we do to a loving father. We ask believing, even though we are not always sure that the request is God's will. But we ask. And we listen to him. We meditate on his Word and ask that God the Holy Spirit open our eyes to the truths of Scripture We desire that he apply those truths to our lives and empower us to live them.. We love God and want him to know how much we love him. And yes, we pray for others, because Jesus said we are to love our neighbors as ourselves. We want God's loving will for their lives as well. Prayer is an expression of our love for God.

As we yield ourselves to God's love, we open ourselves to all the possibilities he has for us. That means that as we pray, we allow God to lovingly transform our lives.

When my wife had cancer, I prayed for her healing. And I believe there are biblical precedents for that. "Are any of you sick?" James, the brother of our Lord asks in James 5:14-15: "You should call for the elders of the church to come and pray over you, anointing you with oil in the name of the Lord. Such a prayer will heal the sick, and the Lord will make you well."

We did just that, as exactly as we knew how. We had a special prayer service in our church. Katri sat in a chair in front of the sanctuary. The deacons came by one by one and prayed. We anointed her with oil. That was when she was first diagnosed. And later, when she was ill from the effects of chemotherapy, when she lost her hair and strength, and she cried out in pain, I prayed that she be delivered from that horrible disease. I prayed that many times. And she prayed many, many times through each day.

I believe I was forever changed by God because of those prayers. I can tell you that I became more humble before God, more attentive to God and others, and I think less concerned with the outward show of things, and more settled and at peace with who I am and where I am at this stage of my life. Of course, the Lord is still working on me; I am a work in progress.

My cry at that time was not for God to change me, although God did indeed do that; my prayer was for her healing. The changes in me were mere byproducts of my main prayer for her healing.

Now, I ask you, did prayer change anything beyond my own attitude, perspective, and devotion to God? Yes, I believe it did. Who is to say Katri didn't experience some form of healing? Dr. James Brooks, the oncologist at Oschner's Clinic in Baton Rouge, La. told me when she was first diagnosed that her situation was so serious that it was possible that she might not survive more than six months and that if she were alive in two years, it would be nothing short of a miracle. She lived six more years. Six more years, and for most of those years she was well enough to care for our children.

Was it because of prayer? I believe it was because of God's mercy and faithfulness. As Oswald Chambers said, "God answers prayer on the ground of redemption and no other ground."[54] You say, "But God didn't completely heal her." I

---

[54] Oswald Chambers, *Prayer, A Holy Occupation*, ed. Harry Verploegh (Nashville, Tennessee: Thomas Nelson Publishers, 1992), p. 30.

know. But I also know we are all going to die, no matter what kind of complete or partial healing we may experience. I believe there are times when God hears the cry of his children and responds in miraculous ways. Why he responds in dramatic ways in some instances and not in others is a mystery. I come up against the limit of my understanding here.

We wrongly assume that because God didn't answer our prayers in the way we thought he would, he didn't answer our prayers at all. From our limited human perspective we just don't see it yet, and we may not until we "see" it from heaven's side. My prayer for Katri's healing was answered, I believe. She was healed, perhaps not completely but healed to carry on in this life for God's appointed time. And, she was healed completely when God took her to heaven. In those ways my prayers were answered.

Theologian J.I. Packer says this: "We must remind ourselves…that since our heavenly Father, who is as wise as he is loving, answers his children's prayers in the best way, what he does or fails to do in our immediate situation may look and feel at first as if he is saying a flat no to us. This is because of our slowness to realize that what we asked for, good and proper as it seemed, my not have been God's best."[55]

Oh, but how difficult it is for us to admit that we do not always know what is best for ourselves and those whom we love.

So, is God sovereign? Does he not know the number of our days and the beginning from the end and the end form the

---

[55] Packer and Nystrom, *Praying: Finding Our Way Through Duty to Delight*, p. 56.

beginning? Yes, I believe that. Then how does prayer change the unalterable plan of God? I do not know. For his own reasons God has chosen to give us the gift of prayer. Somehow the plan of God is actualized in the prayers of his people. As one man said, "Prayer moves the hand which moves the world."[56]

And so I pray believing. I believe prayer changes things. I do not know this side of eternity how much has been changed as a result of prayer. It is a mystery. But, I nonetheless pray, believing God has a plan; and I believe prayer is part of that plan. How prayer alters the sovereign plan of God must remain a mystery.

Karl Barth, the brilliant theologian, saw no contradiction in a sovereign God who is affected by the prayers of his children. "He is not deaf, he listens; more than that, he acts. He does not act in the same way whether we pray or not. Prayer exerts an influence upon God's action..." Barth went on to say, "The fact that God yields to man's petitions, changing his intentions in response to man's prayer, is not a sign of weakness. He himself, in the glory of his majesty and power, has so willed it."[57]

God calls us into a relationship of love and within the intimacy of that relationship of love, God responds to prayer. What I understand in only partial ways does not keep me from acting on his word in complete ways.

I like the simple but true aphorism that goes like this:

"If the *request* is wrong, God says, 'No.'

---

[56] John A. Wallace, cited by George W. Sweeting, ed., Great *Quotes and Illistrations*, (Waco, Tx.: Word Publishers, 1985), p. 208.

[57] Karl Barth, cited in Yancey, *Prayer*, p.143.

If *you* are wrong, God says, 'Grow.'
If the *timing* is wrong, God says, 'Slow.'
And if the *request* is right, and you are right, and the timing is right, God says, 'Go.'"

As David Jeremiah has pointed out, the most difficult part of that little paradigm is not the "no," but the "slow."[58] Isn't that the truth? We want God to answer our prayers now, not later. We forget that God is not on our time-table. He is in fact, above and beyond time itself. He is answering prayer. We cannot always see it from our tiny, human-conditioned perspective. That's where faith becomes a factor. And that's why being in his arms is the absolute perfect place to be in the storms of life. As we look to him in faith, we are assured of his presence in the storms of life.

## Practice Going to Your Safe Place

Not only should you have a place designated as a "safe place," during the storm, but you should practice having everyone in the family go to that place, so that when a storm comes, retreating to the shelter is almost second nature.

I remember having tornado drills at school when I was growing up in Altus, Oklahoma. Usually at the beginning of tornado season, we would practice going out in the hall, sitting down with our backs against the wall, and waiting for the

---

[58] David Jeremiah, *The Prayer Matrix* (Sisters, OR.: Multomah Books, 2004), p., 36.

teacher's instructions. I didn't mind those drills because we got out of class; and I understood, even when I was at Washington Elementary School, that we would be better prepared for a tornado by practicing the drills.

How do we prepare for the storms of life? By Praying. If the safest place we can be during the storm is in the arms of our Heavenly Father, then the way to be secure is to know the strength of those arms. Proverbs 24:10 says that "if you fail under pressure, your strength is too small." The way to increase our strength is to exercise our faith by spending more time in the Father's arms. It is there that he makes us stronger.

That's why when I hear someone saying prayer doesn't work, I know they haven't practiced it much. It's like the person who wants to lose weight and starts jogging. He has read a book on the joy of running, and he wants that runner's "high," not to mention the lean, healthy body. So he decides to try. He gets the running shoes, shorts, and shirt. Early the next morning, he hits the running trail. Twenty minutes later, huffing and puffing home, he virtually collapses on the front porch. The next day, his muscles are so sore he can barely make it out of bed. Ambling to the bathroom scales, he notes that he hasn't lost a pound. He then tells his wife he is through with running because "it doesn't work for me."

We would all acknowledge that he didn't really try it, and so he cannot adequately make a judgment about whether running "works" or not. The same is true about the discipline of prayer. If we want to be strong in the day of adversity, we have to practice exercising our spiritual muscles before the storm arrives.

I have to admit: praying is not always easy. Paul prayed for the believers in Galatia, "Oh, my dear children! I feel as if I'm going through labor pains for you again, and they will continue until Christ is fully developed in your lives" (Galatians 4:19). And remember, after the High Priestly Prayer in John 17, Jesus prayed in the Garden of Gethsemane with such agony and intensity that his sweat fell to the ground "like great drops of blood" (Luke 22:44).

Most of the time, those agonizing moments of prayer are a result of the pressures of life. It's not that the prayer in itself is agony. In fact, though you may prayer diligently, prayer is stress relieving. It's not drudgery. It's not the attitude of, "I have to pray," but of "I get to pray."

We do not face the storm every day. Praying through the difficult times helps me enjoy the smoother days more completely.

It is like any discipline. The intense times of training make the regular routine seem easier. That's why athletes push themselves physically; they can compete better and achieve more. The regular routine isn't so much of a struggle when they've trained through the more challenging ones.

As we are diligent to "always pray and not give up," (Luke 18:1), prayer becomes an adventure; the more I pray, the more I realize I have to learn about it. At the same time, the more I practice genuinely praying, the stronger and more confident I am spiritually. Do I falter and sometimes fail? Of course. And some days it's easier to pray than on others. But the more I discipline myself to stay in tune with God, the quicker I get back up when I get knocked down.

## Have a Supply Kit Ready

The American Red Cross suggests that you have a "disaster supplies kit" ready in your "safe room," or shelter area. The kit should contain such items as a first aid kit, a battery powered radio, flashlight, and extra batteries, canned and other non-perishable foods (and a hand-operated can opener), bottled water, candles and matches, and shoes and work gloves.

We should have a supply kit ready for the storms of life as well. What should it include? The Word of God, of course. In distress, that's usually the first place I turn. I find solace in the Book of Psalms during times of stress and strain. The Book of Psalms is comforting because David, who wrote most of the Psalms, went through so many storms in the roller coaster ride that was so characteristic of his life. Think of the close escapes he had. "O Lord, I have come to you for protection," he wrote in Psalm 31:1. "Be my rock of protection, a fortress where I will be safe," he continued in verse 2. And sometimes it seemed to David that God was absent. "O Lord, how long will you forget me, Forever? How long will you look the other way?" he cried in Psalm 13:1. But David trusted God in the midst of the storm and even sang in it: "I will sing to the Lord because he is good to me" (Psalm 13:5-6). As he acknowledged God's goodness to him, David proclaimed, "I will sing." He didn't say, "I might sing if I feel like it." It wasn't, "I will sing if God orders all life events to my liking." David simply said, "I will sing." It takes faith and courage to say, "Even though it seems like God has forgotten me, even though times are excruciatingly harsh, yet I *will* sing; God is good to me." As I read the Psalms, I find God's servants walking tall in the midst of trials and tribulations.

When we have the Word on our heart, it affects our attitude during the storm. The truth that directs us through life storms and the comfort we receive from the Word of God become almost like a second nature to us. Over a period of time, we find ourselves navigating through the storm with a new confidence, almost as if we had been through the storm before.

One other essential item you need to include in your emergency supply kit: the name and number of someone you can talk to. You probably don't need to write down their number; I'm sure you already have it, if it's a friend's. I hope you have someone you can bear your soul to as you face the trials of your life.

And even if you can't reach your friend the moment the storm strikes, you can always know Jesus our Lord is there. What a friend we have in him!

After the oncologist at Ochner's Clinic gave me the sobering news about the seriousness of Katri's cancer, the doctors decided to perform a surgical procedure called an oophorectomy. During that time, I was alone; only the two of us---Katri and me---had made the trip to the clinic. I prayed, read my Bible, and prayed some more.

But I needed a friend. I recall trying to reach a friend. I called several times, but he didn't answer. (I later learned he was in a meeting.) Then I tried another friend and only got a busy signal. I called him several more times, but got the same response. I finally gave up and walked around the parking lot of the hospital. I simply rested in God. I asked the Holy Spirit to heal my wife but also to comfort me. Somehow in that lonely moment I sensed the presence of God. I was alone, but no longer lonely. I was encouraged and knew that somehow everything would work out because God was in control. I had no supernatural revelation; only the awareness of God's loving presence. The passage that came to my mind was one I had committed to memory, Psalm 34:18: "The Lord is close to the brokenhearted; he rescues those whose spirits are crushed."

In your most hopeless situation he will give you hope; when you are weakest, he will strengthen you; and when you think you can no longer continue in the storm, he will lift you up and carry you through it until you are safely home. In his arms is the safest place you can be.

So, it's essential that you have a safe place, a safe room, during the storm. As you endure the storm, it's very important to know what is happening. For that, you need to stay tuned to a reliable source. We'll explore how you can do that in the next chapter.

*"Jesus looked up to heaven and said, 'Father, the hour has come.'"*

—John 17:1

*"Mayday! Mayday! Mayday! This is the Hannah Boden relaying a mayday for the Andrea Gail."*[59]

—From the film, *The Perfect Storm*

---

[59] www.imdb.com/title/tt0177971/quotes

## Chapter Four
## Know When to Call for Help

THE MOVIE, *THE PERFECT STORM*, WAS AN ADAPTATION of the non-fiction book by the same title. It was about a swordfishing boat, the Andrea Gail, which in October of 1991 got caught in what was called, "The Perfect Storm." At one point in the film, the crew debated about whether to sail through the storm or wait it out. Instead of calling for help, they risk it and attempt to sail through the storm. After the ship loses its antenna, it's too late to call for help. Another ship sends out a mayday call, but by then, the storm is too powerful and a rescue attempt fails. Everyone on board the Andrea Gail perished. It's a sad story. The wife of the Andrea Gail's youngest crew member grieves his death, "I'll be asleep, and all the sudden there he is, that big smile...And I say, 'Hey, Bobby - where you been?' but he won't tell me. He just smiles and says, 'Remember, Christina: I'll always love you; I loved you the moment I saw you; I love you now; and I love you forever."[60]

If you are in a severe storm, your survival may depend on knowing when to call for help. Our problem is that we *think* we can make it through the storm on our own strength or abilities. We overestimate our own power and underestimate the strength

---

[60] Ibid.

of the storm. When Jesus was sharing the Last Supper with his disciples, he warned them of the fierceness of the approaching storm. And Simon Peter boasted, "Lord, I am ready to go to prison with you, and even to die with you" (Luke 22:33). But before it was over, Simon sank beneath the waves of the storm.

Jesus, on the other hand, was ready, even though he would pray if there were a way for the Father to take away the cup of suffering that he would do it. (Luke 22:42) But Jesus knew the time had come. It was his hour.

And in the Upper Room, before he reached the Garden of Gethsemane, he prayed, having looked to heaven, "Father, the hour has come."

This was not the first time Jesus had referred to "the hour." It seems to denote the culmination toward which his ministry was always headed. Like a laser beam tracking its target, Jesus' attention, his focus was directed toward this "hour." In John 2:4, when Jesus' mother informed him that the wine had run out at the wedding feast in Cana, he told her his "hour" had not yet come. And when his unbelieving brothers tried to goad him into going to Jerusalem openly and declaring who he was, Jesus was firm and unapologetic: his time had not yet come. And later, when Jesus did go to Jerusalem and the authorities tried to have him arrested, he eluded them because "his hour had not yet come" (John 7:30). When he began teaching in the temple, none of the authorities laid hands on him because "his hour had not yet come" (John 8:20).

Then in John 12 we read of some Greeks who had come to Jerusalem for the Passover celebration. They were probably converts to Judaism, but the fact remains that they were Greeks.

Though Philip was a Jew, he had a Greek name, so these Greeks went to him and asked to see Jesus. When Jesus heard about it, he said, "Now the time has come for the Son of Man to enter his glory" (v.23). These Greeks represented the first fruits of a vast number of Gentiles who would come to Jesus. And in this context Jesus explained why he must suffer and die, and he declared that he would be "lifted up from the earth," and would "draw everyone," to himself. (v.30). In the Upper Room, Jesus would tell his disciples again that his hour had come, and when he began the High Priestly prayer, he said, "The hour has come."

It was his hour, and he knew it. The time had come. I think of that line in *The Passion of Christ* where John rushes in and in a panic informs Jesus' mother, "They've seized him!" It was Jesus' hour. And Jesus was ready. He had prayed himself into it. He was prepared for "his hour."

We are to pray, as Paul said, "without ceasing" (I Thessalonians 5:17), but we face those times when the hour has come for us, when the storm is upon us or we are already in it, when we are up against superior forces, and we must pray fervently, earnestly, passionately.

**When you are about to enter the storm, it's time to call for help.**

Jesus could pray at his hour with such intensity because he had prayed at other times with consistency. Think about that. A weight lifter doesn't suddenly bench press 500 pounds. A runner doesn't run a sub-four minute mile the first time on the track. Athletes build up to these feats. We learn to pray with confidence in the hour of tribulation when praying isn't something new to us. We've prayed at other times as well.

So it was with Jesus; His was a life of prayer, in perfect harmony with the Father.

Jesus prayed when he blessed the loaves of bread just before he multiplied them. He prayed when he was transfigured on the mountain, "As he was praying, the appearance of his face was transformed, and his clothes became dazzling white" (Luke 9:29). Jesus prayed before he healed a boy who was deaf. He prayed when he raised Lazarus. He prayed before he heard Peter's confession of faith. We get the impression that Jesus prayed often and frequently. In Luke 11:1, it's as if Jesus just happened to be praying, as a normal pattern of his life: "One day Jesus was in a certain place praying. As he finished one of his disciples came to him and said, 'Lord, teach us to pray.'" Jesus prayed so frequently that it led the disciples to desire that kind of lifestyle.

Now, in the Upper Room, Jesus is praying. "The hour has come." Everything had come down to this hour. All that Jesus had done was pointing to this hour. The cross loomed before him. The hour has arrived. He doesn't panic; he is calm. He now prays knowing the storm is about to hit.

I remember that unforgettable scene in the film, *Saving Private Ryan,* when the soldiers are about to hit Omaha Beach. They are still protected in the boats, but in a matter of seconds they will face the horrific onslaught of enemy fire. The driver of one boat shouts, "Clear the ramp, 30 seconds, God be with you." One soldier makes the sign of the cross, another kisses his crucifix. It was the hour.

It was Jesus' hour. This man, who is the very Son of God, prayed that in the time of suffering, God would be glorified. In this day of trouble, he wants his Father to be glorified. In the time of tribulation we reveal who we are, and here Jesus reveals

*Surviving the Storms of Life*

who he is, what's on his heart, and where he is going. And Jesus, we will find, prays for you and me. We are on his heart. He came to save us. He is the Savior of the world. We find all this in John 17.

When your hour comes, pray. And your hour will come. It will come perhaps several times, as it did for E.M. Bounds. For over a hundred years, the books of E.M. Bounds have challenged, encouraged, and taught Christians to pray. Bounds believed in prayer. He was convinced in the power and effectiveness of prayer. "The prayers of God's saints are the capital stock in heaven by which Christ carries on His great work upon the earth...The earth is changed, revolutionized; angels move on more powerful, more rapid wings; and God's policy is shaped when the prayers of His people are more numerous and more efficient," he wrote. [61]

For Bounds, prayer was essential. A sensitive pastor, Bounds experienced more than his fair portion of tragedy in life. He was a Methodist minister and a tremendous prayer warrior. He spent the last seventeen years of his life, from the age of 58 until his death at age 77, reading, writing, and praying. His regular routine for the day was to pray from 4 a.m. to 7 a.m., before he would begin his work of writing. Through the day he would not only write but intercede in prayer for others and study the Scriptures. He so diligently practiced what he preached that he was able to distill for us the essence of what prayer is all about. "Prayer is the language of a man burdened with a sense of

---

[61] E. M. Bounds, *E.M. Bounds on Prayer* (Whitaker House: New Kensington, PA., 1997), p., 11

need," he wrote.[62] Through his books, classics of the subject of prayer, his influence lives on as he still inspires us to live a life of prayer.

What led Bounds to be such life of intense prayer? Read his statement again: "Prayer is the language of a man burdened with a sense of need." Bounds was burdened with a sense of need because of life's storms.

Bounds was born in 1835 in Missouri. He was a bright young man and at the age of 18 passed the bar exam, earning his license as a Missouri lawyer. He, at that young age, began a thriving law practice. He impressed people with his sharp mind and excellent communication skills. He was a Christian, but in 1859 he experienced a spiritual renewal, recommitted his life to Christ, left his growing law practice, and entered the Christian ministry as a full-time pastor.

Then the trouble began in his life. Isn't it interesting how trouble so often begins when we get serious about following Christ? Bounds had just begun pastoring and was enjoying his new ministry when President Lincoln deployed troops to Missouri to prevent that state from seceding from the Union. Bounds happened to serve in the Methodist Episcopal Church, South, which was pro-South, pro-secession. Because he opposed the Union's confiscation of church property, he was branded a traitor and imprisoned, even though he never pledged allegiance to the South. For a year-and-a half he ministered to his fellow prisoners. There he witnessed what hatred can do to a person, but in the midst of it he shared Christian love and compassion.

---

[62] E.M. Bounds, *E.M. Bounds on Prayer*, p. 589.

He was finally released as part of a prisoner exchange but forced to leave his home state of Missouri. When he tried to pledge allegiance to the Union, he was denied that privilege. So, he began to serve as a Chaplain in the Confederacy.

Then he was captured in the Battle of Franklin, TN, and imprisoned again. This time he was able to pledge his loyalty to the Union in exchange for his freedom. He immediately went back and helped bury soldiers who had died in the very battle where he was captured.

After the tragedy he experienced in the war, Bounds served in war-torn Alabama. He then married and moved to serve an affluent church in St. Louis, Mo. But his humble, simple lifestyle led to a clash with the wealthy members of that church, and he left.

He was without work and had a young family to support, which now included three young children. Then, his wife died. Not long afterwards his son, Edward, died at the age of six. Then another son died the next year.

Bounds felt called to be an evangelist. But his denomination abolished that office of ministry. He struggled but eventually found his ministry in writing, and in time he was able to lead a life of writing and praying, and we benefit today from his ministry through his many books.

But it took tragedy for him to experience triumph. Jesus is our triumphant Lord. And it took the cross for us to enjoy his triumph. So often it is that the greatest prayers have met with suffering and sadness in life. It wasn't until the age of 57, that Bounds found his ministry in writing and began to do what would distinguish him in his ministry for Christ. Frequently it is in the school of tragedy that we learn to pray. But those very prayers are what God uses to turn tragedy into triumph.

In one of his books, Bounds said this, "Wise is he in the day of trouble who knows his true source of strength and who fails not to pray."[63] He went on to say that prayer recognizes God's hand in the day of trouble and prays about it. The day of trouble "shows our helplessness," he said. "It brings the strong man low, it discloses our weakness...Blessed is he who knows how to turn to God in the time of trouble."[64] He knew times of trouble, and he prayed through his hour.

When should we pray?

**When we are faced with trouble, we pray.**

Jesus is our supreme example. In John 17 he is entering the greatest day of trouble anyone on the face of the earth had or would ever encounter. And he warns us that we should expect tribulation in this life. It belongs to this world; we cannot escape it. But remember his word of encouragement: "Take heart, because I have overcome the world" (John 16:33).

We do not carry the burden of the cross as Jesus did, but we face "the hour." Just when you think you've got it together, you find it torn apart. The baby you dreamed of having dies in infancy; the child you love—the very apple of your eye, turns from you and everything you stand for; your "ex" uses your child as a pawn to get even in the tit-for-tat messiness of a divorce; the dream house turns out to be a money pit; the person

---

[63] E.M. Bounds, .E.M. Bounds on Prayer, p. 312.
[64] Ibid, p. 316.

you trusted turns out to be a liar; the job you were so glad to get turns sour and then vanishes.

"Life comes at you pretty fast," in the words of Ferris Bueller, "and if you're not careful, you'll miss it." But many times we just want to duck life; just keep from getting hurt, forget about taking it all in.

But remember, Jesus, who in this "hour" prays, also told us to live life to the abundance. (John 10:10). Live it for all it's worth. Yes, we slog through the muck and mire but Jesus assures us we will come through it, our faces mud-spattered perhaps, but we come through it. He is, we learn in this prayer, praying us through the storm. He has overcome the world. He is victorious. And so are we, when we are in him.

### Pray, knowing that God is in control

When Jesus looked to the heavens and prayed, "The hour has come," he wasn't informing the Father of new information, as if the Father didn't know what was happening in the life of the Son. Jesus was acknowledging what the Father already knew, even as Jesus asked the Father to glorify the Son so he can give glory back to the Father. (John 17:1). The whole concept of "the hour" connotes a plan and that has a direction towards a culmination. When that hour comes, remember God still has a purpose, a plan. The trials are intended to be used by God to shape us into the very image of Christ himself. Romans 8:29 says, "God knew his people in advance, and he chose them to become like his Son." "The hour" is used by God to shape us into what God wants us to be. God is not the author of evil. God does not tempt us to evil. But God, because he is in control, turns it around for the believer, so that, as Joseph said to his brothers who had sold him into slavery, "You intended to harm me, but God intended it all for good" (Genesis 50:20).

Sometimes we wonder, "What did I do to deserve this?" We say, "Why would God allow this trouble?"

I'm reminded of the story of the daughter who tells her mother how everything is going wrong. She's failing algebra, her boyfriend broke up with her, and her best friend is moving away.

As the daughter is telling her mother all her woes, the mother is baking a cake. As she is preparing it, she asks her daughter if she would like some of the cake. "Oh yeah," the daughter says. "I love your cake."

"Here, have some cooking oil," the mother says.

"Yuck!" the daughter jerks away from the oil.

"How about a couple of these raw eggs?" Mom asks.

"Gross!" the daughter scrunches up her face.

"Well, take some of this flour or at least the baking soda."

"Mom, what's gotten into you? I can't eat that stuff!"

The mother responds, "All those things seem bad by themselves. But when they're put together in the right way, they make a delicious cake! God works something like that," the mother explained. "Many times we wonder why certain things happen. It seems meaningless and, as you say, 'Yuck.' We just have to trust him and eventually, he makes something beautiful of it all."

When "the hour" comes, remember, God is in control. The great Bible expositor Martyn Lloyd-Jones, reminds us that Jesus prayed out loud. How else would the disciples have heard?

*Surviving the Storms of Life*

The prayer was to God the Father, but Jesus meant for the disciples to hear it. This prayer is our Lord's Prayer, entrusting the disciples into the care of the Father.⁶⁵ He is praying them, as he is us, through the storms of life.

When "the hour" comes, pray. But pray knowing that Jesus our Lord has already prayed for you. It may seem chaotic, but God is in control. The Lord came to the end of his earthly life and he wants to make sure that the disciples knew that they are secure in the hands of the Father. Christ has handed us over to Him.

John wrote about this assurance in I John 5:13: "These things have I written unto you that believe on the name of the Son of God that you may know that you have eternal life." The "hour" you face cannot take your eternal life in Jesus Christ away. It's safe and secure. The Apostle Paul said it another way in Romans 8. "I am convinced that nothing can ever separate us from God's love. Neither death nor life, neither angels nor demons, neither our fears for today nor our worries about tomorrow---not even the powers of hell can separate us from God's love." Why can John and Paul make these statements? Because they are utterly convinced that God is in control.

I can't help but think of the words of that song that was so popular in 1995. Twila Paris sang "God is in Control." Do you remember these words?

"This is no time for fear/This a time for faith and determination." And the chorus began with the words, "There is

---

[65] Martyn Lloyd-Jones, *The Assurance of Our Salvation, Exploring the Depth of Jesus' Prayer for His Own* (Wheaton, Illinois, 2000) p., 175

one thing that has always been true/It holds the world together/God is in control.⁶⁶

Twila went on to sing that "culture can make its plan" and "deception may fly" but in the midst of it all, "God is in control."

As Jesus prayed, he wanted the disciples to hear so they would remember not to lose the vision but to pray with confidence because they (and we) are secure. God is in control.

**In the midst of your storm, God cares about you**

We are confident that God is in control, but we also know that he cares. God cares. Read through this prayer in John 17 and you read the prayer of our Lord to the Father who cares. He doesn't pray to a cold, unreliable, austere God who is too antiseptic to get involved with us. God cares. We sometimes think that Jesus the Son of God cares but not God the Father. Our Father in heaven is tender hearted and compassionate. He cares about you and me.

Often the Lord God had to remind the Israelites that he is a God who cares. "It was I, the Lord your God, who rescued you from the land of Egypt. Open your mouth wide and I will fill it with good things" (Psalm 81:10). "How precious are your thoughts about me, O God. They cannot be numbered" (Psalm 139:17). And we read the words of the Psalmist in Psalm 31:7: "You have seen my troubles, and you cared about the anguish of my soul."

---

[66] http://lyricsandsongs.com/song/479893.html

Years ago R. I. Williams called the newspaper in Norfolk, Virginia to tell them his sermon title. "The Lord is my Shepherd."

"Is that all?" the secretary asked.

"That's enough," he said.

And the church page of that newspaper stated it just like that: "The Lord is my Shepherd---That's Enough."

Williams liked it so much that he changed the direction of his sermon to fit that title and preached about it being enough that our Lord is our shepherd.[67] He is a shepherd who cares.

After my eight year old brother was tragically killed in a car accident, my mother was reluctant to let me, six years old at the time, out of her sight. I was already the youngest of four boys. But after Dougie died, there was a bigger age gap between me and my next closest brother, Mark. That would be ten years difference instead of 18 months, as it had been with Doug. So Mom watched me ever so closely. Oh, I still played and had all kinds of fun as a kid, but she always seemed to know right where I was.

That's why it was so unusual that I would be apart from her at John A. Brown Department Store in Oklahoma City, Oklahoma. Mom was in "the city" as we called it, and was doing some shopping at John A. Brown. It was downtown. These were pre-mall days. I distinctly remember that desperate feeling of realizing I had wandered away from Mom. I looked around, and all I saw was strangers. Where was she? I saw a lady whose back was turned to me. I thought she was Mom. So I tugged on her

---

[67] Paul Lee Tan, ed., *Encyclopedia of 7700 Illustrations: Signs of the Times* (Rockville, Maryland: Assurance Publishers, 1979), p. 498.

skirt and said, "Mom." The lady turned around and of course she wasn't Mom. A few minutes seemed like an eternity to a boy who thought he was lost. It didn't occur to me to ask a department store clerk. I just stood there, looking. Within just a few minutes, Mom rushed into my presence. "David! Where have you been? How did you get over here?" I don't recall what I said; I was content to have been found.

It's good to have been found. We know someone cares enough to look. The Psalmist concluded Psalm 119 by making this appeal to God: "I have wandered away like a lost sheep; come and find me, for I have not forgotten your commands." (v.176) He is a God who cares. Psalm 107 recounts God's mercy toward his people. When some were in danger in the storm of the sea, when "their ships were tossed to the heavens and plunged again to the depths," they cried for help, and God, "calmed the storm to a whisper and stilled the waves" (v. 29).

But it's that space between the raging of the sea and the calming of the storm that frustrates us and fills our hearts with fear and doubt. And that's when we must trust God and as the Psalmist put it, "see in our history the faithful love of the Lord" (Psalm 107:43).

The Scriptures also remind us that God has precious thoughts for us that are so numerous they cannot be counted (Psalm 139:18), that he keeps track of all our sorrows, and even knows the tears we shed (Psalm 56:8), and that we need not worry because if God provides for the grass of the field and birds of the air, he will certainly take care of us. (Matthew 7:30)

God's care certainly extends to the darkest of days and most violent of storms.

## A benefit of the storm?

One of the unforeseen benefits of being in "the hour," is the sense of desperateness for God it can create in us. David certainly knew that. We can sense his desperation in the Psalms. In Psalm 63 he wrote of searching for God and longing for him, "My soul thirsts for you, my whole body longs for you in this parched and weary land where there is no water" (Psalm 63:1). Perhaps David wrote this Psalm when he was in the wilderness during Absalom's rebellion. David is praying earnestly for God's help in a time of trouble.

In the introduction of his commentary on this Psalm, James Montgomery Boice notes that there are three types of people in any Christian gathering. There are those who are Christians in name only. "They seem to be following after God and Jesus Christ and say they are, but theirs is a false following." The second class are those who are following Jesus but are following "at a distance," like Peter at the time of Jesus' arrest. Then Boice point to the third group. Quoting Murdoch Campbell, Boice says these are the ones who '"in storm and sunshine, cleave to him and enjoy daily communion with him.'" These are the ones, Boice says, who "want God, and...want him intensely, because they know that he and he alone will satisfy the deep longing of their souls."[68]

In our times of desperation, cling to God. When you've had the presence of God, you know how frustrating it is not to have that sweet communion. Circumstances take us away; our own pride takes us away; our distractions take us away. And

---

[68] James Montgomery Boice, *Psalms*, vol.2, 42-106 (Grand Rapids, Michigan: Baker Books, 1996), p.516.

when God seems to be away, despite our efforts to find his presence, we become desperate.

What if you're in one of Boice's first two categories? How can you cultivate a spirit of desperateness for God? It sounds too simple, but here it is; discipline yourself to communicate with God. If you won't carve out the time for God, don't expect to know God. It takes action; it means saying "no" to some things so you can say, "yes," to other things. Here's what's interesting: when you do want God wants, when you spend time in his presence, he changes the desires of your heart so that what he wants becomes what you want. "Take delight in the Lord, and he will give you your heart's desires" (Psalm 37:4).

You and I know what our trouble is. We feed on spiritual fast food and think we will have healthy spiritual lives, strong and able to withstand the desert winds. We are, of course, wrong. A quick drive-through on Sunday morning won't make up for an imbalanced spiritual diet. Then, we get so very busy that we forget to eat altogether. We starve ourselves by filling our spiritual nature with cheap substitutes. But we fail when we substitute for God. H.G. Wells said that every person has a "God-shaped vacuum in his heart---a void only God can fill." And St. Augustine said it like this, "My soul is restless until it finds it rests in Thee."

Sometimes it doesn't seem possible, but the God who promised he would be there will show up. David cried out; God brought him through it. It wasn't on David's time-table perhaps, but God made good on his promises, and he will for you too. When you desperately seek him, you will find him. That's the promise of our God. And when you get desperate, all that matters is him.

In our desperation we seek God and in finding him discover he was always there.

God wants to see our heart. He wants our heart to seek him. He desires our affection, our love. It is only as we become desperate that we truly discover that he was always there for us. It is as we respond to the call that we realize he had been speaking all the while.

But, we must get to that point where he is all in all; where he is the one we desire the most, more than any relationship or any living thing. When we settle for anything less, our prayer life becomes shallow, and we try to fill in the words with an occasional "fill-up" at God's house. In between we are searching and starving for something real, something that lasts more than a few brief moments. But it is going to take some discipline on our part.

How do you describe that intensity, that desperateness? Jesus talked about it. He described what it is for us to seek him and his kingdom. The Kingdom of heaven is like a treasure that a man discovered hidden in a field. In his excitement, he hid it again and sold everything he owned to get enough money to buy the field---and to get the treasure, too! Again, the Kingdom of Heaven is like a pearl merchant on the lookout for choice pearls. When he discovered a pearl of great value, he sold everything he owned and bought it! (Matthew 13:44-46). Again, there is a price for those who are truly desperate. But there is also a benefit: the Kingdom of God, the joy of Jesus in our lives, the glory of God.

He truly wants the best for us. The dark clouds and lightning of the storm make it seem like he is not there and that there is no need to call on him. We hang on to what we have, forgetting that he will not only rescue us but will bring us the best, too.

I love the story about the little five year-old girl. She's at the check-out counter at store. She sees some pearls in a little plastic box. "Mommy, can I have them? Please? Please?"

The mother looks at the back of the box. $3.95. "If you really want them, I've got some extra chores you can do."

So, after supper that night, she clears the table. Then she helped Mom load the dish washer. "Is that enough Mom?" she asks.

"Not yet," Mom says. "I've got a few more things."

She helped Mom fold some clothes. Actually, Mom had to redo most of them, but the little girl tried. Then, she swept the kitchen floor. "I suppose that will do it."

Little Jenny loved her pearls. They made her feel so dressed up and grown up. She wore them to church, to school, even to bed.

Jenny had a very kind and loving daddy. Every night he would sit on the edge of her bed, usually read her a bedtime story, and pray. One night, after prayers, Daddy asked, "Jenny do you love me?"

"Oh, yes, Daddy, I love you."

"Then give me your pearls."

"Oh, Daddy, not my pearls. I just got them. Maybe after I've had them longer you can have them."

"That's okay." Daddy said. "I love you. Good night."

About a week later, after prayers, Daddy asked again, "Do you love me?"

"Of course I love you."

"Then give me those pearls."

"Oh Daddy, not my pearls. But Daddy, you can have my baby doll, the one I got for my birthday."

"That's okay." Daddy said. "I love you."

A few nights later, when Daddy came in for prayers, Jenny was sitting on the edge of her bed, with her legs crossed, Indian style. As Daddy got closer, he noticed her eyes were red. She had been crying. There were tear stains on her cheeks.

"What's the matter?" Daddy asked.

Jenny didn't say a thing. She only lifted her little hand up to her daddy. And when she opened it, there was her little pearl necklace. With a little quiver, she finally said, "Here, Daddy. It's for you."

With tears welling up in his own eyes, Jenny's loving and compassionate daddy reached out with one hand and took the fake, dime-store, pearl necklace, and with the other hand reached into his pocket, and pulled out a blue velvet case with a strand of genuine pearls and gave them to Jenny. He had had them all the time. He was just waiting for her to give up cheap ones, so he could give her the genuine pearls, the true treasure.

So it is with us. We hang on to the cheap stuff that tarnishes and fades with time. It's only as we get desperate, it's only as the hour comes, when we look with empty hands to the heavenly Father, giving all to him, it's in that moment of desperation that we receive the real thing, the genuine treasure, the kingdom of God itself in Jesus Christ. It's then that we realize it was there all along.

If only we would call on him for help.

*"And this is the way to eternal life---to know you, the only true God, and Jesus Christ, the one you sent to earth."*

—John 17:3

*"I'm very angry, because I feel they didn't do their job like they supposed to. My man would still be living if they'da did they job like they was supposed to . . . They took somebody that I love away."*

—Sharon Edge[69]

---

[69] Dan Nephin, "Pa. man dies during storm when 911 calls unheeded," http://news.yahoo.com/s/ap/2010/0228/ap_on_re_us/us_snow911_death

## Chapter Five
## Stay Tuned to a Reliable Source

IN THE EARLY MORNING HOURS OF February 6, 2010, Sharon Edge made a 911 call to the Pittsburgh, Pennsylvania EMS. A storm had dumped nearly two feet of snow on the city, and Sharon's boyfriend was having severe abdominal pain. Because of the storm, the 911 system was overwhelmed with twice its normal amount of calls. But that was no excuse for what *didn't* happen.

It took nearly 30 hours and 10 calls from the couple to 911 before paramedics arrived. By then it was too late. Sharon's boyfriend, Curtis Mitchell was dead. Apparently the couple's calls weren't passed on to each 911 operator at the beginning of each shift, so each time the couple called, it was treated as a new one. In all, three ambulances were dispatched at separate times, but in each case, Mitchell was told he'd have to walk to them, and because of his physical condition, he canceled the calls. When paramedics finally walked to Mitchell's residence, he was dead. "We failed this person," said Michael Huss, Pittsburgh's public safety director.[70]

Here is a situation where someone knew when to call for help. But what they thought was a reliable source wasn't. It was

---

[70] Ibid.

a tragic breakdown in the EMS system and reminds us that not only must we know when to call for help in the midst of a storm, we must contact the right source, the one that can come to us and guide us through the storm.

And we have to *stay* in contact. Whether it's the danger of a hurricane or tornado, staying tuned to a reliable source of information during a storm is essential. "It's important to stay tuned to weather reports even if it seems a hurricane will make landfall somewhere else," said Michael Cline, state coordinator for the Virginia Department of Emergency Management.[71] The storm can still pose a powerful and destructive force. It's equally important to stay tuned during a tornado. Listening to a local radio or television station can keep you updated on whether it's a tornado watch or warning, the possible path of a tornado, and whether it's once again safe to emerge from shelter.

What about the storms of life? How do we know we are in touch with the right source, the one that can come to us and guide us? And how do we stay tuned with this reliable source during these life changing events? Just who or what is our reliable source?

## What's your image of God?

Your immediate response is, "God, of course," and that's certainly correct. We've already discussed praying to God. But, just who is the God to whom we pray? What's your image of God? Are you praying to a false image of God?

---

[71] www.spotsylvania.va.us/2614/147/2742/183/996.aspx

*Surviving the Storms of Life*

In his book, *The Papa Prayer*, Larry Crabb identifies ten common images he believes people have of God when they pray. These mental pictures of God include: (1) the Smiling Buddy, (2) the Backroom Watchmaker, (3) the Preoccupied King, (4) a Vending Machine, (5) the Stern Patriarch, (6) a Kindly Grandfather, (7) an Impersonal Force, (8) the Cruel Tyrant, (9) a Moral Crusader, and (10) a Romantic Lover.[72]

Maybe one of those fits your image of God, or more likely, you have a blend of several. Do you have an image of God when you pray?

Do you remember the story of *The Wizard of Oz*? A little farm girl from Kansas, Dorothy, and her dog, Toto, are blown away in a fierce tornado. Dorothy is struck on the head by a window frame and finds herself and her dog in the fairyland of Oz. There they meet the Scarecrow, the Tin Man, the cowardly Lion, and together they go on a quest to see the Wizard of Oz, each of those characters seeking what they want most. Through many hair-raising adventures they travel the Yellow Brick Road to the Emerald City. The Guardian of the city gates confronts them. When asked to state their business, Dorothy blurts, "We want to see the wizard!"

"The Wizard," the gatekeeper condescendingly says, "But nobody can see the great Oz, nobody's ever seen the great Oz…even I've never seen him!"

---

[72] Larry Crabb, *The Papa Prayer* (Brentwood, TN, Integrity Publishers, 2006), pp., 104-114.

And you've got to love what Dorothy says next. It's something we want but are perhaps afraid to ask about God. "Well, then," she demands, "how do you know there is one?'

Yes, indeed Dorothy, sometimes we feel the same about God: "How do we know there is one?" They do discover that Oz exists. But they are deeply disappointed. He is just a bumbling fraud---a likeable fraud, but a fraud nonetheless.

Is that the way it is?

No. We must come to the revelation God has given us of himself. I am not going to attempt to prove the existence of God. I could point to the reasons we maintain God exists. But this is not a book on apologetics. You may have doubted God; you may have been angry at him. You may have been disappointed in him. But by faith we believe God exists, just as by faith I believe my wife loves me, or the doorway I walk through will not collapse, or that the world will continue to spin. Ours is not blind faith; it's a reasoned faith, yet faith still.

To keep myself from having inaccurate images of God, I often visualize Jesus when I pray. After all, Hebrews 1:3, says that the Son, Jesus Christ, "is the radiance of His glory and the exact representation of His nature, and upholds all things by the word of His power. When He had made purification of sin, He sat down at the right hand of the Majesty on high." (NAS).

So there is Jesus my Lord, the exact representation of God the Father, seated at the Father's right hand, interceding for us and receiving our prayers. Why not visualize the Son?

In Revelation 1:10-18, John describes his vision of the risen Savior. His voice was like a "trumpet blast," (v.10), and as he appeared to be someone like, "the Son of Man" (v.12), which would seem to indicate that John recognized him not only as the mighty Son of Man but as the Jesus he knew in Galilee some 60 years before this vision on the Island of Patmos. Johns sees the Son of Man dressed in a long robe with a golden sash around his chest (v.13), his head and hair "white like wool, as white as snow" (v. 14), his eyes "like flames of fire," (v.14), his feet "like polished bronze refined in a furnace," (v.15), his voice thundering "like mighty ocean waves," (v.15), and his face shining "like the sun in all its brilliance" (v.16). In addition, John's vision of Jesus has him holding seven stars in his right hand and brandishing a two-edged sword in his mouth. (v. 16)

Seeing and hearing such a powerful revelation of Jesus drove John to his knees. In fact, he fell at Jesus feet as if dead. (v.17) When Jesus was with the disciples in the Upper Room the night he was betrayed, John laid his head on the Lord's chest. But now, the Apostle was driven to his knees.

In that moment, Jesus, the Son of Man, placed his right hand on John and said, "Don't be afraid" (v. 17). The Master's touch of assurance and words of comfort was all it took for John to be at peace in the presence of Jesus.

What does John's image of the risen Savior do for your concept of God? It should remind us of the necessary healthy balance between a fear of God on the one hand and a casualness that is indicative of a lack of respect on the other.

*The Chronicles of Narnia* is a series of seven novels written by C.S. Lewis. They are classics of children's literature and have sold over 100 million copies and have been translated in 41 languages. They've been adapted to radio, television, and the cinema. In this series Lewis writes about the adventures of children in a fictional land called Narnia. It's a place where animals talk, magic is part of life, and where good is battling evil.

One of the central characters in the books is a lion named Aslan. Aslan is a noble lion who is king of Narnia. Lewis presents Aslan as a Christ-figure in the Chronicles. Aslan is put to death in place of a traitor, and then Aslan is resurrected.

When the children first meet Aslan they are apprehensive, and with good reason. Aslan is powerful and can be dangerous. When they are about to be introduced to him, one of the children named Susan confides in Mrs. Beaver, "I'd thought he was a man," Susan says. "Is he---quite safe? I shall feel nervous about meeting a lion."

Mrs. Beaver tells Susan that she should be a bit nervous. "If there's anyone who can appear before Aslan without their knees knocking, they're either braver than most or else silly."

Then another child, hesitatingly questions, "Is he...safe?"

At that point Mr. Beaver says: "Safe? Don't you hear what Mrs. Beaver tells you? Of course he isn't' safe...but he's GOOD...He's the King."[73]

God wants us to know him. We can by the grace of our Lord and God Jesus Christ call him "Father." But we must approach him in the right manner. We must come to him through the Son, who is very God and very man, and who died that we might come to the throne of God's grace. He is good; he is the King of all kings.

---

[73] C.S. Lewis, *The Lion, the Witch and the Wardrobe* (New York, NY: HarperCollins Publishers, 1978), p. 86.

*Surviving the Storms of Life*

And he is our very reliable source of guidance and direction, capable of perfectly navigating us through the storms of our life. In fact, his words to John in his revelation were, "I am the living one. I died, but look---I am alive forever and ever! And I hold the keys of death and the grave" (v. 18).

Our future is in his hands; he holds the key to death and the grave, and has the power to instill us with confidence as we face the storm. Billy Graham said, "Whatever suffering and agony we must endure, either in our own body or for someone we love, we are assured of His presence. And ultimately we will be resurrected with a body free of pain, an incorruptible and immortal body like His. This is our future hope."[74]

So we can have confidence in God as our Reliable Source at all times, and he is there in the midst of the storm. He holds "the keys of death and the grave" (Revelation 1:18), and "he sustains everything by the mighty power of his command" (Hebrews 1:3). He is no bumbling fraud; he is the creator of the heavens and the earth, and the sustainer of all creation.

### He is a God who invites us into a relationship of love

God invites us into his presence; he yearns for us to know him. That's great news! Unlike the Wizard of Oz, or the gods of many other religions, our God invites us to know him. In fact, Jesus clearly states that the way to eternal life is to know God. "And this is the way to have eternal life---to know you, the

---

[74] Billy Graham, *Facing Death and the Life After* (Waco, TX: Word, Inc., 1987), 119, cited in David Jeremiah, *Escape the Coming Night* (Dallas, London, Vancouver, Melbourne: Word Publishing, 1990, 1997), p. 50.

only true God, and Jesus Christ, the one you sent to earth" (John 17:3).

But if we are to get to know this God, which is what he wants, we must approach him in the right way. In Exodus 19, God revealed himself at Mt. Sinai. He spoke to the people of Israel, "You know how I carried you on eagles' wings and brought you to myself. Now if you will obey me and keep my covenant, you will be my own special treasure from among all the peoples on earth." After Moses returned from the mountain, God told him to prepare the people. Why? God himself wanted to speak to them. The people were to follow strict instructions, which included a three day regimen of keeping their distance from the mountain, washing their clothes, and abstaining from sexual intercourse. After the Ten Commandments were given, there was a display of God's power, flashes of lightening, smoke rising from the mountain, and the loud sound of a ram's horn. The people in fear told Moses in Exodus 20:19, "You speak directly to us, and we will listen. But don't let God speak directly, or we will die!"

To me this is one of the saddest verses of Scripture in the word of God. It wasn't God's idea to speak through another, a mediator. God would have spoken directly to the people. But in fear they didn't want that. They were content to let someone else speak to God and then get the word from that person. In this case, of course, that's Moses.

Does this describe you? Do you let someone else experience God for you? Are you afraid to know God yourself? "Well," you say, "isn't that what the preacher is for? Our Pastor gets to know God, and then tells us what we need to know."

Getting to know God is not something someone else can do for you. It may work for a test where you can get the Cliff Notes version to a book and not actually read the book. But that doesn't work when it comes to relationships with family, friends, or God.

I love the story of the neglectful husband who takes his wife to the doctor. Now, this guy is a real "bubba" who doesn't take time for his wife. But he is concerned because she just doesn't seem to have energy for him. She is tired, run down, lacks color in her face, and frequently complains of having no zest for living. She barely has strength to shuffle into the doctor's office. Her husband is with her as they await the test results. The doctor walks in, sits down, and looks her face to face. He takes plenty of time to visit with her. He really pays attention to her. He tells her among other things that the test results showed nothing. But then he continues to talk and listen to her. Then he listens to her some more. All of a sudden he kisses her passionately. I mean he really lays one on her. For the first time in months she smiles, her color returns, she comes to life. Then the doctor turns to the husband and says, "That's all she needs."

The husband shakes his head, looks at the doctor, and says, "I don't get it, but if that's all it takes, I'll bring her in once a week!"

Getting to know God is not something you can have someone else do for you once a week. Jesus said, "Father." Jesus was in relationship with his Father.

This can be frightening to us, just as it was with the Israelites. We make ourselves vulnerable to God. I heard about a church that had these words carved in wood over the front entrance of the sanctuary: "Enter at your own risk."

Whenever we enter the presence of God we make ourselves vulnerable to the possibility that we might experience transformation. And that can be frightening. But if we believe prayer changes things, then we must also believe change might begin with us. After all, like Lewis' Aslan, our God is not tame. He is God. And he is supremely good and perfect love and infinitely merciful.

And he invites us in.

Jesus told a parable about a man who sent a very important invitation. The story, in Matthew 22, is about a king who sent out a notice to all who had been invited to his son's wedding feast. He sent three invitations, to be exact. The first invitation, as was customary in that culture, was to ask the guests to attend. The second was to announce that the banquet was ready. Not only did they ignore the invitation to come, they insulted, beat, and even killed some of the messengers. No one would accept the invitation. So the king sent out other messengers to anyone, good or bad, who would come to the banquet. And the hall was filled with people, all kinds of people, "good and bad alike" (v.10). But even then, someone showed up with improper clothes, and they threw him out. It's a story in part about the kind of God our God is. He is a God who wants to have a relationship with us. He loves us. But when we reject him, he becomes our adversary. He loves us the same, but he appears to us in his justice. That's because, although he loves us in our sin, he does not approve of our sin. Yet, the invitation is there.

The king in the story represents God. The son is Jesus Christ. The messengers are the prophets. God first invited his chosen nation, Israel. When they refused, God opened the invitation to the rest of us. But if we respond, we must show up wearing the proper clothing: the righteous robe of Jesus Christ, which we receive when we take Jesus as our Lord and Savior. God loves us so much he sends us an invitation to a banquet, and he even provides the proper clothing. We just have to be humble enough to receive the robe. It was customary for a host to provide the outer clothing for the guest. The man who was thrown out in the parable was too proud to wear what the host had for him. He showed up with his own.

We can show up with our own plan. We can do things our way. We don't have to receive what our heavenly Father wants to give us; we can work it out on our own.

But heaven is God's party. If we want in, we must humble ourselves and enter on his terms.

In the Old Testament, in Hosea 6, we read about this same God inviting us in. God has sent the invitation to the people of Israel. They have rejected God. And God chastises his people. He does this to get their attention, so they will come to him. In verses 1-3 of Hosea 6 we have a prophetic picture of Israel's repentance and restoration. They look to home for healing and new life.

I think we can see in both of these biblical stories that when we pray, we are praying to a God who invites us in. He sent the invitation. And furthermore, this God will use the trouble in our life to get us to trust him, to receive his invitation. And we must come on his terms not ours.

## God is waiting for you to come to him

Though God is infinitely complex, above our total comprehension, the terms for coming into his presence are quite simple. It begins as we admit that we need God, that there is a God, and *we* are *not* God. Most of the people in the parable of the King's party thought they were so righteous that they could ignore the invitation; they didn't need God.

God says in Hosea 6:6: "I want you to show love, not offer sacrifices. I want you to know me more than I want burnt offerings." Jesus quoted this very passage in Matthew 9:13 when the Pharisees were accusing him of hanging out with the wrong kind of people, "scum."

It was the love relationship that Jesus was after. And in the parable, the people who rejected the invitation did so in part because they didn't think it was necessary at the time.

Here's what you need to know about this God. He is much more concerned *that* you come to him than he is in how you look or appear when you come.

In the parable of the prodigal son in Luke 15, Jesus described the father like this, "Filled with love and compassion, he ran to his son, embraced him, and kissed him" (v.15). The father was waiting for the son. And when he saw his son, the father ran to welcome his boy. The father didn't say, "You can't come because you have been in a pig sty and you smell like it." Did you notice he put a robe on him? It's your heart God wants. He wants you to have a heart that wants to know him.

Tradition and ritual are fine. They can actually help us worship. But when we worship the tradition or are more concerned about the form of worship than the God to whom we are supposed to be worshipping, then something is wrong. Tradition and even ritual can carry important meanings to us. That can be a good thing. But, it is an avenue to help us worship. Whenever we worship the avenue rather than the one to whom the avenue takes us, we have missed what God wants.

William Willimon, former Dean of the Chapel at Duke University tells about how we very subtly, without realizing it, put ourselves before God in worship: "When asked, 'Why worship?' we are quick to point out all the valuable benefits of worshiping God. While few enlightened Christians admit to the crudity of expecting God to give them a Mercedes in appreciation for an hour in church, they nevertheless do expect 'inspiration' or, at a minimum, 'a warm feeling' on Sunday morning." Willimon's point is that we still make ourselves the focal point. "The focus is on **me**, my feelings, my thoughts, my commitments, my guilt, my needs. I am the center of worship, the focus of a carefully orchestrated series of Sunday morning activities that are designed to do something to or for **me**."[75] If Willimon is right, it is no wonder we miss God.

God wants you, your heart. When we focus on him rather than ourselves, we are moving into the heart of worship, because it truly is all about God and not ourselves.

---

[75] William H. Willimon, *The Bible: A Sustaining Presence in Worship* (Valley Forge: Judson Press, 1981), pp. 30-31.

## God is more concerned about your commitment to Christ than your conformity to laws

What the king in the parable wanted was for those to whom the invitation had been sent to honor his son by attending his wedding banquet. That's commitment to Christ. What God let the people know in Hosea's day was that it was not the keeping of law but the love of God that mattered most. Of course, if we love God and want to please him, we will want to abide by his laws. We will love the law because abiding by it pleases the Father. But conforming to it doesn't place us in a right relationship with God.

God is not as interested in your conformity to laws nearly as much as in your obedient heart. He wants you to commit yourself to the Son, Jesus Christ. That's the obedience he wants. Why? That's the condition for coming to his party. Remember Acts 4:12: "There is salvation in no one else! There is no other name in all of heaven for people to call on to save them."

We are not made worthy by the keeping of the law; we are made worthy by the grace of Jesus Christ. The man who was kicked out of the wedding feast wore his own clothing. That represented his works. He needed the righteousness of Christ and that comes by grace through our faith in Jesus Christ.

I laughed at the story of the little three year old girl. Her mother had been teaching her the traditional fairy tales. Her mind was taking it all in, all those fairy tales. Her two favorite stories were the stories of Goldilocks and the Three Little Pigs. One day her mother read to her Chapter 3:20 of the Book of Revelation. Jesus said, "Behold, I stand at the door and knock. If anyone will open the door, I will come in..." She then asked her daughter, "If Jesus is knocking at your heart's door, will you open the door and let him in?" Without a moment's hesitation, the little girl responded, "Not by the hair on my chinny-chin-chin."[76]

The most important thing you can do is receive Jesus Christ. This is not a fairy tale. Christ really did come. He really did live. He really did die. He really did rise from the dead. He really did ascend into heaven. He really is at the right hand of God the Father. He really will return. The question is, will he return for you? It all depends. Have you let him into your life? In letting him in, you get ready for the greatest banquet of eternity.

What's sad about Revelation 3:20 that it is addressed to the church. Can you imagine it? Jesus is knocking at the door of a church. You see, we can become so indifferent to Christ that he is unable to dwell in our hearts.

If we want Jesus to guide us through the storm we have to let him guide the ship. He has to be our only Reliable Source. We can't function as thought our relationship with him doesn't matter and expect to stay in tune with him. Donald Grey Barnhouse tells of a mother who drew her little two-year old close and tenderly whispers in the little child's ear, "I love you." The little girl draws away and aloofly says, "I know." Barnhouse says that is love that is taken for granted. It is much more tragic, Barnhouse points out, when God says from Calvary's Cross, "I

---

[76] Michael Hodgin, *1001 Humorous Illustrations*, ed., Michael Hodgin (Platteville, Co.: Saratoga Press, 1992), p. 215.

love you," and is answered with indifference. "Most of life's sadness flows from such an attitude."[77]

Life is not meant to be that way. Our God is a loving God who invites us in. You only have to say, "Yes."

Will you?

So, to whom do we pray? Just what kind of God is this God to whom we pray? He is a God who has come to us. He intervenes in our lives by coming to us. The cross of Christ is proof that God, although the God of justice, is also the God of mercy. You see both justice and mercy perfectly demonstrated at the cross. And that changes everything.

Theologian Alister McGrath has said, "Christianity is not just about the historical fact that Jesus was crucified; it is about the astonishing and thrilling truth that he died in order that we might be forgiven."[78] This is what Jesus is referring to when he says, "I brought glory to you here on earth by completing the work you gave me to do" (John 17:4). He is talking about the cross. From his time perspective---which is beyond mere time, our time---Christ's victory was an accomplished fact. It's just like he said in John 16:33, "I have overcome the world." He has already done it although we don't see it until Sunday after the crucifixion.

So, when we pray, we pray to a God who loves us enough to have a relationship with us that lasts forever. But the fact of our sin had to be addressed. We couldn't take care of that.

---

[77] Donald Grey Barnhouse, *Let Me Illustrate* (Grand Rapids, MI.: Fleming H. Revell, 1967), p., 217

[78] Alister McGrath, *"I Believe," Exploring the Apostles' Creed* (Downers Grove, Illinois: InterVarsity Press, 1997), p. 61.

That is the point of what the passage from Hosea 6:6 is saying. All of our sacrifices and human efforts to appease God fail and fall short. God wants our heart. And the only way to give it to him is by receiving his only begotten Son, Jesus Christ. You see, Christ came, and having died for us, leads us to the relationship with God the Father. The Son leads us to the Father. But the Son died as a sacrificial atonement for our sins. His coming to us would not have had an eternal meaning if he had not died for us.

Our God is a God, therefore, who not only invites us into a relationship, but intervened for us at the cross so we would still be left in our sins.

### Your response to God's love

When you pray to God, you are responding to a God who loves. He loves us through the storms of life. He came to us for that reason, for apart from him we are helplessly drowning in the most devastating storm of any life, the storm for your soul.

Christ has won the victory on the cross. Look again at John 17:4: "I brought glory to you on earth by completing the work you gave me to do." Jesus brought God glory. God's glory is the revelation of who he is, his essence. For a moment, Jesus revealed some of the fullness of that on the Mount of Transfiguration when he took Peter, James, and John up there. It was so glorious that Peter wanted to build three tabernacles, one for Jesus, one for Elijah, and one for Moses. "But as he was saying this, a cloud overshadowed them, and terror gripped them as the cloud covered them" (Luke 9:34). It was so awesome that they couldn't take it in; they were terrified. And this was just a portion of God's glory. By coming to us, in this act of intervention, Jesus is revealing to us who God is. If you want to know the kind of God you are praying to, look to the cross. There you see mercy and justice. The glory is hidden on the cross. But Jesus is bringing his Father glory by his obedience, even his death on the cross.

This God wants us to listen to him. If we want to stay in touch with our Reliable Source, God, we have to be still enough to hear him. David prayed, "My soul finds rest in God alone" (Psalm 62:1, NIV). And in that same Psalm he wrote, "Find rest, O my soul, in God alone" (Psalm 62:5, NIV).

Near the entrance of the Abby of Gethsemani these words from Psalm 62 are placed over a gate as a gentle reminder to everyone passes. It simply says, "IN GOD ALONE." It's saying, "Be still. Listen to the voice of God in this place." And that's what attracts me and many others to that place. We really do long for the voice of God.

When we pray, we are praying to a God who intervenes in the messiness of life. He is a God who cares enough to show up. He has shown up in Jesus Christ. Even though there are times, no doubt, when we experience the hiddeness of God, that "dark night of the soul" in which it appears to us that God has removed himself from our situation, he is there, behind the scenes maybe, but he is there.

And suddenly, like a parent who has been watching that child on the brink of danger, at just the right moment, he pounces upon the scene. Sometimes we are the only ones who are aware of his mighty presence. The eyes of the blind are unaware of his powerful reality. But it makes no difference to the faithful, for we are strengthened and comforted and made ready for the uphill climb or walk through the valley. And those who know him also know he will one day make his presence known with such an exclamation mark that even the God-deniers will have to admit that God is after all God.

He can guide you through your storm; he is the one source we absolutely must stay connected with in the midst of life's storms because he is not only "out there," giving us the right directions, he is on board the ship with us, placing his hand of assurance over ours.

A little boy came to his Daddy. "Dad, can I ask you something?"

"Sure, son," answered Dad.

""Is the Devil stronger than I am?"

"Yes, son he is."

"Is he stronger that you, Dad?"

"Yes, son, I'm afraid he is."

The little boy was quiet for a few moments as he appeared to be thinking hard. Then he asked, "Dad is he stronger than Jesus?"

"No, son, he's not. He is not stronger than Jesus."

"Good," said the little boy, "then I'm not afraid, because I'm a friend of Jesus."

Become a friend of Jesus and let him take over the controls as you find the way through the storms of your life.

Staying tuned to a reliable source will also give you confidence in the storms of life. Your confidence grows as you understand why our Reliable Source will never lose the connection with us unless we choose not to listen. Knowing why Jesus prays for us helps us understand why we can trust him. To discover that, turn to the next chapter.

# Section Two: Jesus is Praying for You

*"I have revealed you to the ones you gave me from this world...I have passed on to them the message you gave me. They accepted it...and they believe you sent me... Now protect them by the power of your name..."*

— John 17:6, 8, 11

*"We were really excited."*

—Don Priest, father of Donnie Priest, upon hearing the news that his 10-year-old son was alive

## Chapter Six
## Faith: It Comes by Hearing the Message

IT WAS ONE OF THE WORST SNOW STORMS ever to hit Northern California. The confluence of two fronts stalled over the region, creating a nightmare of a winter storm. And on the 3$^{rd}$ of January, 1982, at the Mammoth Airport, just east of Yosemite National Park, as the storm continued to gain strength, Ronald Vaughan, stepfather of Donnie Priest, made a terrible decision.

Vaughn, piloting a single engine Grumman AA-5B, had his wife Lee, also an experienced pilot, sitting next to him, and Donnie, his 10-year-old stepson, sleeping in the back seat. Ground controllers at the airport refused Vaughn's flight plan, which was to take him across Yosemite's Tioga Pass. Vaughn filed an alternate plan. But shortly after taking off, he radioed flight control and informed them he was heading for Tioga Pass after all. There was nothing the air controllers could do. The plane later crashed into a snowy slope on the northeastern edge of Yosemite National Park.

For four days the search and rescue teams found no sign of the plane. Hope was diminishing with each passing hour. By the fifth day, no one was expecting survivors. But it was on that day that Jim Sano---a Yosemite Park Ranger who had been asked to assist in the rescue---noticed something unusual while the rescue helicopter he was in passed over the eastern slopes of White Mountain. It was a shadow on the snow. And it was formed by the tip of a plane's tail. The dramatic rescue effort that followed the sighting was too late for Ron and Lee Vaughn. They died, probably upon impact. But Donnie was still alive. His body temperature was only 84 degrees, and his two feet would have to be amputated just above the ankles. But he was alive; he had survived.

His dad and stepmom had been desperate for good news. "It was very close to his not making it," his dad, Don Priest, said. Then the Priests heard the beautiful news that Donnie had been rescued. "We were," he paused, choking back tears, "really excited."[79]

Sometimes the news is so wonderful that we can only respond with a few inadequate words. "We were really excited," doesn't capture the depth of emotion Don Priest must have felt upon receiving the good news about his son. But he said what he could. And, he said it all.

Sometimes saying a few simple words is our best response to incredibly good news.

---

[79] www.weather.com/weather/videos/on-tv-43/storm-stories-352/storm-stories-aerial-rescue-13734#loc=43/352/13724; John Flynn, "Emotional Trek to Sierra crash site for a man who lost legs at age 10," www...articles.sfgate.com/2007-11-25/news/1726966_1_white-mountain-plane-crash-prosthetic/2, and Cyndee Fontana and Mark Grossi, "10-year-old survives plane crash, bitter Sierra cold," www.finalflightthebook.comFresnoBee-LostFlightsSeries/859359_DonniePriest_Sept10-08.html.

Something like that must have happened in John 2, when Andrew told his brother, Simon Peter, about Jesus. Andrew had been a disciple of John the Baptist. The day after Jesus' baptism, John was standing with two of his disciples when Jesus walked by. Both disciples left John to follow Jesus that day. And Andrew hurried to tell his brother, Simon Peter, the good news. "We have found the Messiah," Andrew told his brother.

"We have found the Messiah," doesn't communicate the thrill Andrew must have had in his heart when he shared that bit of good news. They had been waiting on the Messiah; they had been earnestly anticipating him. And Andrew was ready to leave his teacher, John the Baptist, because Jesus of Nazareth, Andrew was convinced, was indeed the long awaited Messiah.

One by one each disciple heard the Good News of Jesus' message and decided to follow him. Philip and Nathanael seemed more animated than Andrew. Philip told Nathanael. "We have found the very person Moses and the prophets wrote about!" (John 1:45). And when Jesus displayed superhuman power, Nathanael responded, "Rabbi, you are the Son of God---the King of Israel! (John 1:49)

We have no record of what most of the disciples said when they first believed and decided to follow Jesus. We don't even know what Simon Peter's first words were in response to Jesus affirmation, "Your name is Simon, the son of John---but you will be called Cephas" (John 1:42).

But all of them received the Good News of Jesus. In John 17:8, Jesus prays to the Father," I have passed on to them the message you gave me. They accepted it and know that I came from you, and they believe you sent me."

It's difficult to imagine how mere words could capture the thrill they felt in hearing the Good News. They responded by faith and followed. And Jesus prayed that his disciples would be protected by his name.

This brings us to a new division in Jesus' prayer. Jesus first prayed for himself in verses 1-4 of John 17. Then he prayed for the twelve in verses 6-19. And finally he prayed for future believers in verses 20-26. In section one of this book, I took Jesus' prayer for himself and applied it to questions of how, when, and to whom we pray. As we face the storms of life, those are important questions to answer.

In this section, I am taking Jesus' prayer for his disciples and relating it to his followers today. Jesus prayed specifically for the original twelve, also known as apostles. I am simply applying what Jesus prayed for them to current believers. He was praying for the twelve in their unique situation. But this portion of Jesus' prayer can also apply to us as well.

Like the disciples, we must receive the Good News by faith. They heard it from Jesus. "I have passed on the message you gave me," Jesus prayed in John 17:8. Paul would later write to the Christians in Rome, "Faith comes by hearing and hearing by the Word of God" (Romans 10:17). These earliest disciples heard the message through the Messiah himself, who was the living message. Jesus revealed to them the Word; he himself is the living Word. And the Word penetrated to their hearts. They had reason to believe Jesus was the promised Messiah. Their response was an act of faith, evidenced by their following Jesus. These verses, 17:6-12, tell us why Jesus prayed for them, and why he prays for his followers today.

## We are family

If you pray at all, you probably pray for your family. They are closest to you. Jesus loves *everybody.* But during his earthly ministry, he was closest to the twelve. He intercedes for them and prays that they will be protected by his name. They are family.

Why were the disciples part of the family? Read again Jesus' words in John 17:6: "I have revealed you to the ones you gave me from this world. They were always yours. You gave them to me..." Who gave who to whom? God the Father, to whom Jesus is praying, gave the disciples to Jesus. When did he do this? "They were always yours."(v. 6) What does that mean?

We get some help from Ephesians 1:4-5: "Even before he made the world, God loved us and chose us in Christ to be holy and without fault in his eyes. God decided in advance to adopt us into his own family by bringing us to himself through Jesus Christ."

How do you know if he chose you? How do you know if you are part of the family? If you are a follower of Jesus, you are in his family. If you are not a follower of Jesus, do you have a desire in your heart for God? Do you want to know God? Would you like to be a part of his forever family? If so, God is moving in your heart. Act on the truth you know.

What about not being chosen? We shouldn't be concerned about *not* being chosen. Like I said, act on the truth you know. God loves you and wants you to know and love him. Respond to him by choosing to follow Jesus Christ. Paul said, "God loved us and chose us in Christ" (Ephesians 1:4). You can assure your family ties by accepting your acceptance in Jesus Christ. There is a mystery here that I cannot completely grasp. All I can say is God chose me to be in his forever family. I say, "Forever family," because it lasts forever.

John Chrysostom, who lived in the fourth century, actually dying in 407 A.D., was Bishop of Antioch. Chrysostom said, "Christ chose us to have faith in him before we came into being, indeed before the world was founded." [80] Notice he said God chose us to have faith in him. I must respond to him by faith. That is my part. But I wouldn't have responded by faith, according to Chrysostom, had God not first chosen me. Again, I can only act on the truth I know.

Our faith is not a blind faith. Based on what they knew, the disciples believed Jesus to be the fulfillment of prophetic statements concerning the promised Messiah. After his death, they were despondent. But after the resurrection, they cannot help but tell others the Good News of the Messiah. That's because they were convinced the resurrection really occurred. Their faith in Jesus as the risen Savior was based on knowledge and experience.

As we act on the truth we know, we can rejoice that God chose us simply because he loves us and not because of anything we've done or because of who we are or are not. You see, I might mess up, in fact I have many, many times, and I am not

---

[80] , Thomas C. Oden, gen. ed., *Ancient Christian Commentary on Scripture,* New Testament, 12 vols. (Downers Grove, Illinois: InterVarsity Press, 2007), vol. Viii: *Ephesians,* ed., Mark J. Edwards, p. 110

exactly the same person I was when I first came to Christ. But his love is the same. It's constant. And his love won't let me go.

We are family when we you receive his gift of adoption. He loves us simply because he is love. Our significance is grounded in his love and not on our behavior or looks or status in the world. We are important to God because God loves us with a love that takes us in, just as we are.

Of course, as we will see in this section of the Scripture, he will pray that we will be transformed by that love, that we will be shaped into the image of the Son and that we will, by our lives, give him glory.

Teacher Debbie Moon's first graders were discussing a picture of a family. One little boy in the picture had a different color of hair than the other family members.

One child suggested that he was adopted and a little girl named Jocelyn Jay said, "I know all about adoptions because I'm adopted."

"What does it mean to be adopted?" another asked.

"It means," said Jocelyn, "that you grew in your mother's heart instead of her tummy."[81]

God is described as a father. Although I have earthly parents, I grew up in the heart of my heavenly father from eternity. I mean that much to him. He wants me, yes, even me, in his family, to enjoy all the privileges of a child of God. And he wants the same thing for you. I know Jesus is praying for me through every storm because I am part of his family.

---

[81] Jack Canfield, Mark Victor Hansen, Patty Hansen, *Condensed Chicken Soup for the Soul* (Deerfield Beach, Florida: Health Communications, Inc., 1996), p. 69

## We are Believers

It is a great mystery of our faith that although God chose us from eternity, we still have freedom of choice. We had to choose our chosenness. On the other hand, we could reject God's choosing of us.

It has been said that before being converted to Christ one could read over the entrance to the narrow way that leads to salvation and read the words, "Whosoever will may come." But after entering, a person can look back and, to his or her amazement, see on the other side of the door that leads to eternal life the words, "Chosen in him before the foundation of the world." The Bible teaches both divine sovereignty and freedom of choice.

True love cannot be forced. If we did not have the freedom to say no to God, we would not truly love him. But having a choice also means that we could choose something or someone else to love other than God. We could replace love for God with a love for someone or something else.

In these verses Jesus is saying he is praying for his disciples first of all because God chose them from eternity, but also because they chose Jesus.

It's a mystery. Jesus prays for us because we are family. We are part of his family. We have only him to thank for that since he did the choosing. But we had to respond. That positive response to him, that "yes," to Jesus Christ, cements our relationship. We know that our Savior prays for us; we have received his love.

I have four children. Two are biologically my children; two are adopted. All had to accept or reject me as their father.

*Surviving the Storms of Life*

I've chosen all of them. I'm thankful they've received my love and are proud to be part of our family.

A child, at some point, must receive or reject the love of a parent. I know there are times when children will say, "I hate you," or "You're not my daddy!" and later realize they were just angry; they didn't mean it. We must look beyond that in children, just as, thankfully, God does with us. But, it is very possible for a child to disown the parents. Maybe you've seen that happen.

In Philip Roth's novel, *The Human Stain,* the central character, Coleman Silk, is a black man who looks very much like a white man. He grew up in the era of the 1940s. Coleman was a very intelligent and talented young man. At one point he decides to hide the fact that he is a black man. He tells his mother that he will never acknowledge her as his mother. He will hide his blackness. He disowns her, and it breaks her heart. The tragedy is that by doing that he enslaves himself by living a lie.[82]

We must choose back, or deny God the Father. When we deny who we are---God's children loved by him, we in effect live a lie and enslave ourselves to a false self.

We can know that we are family when we believe in Jesus and the message he brought. This confirms our relationship of love. In another place John wrote, "I have written to you who believe in the name of the Son of God, so that you may know you have eternal life" (I John 5:13). So, we have this assurance that as believers we are being prayed for by Jesus himself. Recall

---

[82] Philip Roth, *The Human Stain* (New York, New York: Houghton, Mifflin Co, 2000).

Romans 8:34, where it says that Jesus has been raised to the right hand of God the Father and is interceding for us.

The majority of religious leaders of the day hounded Jesus until they nailed him to the cross because of the amazing claims he made about himself: He claimed to be the Messiah, the Son of Man; he claimed to have the power not only to heal but to forgive; and he claimed that he would die, rise again, and return in power to be the Judge in the Last Days. According to John 17:8, the disciples accepted Jesus' claims about himself. They believed him.

If what Jesus said about himself is true, and we believe it, our lives cannot remain the same. Jesus must become the most important person in our life. As C.S. Lewis said, "One must keep pointing out the Christianity is a statement which, if false, is of *no* importance, and if true, of infinite importance. The one thing it cannot be is moderately important."[83]

I read some years ago that there are only two ways out of a street gang: either to be killed in the loyal defense of your gang or be "jumped out." Being "jumped out" means you take a brutal beating which can leave a gang member crippled or near dead. But those who have studied these gangs discovered a third way. A member can get out by making a sincere decision to follow Christ. Because the young people from these gangs come from cultures that have or once had deep religious convictions, they see Christ as a sort of neutral turf. If you accept Christ and mean it, you're out of the gang. But here's the hitch: if you only say it

---

[83] C.S. Lewis, *God in the Dock, Essays on Theology and Ethics*, ed., Walter Hooper (Grand Rapids, Michigan: William B. Eerdmans Publishing, Co., 1970), p. 101.

and don't mean it, and the word gets back that you are only saying you are a believer and not truly living it, you're as good as dead.

While that may not be the practice of gangs today, it prompts a question for those in Christ: What if you could die for not living up to your verbal claim to be a follower of Jesus? What if you had to be so serious about your confession of Jesus as Lord that failure to walk the talk could result in death? Think of the difference it would make for Christianity. "The one thing it cannot be is moderately important."

More damage has been done to the cause of Christ by those who give mere lip service to Jesus' words than by all the atheists put together.

Based on what they knew of God's Word---the prophetic passages about Jesus,and what they saw in the life of Jesus---the miracles, the perfect life demonstrated by perfect love---the disciples believed. They believed for these reasons and chose to follow Jesus, at least this far. Jesus would pray them out of the storm of their doubt, disbelief and despair during that time in-between Jesus' death and Resurrection. Jesus prayed them through it, just as he promised he would pray for Peter, that after Satan had "sifted" him like "wheat," Peter would turn back. (Luke 22:31-32).

Jesus knows us in our weakness. He gives us the grace to believe. It is a gift. As he told Peter when he confessed Christ as the Son of God, "You did not learn this from any human being" (Matthew 16:17). We are believers. The word Jesus used to describe what the disciples did is the Greek word *pisteou*. It means "to believe," "to trust," and even "to obey." True belief results in action, works. It means you are willing to step out from the crowd in order to exercise faith, which the writer of Hebrews describes as "the evidence of things hoped for, the assurance of things not seen" (Hebrews 11:1). As Alistair McGrath notes, "Faith realizes that God loves us, and responds to that love. Faith is saying yes to God. It is a decision, an act of will to trust God."[84]

The first of many tightrope walkers to cross Niagara Falls was a Frenchman by the name of Jean Francois Gravelot, who went by the stage name, "The Great Blondin," because of his blond hair. His first attempt to cross Niagara Falls came on June 30, 1859. Midway across, Gravelot stopped, dropped a bottle tied to a piece of twine to the Maid of Mist tourist boat below, had it filled with water from the Niagara River, hauled it up and drank it. He resumed his tightrope walk, made it across, accepted a glass of champagne, drank it, did a little dance on the rope and walked back across. Over the next two summers he would cross the Falls at night, on stilts, and on a bicycle. One time he pushed a stove on a wheelbarrow and cooked an omelet. Another time he crossed blindfolded. But it is said that his greatest feat was to carry a man across on his back. On that occasion he persuaded his manager, Harry Colcord, to climb on the Great Blondin's back and trust him not to make a mistake. Colcord trusted Gravelot with his life. Colcord later described Gravelot as a "piece of marble, ever muscle tense and rigid." They made it to the other side. When they reached the Canadian side, according to the story, the audience cheered. Gravelot then asked if they

---

[84] Alister McGrath, *"I Believe," Exploring the Apostles' Creed* (Downers Grove, Illinois: InterVarsity Press, 1991), p.20.

believed he could do it again. And of course, many applauded and cried for them to do it. Then Gravelot said, "Mr. Colcord is a bit tired, who will go in his place?" And of all those who said they believed he could do it again, not one volunteered to get up on the tightrope with him.

Many believe Jesus, like the crowd at Niagara Falls, believed Gravelot. It's a belief that Jesus did the things he did, and maybe even that he is a miracle worker today. But that's as far as it goes. The evidence that we believe is that we will step out in faith. We will get on the tightrope. We will take up our cross and follow Jesus.

And so we trust and follow him; we often do not know where he is taking us; we only know we are to follow. I read about the pilot of a military plane who was forced to parachute into a jungle in Southeast Asia. How could he possibly find his way out? A local man saw what had happened and came to the pilot's rescue. He slashed through the tangled underbrush and was face to face with the frightened pilot. The frantic pilot cried out, "Where's the road? Which way out?"

The villager simply said, "No road! I'm the way! Follow me!" And the pilot followed him through the jungle to safety.

While he was in the Upper Room, shortly after he had shared the Last Supper with his disciples but before he prayed the prayer of John 17, Jesus said, "I am the way, the truth, and the life" (John 14:6). The disciples must have believed, but soon they would feel lost, abandoned, far from God's presence, and cheated of his victory. This place, like that Southeast Asian jungle whose entangled underbrush could hide the very light of day, would become—as the disciples followed the Son of God—a brightly lit open road to new life. But it would take the bleakness, the barrenness, the blackness of that God-forsaken hill called Golgotha for them to see the light of life in the resurrection. And so, following him to that other place—the far side of Easter, the place where he promised to meet them in Galilee---they would find him in due time, realizing in the finding that it was him all along, praying them through the storm, securing them safely to shore. And we must go there too; for it is there that we meet the risen Savior, we who are family— we, his children, children whom he prays through the storm.

**We are followers**

It's been said that there are three kinds of people: Believers, non-believers, and make-believers. Now, the problem with make-believers is that they haven't experienced the inner transformation necessary for Christ to bear fruit through them. They proclaim one thing but their fruit shows something contrary to what they publicly profess. An apple tree is an apple tree because it produces apples, not oranges or cherries. If it could talk, an apple tree might try to convince you that it's an orange tree. But the apple tree bears apples, not oranges. That's how you know it's an apple tree.

Here, in John 17, Jesus is praying for us. As we read this section we can see why Jesus prayed for his disciples, and by extension, why he prays for us: we are family (he chose us); we are believers (we chose or accepted our chosenness); and we are followers (we walk after him). The following or walking in the steps of Jesus is the evidence of being in the family; it's in the following that the fruit of believing is produced. A make-believer may claim Jesus Christ, perhaps verbally, but the evidence of true faith is in the actual following of Jesus Christ. No fruit is produced apart from the following; it's in following that we find fruit. In other words, it's in the following of Jesus Christ the Lord that he produces fruit through us; it's in the following that we demonstrate our faith.

In June, 2006 1st Lt. Ehrem K. Watada faced court martial charges because he refused to serve in Iraq. He had volunteered to serve in the military in 2001. All was fine as long as he was working behind a desk. But when he was called to Iraq, he refused. As a result the military tried to court martial him.[85] The case ended in a mistrial, and he was discharged in 2009.

Now, regardless of your personal views of the war in Iraq, to have military personnel pick and choose when and where they will respond to orders simply won't work, will it? When it comes to serving Jesus, we are a bit like the person who joins the military but wants to determine when and where he or she will serve. This is exactly what happens in the church every day: We've got our uniform; we want the benefits; we get our orders. And we simply won't go. But going is the mark of being in the family. That's the evidence of being a believer. Being in Christ carries with it a commitment; it is supposed to mean something when you say you are a "follower of Christ." Faith, true faith, is expressed in action.

Perhaps Jesus in some way prays for everyone. Who am I to place limits on the prayers of our Lord? But I do know for **certain** he is praying for his followers in the way we hear it in

---

[85] "Officer charged after refusing to serve in Iraq," *The Courier Journal,"* July, 23, 2006, p., A7.

John 17. In John 17:9, he says he is not praying for the world. The "world" as John uses it, is all that is against God. This is not the prayer of Jesus praying for the world; this is a prayer of Jesus for his followers. He continues to pray today. Recall again Romans 8:34 where is says Christ "died for us and was raised to life for us, and he is sitting in the place of honor at God's right hand, pleading for us."

This is my question: Are you one of the followers? It's easy to claim you are in the family: "Sure I'm in the Jesus family. Oh yeah, I'm in." And, "Of course I'm a believer. I believe it all. Sure I do." Be honest enough with yourself to ask yourself, "Where's the evidence in my life? Am I following?" If you are truly a part of the family, if you are a believer, it will be evidenced by your following him. The book of James reminds us that faith without works is dead. "Even so faith, if it has no works, is dead, being by itself" (James 1:17, NAS). He goes on to say that "a man is justified by works and not by faith alone" (James 1:24, NAS).

I want to encourage you to ask yourself why you say you are a follower of Christ. John himself says in I John 2:3, "By this we know that we have come to know Him, if we keep His commandments." (NAS) Take a look at why you say you are in the family of God. Is it because you show up and nod in agreement with the preacher? Is it because you are there when the church doors open? Is it because you filled out a membership card?

Perhaps you are a follower but just aren't showing it at this point. Maybe you are in God's family---the church, the body of believers,but you are not evidencing it by following him at this time. I am not saying you are not of Christ; I just don't want you to miss out on the joy of experiencing the journey with him.

As we read Jesus' prayer for his disciples in John 17:7-9, it is clear that his followers bring glory to Jesus. That means it's not about us; it's about him. We let him shine through us. As Eugene Peterson translates Jesus' words in John 17:10b: "My life is on display in them."[86]

Is Jesus life on display in you?

How do we give Jesus the glory? By letting him be on display in what we say and do.

So, when we live by faith in God, we are bringing him glory; when we live pure lives, we are bringing God glory; when we live our lives by his Word, loving him with all we are, then we are bringing God glory. Since the first and greatest commandment is to love the Lord with all our heart, mind soul and strength, the most powerful way we can bring God glory is to love God and point people to his love.

St. Benedict said, "Prefer nothing to the love of Christ." What a wonderful motto for your life, "Prefer nothing to the love of Christ." The love of Christ is paramount in our lives. Should we live like that, the glory of Christ would be evident in every aspect of our lives.

A family was having their evening devotions and each of the family members took turns reading the Scriptures. One night the four-year-old insisted that she be allowed to read the Bible. The other children didn't like that because they said the younger

---

[86] Eugene H. Peterson, *The Message, the Bible in Contemporary Language* (Colorado Springs, Co.: NAV Press, 2002), p. 1955.

sister could not read. But the mother intervened, and the youngest was allowed to try and read the Scriptures.

She opened to Bible to the book of Genesis, looked at the page, and then quoted a verse she had learned in Sunday School, "God is love," she proudly said. Then she turned to the book of Psalms, looked at a page and said, "God is love." After that she flipped the pages to the Gospel of Mark and pretending to quote a verse said, "God is love."

This was more than the older brothers and sisters could take. "See," they said, "we told you she couldn't read the Bible."

The mother wisely replied, "Yes, she can, for when we really learn to read the Bible, it says, 'God is love,' on every page."[87]

When we learn to truly live our lives as they should be lived, our life will say, "God is love," in our every action and thought. If we live our lives as followers for the glory of God, "God is love," will be written on every day of our lives, and when it is not, we as his followers, ask for forgiveness and strength to love more truly and authentically.

It is also evident as we read this portion of Jesus' prayer that his followers will claim and carry his name. Jesus said, "You have given me your name, now protect them by the power of your name" (v 11). There is power in the name of God. Jesus' followers would take his name.

St. Gregory Nazianzus, one of the fathers of the church, defended the faith when he as Bishop of Nazianzus Gregory said, "Different men have different names, which they owe to their

---

[87] *Brian's Lines*, Vol.4, no. 9, September, 1998, p.13

*Surviving the Storms of Life*

parents or themselves, that is, to their own pursuits and achievements. But our great pursuit, the great name we wanted, was to be Christians, to be called Christians."[88] These disciples would eventually be called by the name they carried.

Would they fail? Oh yes, for we see in just a few moments, with the flip of a few pages in our Bibles, that they all run and scatter like frightened chickens fleeing from a dog in the chicken coop. But they would come back. And when they did, they became strong and courageous, even to the point of being willing to die for the name of Jesus.

But doesn't Jesus say here that the power of this name will protect them? How then were they protected?

We have to remember that to the Semitic mind, the name of a person revealed who that person was, that is, their character, their attributes. To be protected by the name of Jesus the Messiah would be to be protected by a loving, holy, sovereign, wise, compassionate Lord. All of the attributes of our Lord are wrapped up in that name.

How do we then account for the fact that these disciples all encountered trouble because of the name of Jesus? The promise was not that they would never encounter difficulties, but that within those trials, they would be protected and secured by the love of God.

In Romans 8:35, Paul asks, "Can anything ever separate us from Christ's love? Does it mean he no longer loves us if we have trouble or calamity, or are persecuted, or hungry, or destitute, or in danger, or threatened with death?" The answer

---

[88] Cited in *The Liturgy of the Hours,* vol. I: *Advent Season, Christmas Season* (New York: Catholic Book Publishing Co., 1975), p. 1287.

Paul gives is an unequivocal "No." Absolutely nothing can separate us from the love of God.

And our faith, when it is grounded in Jesus, will hold. "Whatever storms life may bring, the anchor of faith will hold us firm to God."[89]

As we face those frightening storms of life, we are assured that Jesus himself prays for us, and he gives us the name that keeps us, not from the storms of life, but from any power that could take his name from us, for it is by his powerful name that he will finally bring us to shore. We follow him and in so doing we are carrying the name of our Lord, the name of the risen Christ, who died that we might live, was weak that we might be strong, endured rejection that we might be accepted, and yes, is with us right now, at this very moment for whatever trial or temptation we may be encountering.

It was in David Livingston's sixteenth year in Africa as an explorer and missionary that he faced his gravest danger. He was surrounded by angry, hostile African tribesmen. They were threatening him with his life. Late one night he contemplated fleeing, but that too was fraught with danger. Late that night, he decided to stay. He was given a great peace about it. What gave him that peace in this trying situation? Here is what he recorded in his diary, dated January 14, 1856: "I read that Jesus said: 'All power is given unto Me in Heaven and in earth. Go ye therefore, and teach all nations, and lo, I am with you always, even unto

---

[89] McGrath, "I Believe," p.20.

the end to the world.' It is the word of a gentlemen of the most strict and sacred honour, so there's an end to it! "[90]

"There's an end to it," may not capture the depth of determination and complete peace Livingston felt that night. But his words, like those of Don Priest, or Andrew, said enough. And they were followed by actions.

We too have the word of the same gentleman Livingston followed, a gentleman, as he said, of "the most strict and sacred honor." If Jesus says he is praying for us, we had better believe it. If he says he will protect us, we can count on him. If he says the power of his name will be with us, then we must be going.

---

[90] Paul Lee Tan, ed., *Encyclopedia of 7,700 Illustrations: Signs of the Times* (Rockville, Maryland: Assurance Publishers, 1979), p. 507.

*"I told them many things while I was with them in this world so they would be filled with my joy."*
—John 17:13

*"We can do nothing but trust in the Lord."*
—-Elvira Smith, speaking to her four children as a tornado destroyed their home in Louisville, Kentucky, March 27, 1890[91]

---

[91] Keven McQueen, *The Great Louisville Tornado of 1890* (Charleston, SC: The History Press, 2010), p., 71.

## Chapter Seven
## How to be filled with Joy in the Midst of the Storm

JOY IS MORE THAN A FEELING; IT'S A GIFT we receive as we trust in the Lord. When all we can do is trust the Lord, we have done enough. And it time, joy will come.

More than 100 people were killed, according to historian Keven McQueen, when a deadly tornado struck Louisville, Kentucky on March 27, 1890. There were no warning sirens in those days, and by the time the storm approached Louisville, it had blown down telegraph lines, preventing any kind of warning. The devastation and loss of lives was horrific.[92]

The tornado hit Louisville during the season of Lent, and the Palm Sunday following the tornado, a Sunday normally characterized by joy, became known in Louisville's history as "the Sunday of funerals."[93] And the celebration of Easter was dampened by the grief left in the storm's wake.

Storms don't consult our calendars before they wreak havoc. Tornadoes may touch down on your birthday or anniversary; hurricanes might thrash a community on Christmas Day or Easter Sunday.

---

[92] Ken Neuhauser, "Author sheds new light on lethal storm," *The Courier-Journal,* January 31, 2011, D1, 3.
[93] McQueen, p., 71.

Jesus prayed while he was in this world, not another one but this one, a world with tragedies and trials and unexpected storms, storms that destroy communities on an Easter Sunday or take a life on Christmas Day. How can anyone be filled with joy when something like that happens? Surely Jesus didn't mean we are to be filled with joy in the midst of life's storms, did he?

I believe he did. We can actually be filled with joy in the midst of pain and difficulty.

I didn't say, happy; I said joy-filled.

We tend to confuse joy with happiness. Happiness depends on what happens to us. It's a feeling. Joy is not necessarily a feeling. The English word for happiness is derived from an Old English root word, *hap*, which means chance. Happiness is dependent on our circumstance. And the word, circumstance, is the combination of two Latin words, one of which means "to stand" and the other, "around." Our circumstances are those things standing around us. If they are pleasant, then we are happy. If not, we are sad.

Joy is altogether different. Joy is not the result of our circumstances, those things standing around us, but instead has to do with what stands within us. In the last chapter, I noted that we are chosen by God in Jesus Christ; we are adopted into the family of God, having been placed in a right standing with him. Because of that, we have "peace with God through our Lord Jesus Christ" (Romans 5:1 NAS), and now are in a "place of underserved privilege" where "we confidently and joyfully look forward to sharing God's glory" (Romans 5:2). Even as we face trials, "we can rejoice" (Romans 5:3), knowing "how dearly God loves us, because he has given us the Holy Spirit to fill our hearts with his love" (Romans 5:5).

Where God's love is, there is joy as well. Love gives rise to joy. As we face the storms of life, God continually pours out his love into us through the Holy Spirit. It overflows in us, bursting forth like water from a fountain. We are filled to overflowing with joy.

Of course we don't like storms. If we are smart, we try and avoid them. But when they come, we can still be filled with joy.

The Biblical word for joy isn't the same thing as what we call happiness. It can include that, but it's more than that. It's interesting that the Hebrew language of the Old Testament has ten different terms for joy. One Hebrew scholar states that no language has as many words for joy and rejoicing as Hebrew.[94] I wonder if it's because the Hebrew people could find so many reasons to rejoice. After all, as God's chosen people, they knew that when they rested in God's embrace, trusted his promises, and followed in his paths, he would bring them joy. The Psalmist wrote, "May all my thoughts be pleasing to him for I rejoice in the Lord" (Psalm 104:34).

Sometimes joyful people look like what we would interpret as happy, and often they are. There is certainly nothing wrong with being happy. But, in the New Testament joy is something above and beyond and deeper than happiness. It's considered a gift from God and a fruit of the Spirit. In the midst of pain and suffering, we can still rejoice. Paul's list of the

---

[94] Everett F. Harrison, ed., *Baker's Dictionary of Theology* (Grand Rapids: Baker Book House, 1979), p., 299.

tribulations he had personally endured for the cause of Christ included being slandered, whipped, imprisoned, stoned, shipwrecked, as well as hunger, and thirst. And yet, though his heart ached, Paul could say, "we always have joy" (II Corinthians 6:10).

The joy that Jesus is praying for us is more than a feeling; it's a fruit of the Spirit that comes to us as we abide in him and receive the joy he prays for us.

**Finding Joy in the Darkness**

Fanny Crosby was one of the greatest hymn writers the Christian faith has ever known. Before her life was done, she had written some 9,000 hymns. She was talented but her words were written in the dark because Fanny Crosby was blind.

Somehow she managed to find joy in the darkness.

When she was about six weeks-old, her parents noticed with some concern that something was wrong with her eyes. Her parents thought a cold had set into her eyes. The local physician was out of town, so another country doctor was called. The year was 1820, and in those days it was easy for a man to charade as a physician. Such was the case with the man who made the house call to the Crosby home. By the time they discovered he was not a real physician, it was too late. He had left the area. This man had prescribed a hot mustard poultice to be applied to her eyes. It cleared up the infection but left white scars, and in the months that followed, baby Fanny did not respond when objects were placed before her. She would be totally blind.

*Surviving the Storms of Life*

No one reports Fanny Crosby ever having expressed any resentment toward her parents or the charlatan physician. She believed it happened as a part of God's plan. When a well-meaning minister remarked that it was a pity that she had been born blind, Fanny, without hesitating, responded, "Do you know that if at birth I had been able to make one petition, it would have been that I was born blind? Because," she continued, "when I get to heaven, the first face that shall ever gladden my sight will be that of my Savior."[95]

In 1858, Fanny married a teacher at the New York Institution for the Blind. Like Fanny, he too was blind. And he was also a composer. Their only daughter, Frances, died in infancy. It was a deep pain for Fanny. A relative, Florence Paine, lived with Fanny for six years and could never get her to talk about it. Fanny could forgive the man whose remedy blinded her, and apparently even in the tragedy of losing her child, Fanny carried no resentment towards God. Yet, privately she seemed to carry a deep hurt in her heart. But as far as we know, she never lost her joy, even though she didn't always feel happiness.

In 1868, almost ten years after the death of her only child, musician Howard Doane knocked on the door of Fanny's apartment in Manhattan. He had a tune and asked Fanny to put words to it. But Doane had less than an hour before he had to catch his train to Cincinnati, Ohio. Fanny took the tune, quietly retreated to another room in her tiny apartment, got on her knees, prayed to God to give her the words, and within an hour

---

[95] www.christianitytoday.com/ch/13/christians/poets/crosby.html

composed a poem in her mind, then dictated it to Doane, who hurried out the door and down the street to catch his train.

The hymn she wrote was later named, "Safe in the Arms of Jesus," and it became one of Fanny's best loved hymns. She claimed she had written it for grieving mothers who had experienced what it was to have lost a child. One Presbyterian minister claimed the hymn had given more peace and satisfaction to mothers who had lost a child than any hymn he had ever known. As the title suggests, she wrote of being "safe in the arms of Jesus," where she was "free from the blight of sorrow, free from doubts and fears." [96]

Fanny overflowed with joy in the midst of her storm of pain and hurt and loss. She found joy in her darkness.

**It's time to rejoice**

Rejoicing isn't something we happen to do. We choose to be joyful. Paul wrote, "Always be full of joy in the Lord. I say it again---rejoice!" (Philippians 4:4) If we are to rejoice always, then being full of joy simply cannot be determined by our circumstances. That means we must choose to be joyful. "Joy does not simply happen to us," wrote Henri Nouwen, "we have to choose joy and keep choosing it every day."

Paul spoke of being full of joy "in the Lord." Our joy comes from the Lord. It is a gift from him. In John 17:13 Jesus talked about telling the disciples "many things" so they would be filled with joy. "Many things" of course refers to all that he had taught them, but in this context, as they were in the Upper

---

[96] Robert J. Morgan, *Then Sings My Soul* (Nashville: Thomas Nelson Publishers, 2003), p. 164

Room, I believe it has special reference to something he had just shared with them. It's recorded in John 16:19-24. There, we read of Jesus preparing the disciples for his death. They would grieve, but their grief would turn to wonderful joy: "You have sorrow now, but I will see you again; then you will rejoice, and no one can rob you of that joy" (John 16:22). Jesus went on to say that when the disciples ask, using his name, they would receive "abundant joy" (John 16:24). Jesus was telling the disciples they would grieve in his absence, but he would return. He was of course referring to his death and resurrection. They were to rejoice because he would return. And abundant joy would be a gift he would give them.

Too often we live like we are stuck in between Christ's death and resurrection. We live as though Christ is in the tomb. But the fact that he is alive should make all the difference in the world. We are to be joy-filled people. He is alive!

Jan Willem van der Hoeven was the Custodian of the Garden Tomb in Jerusalem from 1968 – 1975, and he had the opportunity to speak to thousands of people at the site of the Empty Tomb. He told of a young skeptic who listened to Jan's talk about Jesus' death and resurrection and how we find forgiveness and eternal life in him today. The young man, who was traveling the world searching for peace, listened attentively. Then, when Jan concluded his message, the man could no longer restrain his emotion. He shouted from the crowd, "Mister, if what you say is true, there should be singing and dancing for joy at this site every day of the year!"[97]

---

[97] *The Pastor's Story File*, vol. 11, num. 6, April, 1995, p. 3.

Why don't we? The problem is that we focus on the storm or the perceived threat of one. We think about the storm; we talk about the damage it has inflicted on us and how and why it can harm us again; we live in anxiety and descend into anger. Our joy is sapped. We have no room for it. It's impossible to sing and dance for joy when your feet are stuck in the mud of despair and your voice is strained with worry.

**Abiding in Jesus**

How then can we live a joy-filled life? Experiencing joy involves a confident taking hold of the promises of God. It is believing that through the Holy Spirit we can find true rest in God. The biblical word for this is "abiding." It's a word that's often used to describe having a personal relationship with someone. It connotes living in close community with another or literally being joined with someone in an intimate relationship. Joy springs up within us as we rest or abide in Jesus. Joy is not something we struggle to keep, as if we are on the defense to do so, but rather joy is something we intentionally cultivate with intensity.

Jesus made it clear that unless we abide in him, we can do nothing. "Apart from me you can do nothing" (John 15:5). He didn't say we can do some things fairly well or a few things that are at least average. He said we can do nothing. But as we abide in him he produces much fruit: "Those who remain in me, and I in them, will produce much fruit." Since joy is a spiritual fruit, the only way it will be produced in our lives is as we abide in Jesus.

The key to a joy-filled life is abiding in Jesus. We fall in love with Jesus and can't help but want to spend time with him. Joy doesn't come as we pursue joy in and of itself. It is a by-product of staying connected with Jesus.

The better we become at abiding with Jesus, the more of his joy will be ours. The less we abide in him, the less of his joy we will have.

Dr. George Beasley-Murray used to point out that the root meaning of abide is to lean back against something with all your weight---like sitting down in a forest and placing your back against an oak tree and resting against its stout trunk, or lying down in a bed and sinking into its softness until you are completely at rest.[98]

How does that happen? How do we place our full weight against Jesus? How do we rest in him like a person resting in the comfort of a bed?

In John 15:9-12, Jesus talks about it. He associates remaining or abiding in his love with obeying his commandments. Just as he obeys the Father's commandments and therefore abides in his love, so must we obey Jesus' commandments. Then he gives the disciples a new commandment: "Love each other in the same way I have loved you" (John 15:12).

Earlier Jesus had responded to a man who asked him what was the greatest of all the commandments. And Jesus replied, "'You must love the Lord your God with all your heart, all your soul, and all your mind, and all your strength'" (Mark

---

[98] Scott Walker, *Daily Guideposts, 2008* (Carmel, New York: Guideposts, 2007), p., 85.

12:30). Then Jesus went on to say in the next verse, "A second is equally important: 'Love your neighbor as yourself."

The key to resting, abiding in Jesus is in that command. As we love the Lord with all our heart, mind, soul, and strength, and love others as ourselves, we are abiding in him. And he will produce joy in our lives. And that joy will inevitably show itself in our words and actions. As Mother Teresa said, "One filled with joy preaches without preaching."

**Mr. Glory-Face**

It might even affect our countenance.

When missionary Adoniram Judson arrived in Rangoon, Burma on July 13, 1813, he didn't have very much to smile about. It was wretchedly hot; their accommodations were horrible; and no other missionaries were there to help them. In fact there were *no* Burmese Christians nor was there religious toleration. The great missionary William Carey in India had told Judson not to go to that hostile country.

Judson, who was only 24 years old and his wife of 17 months just 23, later wrote about that first day in Burma: "Instead of rejoicing…in having found a heathen land from which we were not immediately driven away, such were our weaknesses that we felt we had no portion left here below and found consolation only in looking beyond our pilgrimage, which we tried to flatter ourselves would be short, to that peaceful region where the wicked cease from troubling and the weary are at rest." Ann, his wife reflected on their first night there: "We felt gloomy and dejected...in view of the prospects."[99]

Despite such grim circumstances, Judson and his wife regrouped, and soon after he arrived, not yet knowing the language yet anxious to reach out in love to the Burmese people, Judson walked up to a man and embraced him. Later, Judson was told the man had gone home and told his family he had seen an angel.

The Judsons faced many hardships: It was six years before he baptized the first Burmese convert; he was falsely accused of being a spy and was imprisoned for 20 months; Ann gave birth to three children, none of which survived infancy, and she died at the age of 36, having served with Adoniram for 14 years. Yet, despite all these tribulations, historical accounts portray Judson as a kind, affectionate, and loving man who embraced the Burmese people. In fact, his countenance so radiated Christ that he became known among the people by the sobriquet, "Mr. Glory-Face." And before his ministry was completed, there were nearly 8,000 Christians in Burma united in 63 churches.[100]

Judson could maintain a glory-face amidst all of his pain because he remained close to Jesus. He had a deep love for the Lord. According to his biographers, in his letters Judson spoke frequently of his love for Christ.

"The love of Christ!' he wrote again and again, "the breadth and length and depth and height of the love of Christ! If

---

[99] Basil Miller, *Ann Judson, Heroine of Burma* (Grand Rapids, MI., Zondervan Publishing House, 1947), p., 39.

[100] K.P. Mobley, "Judson, Adoniram, Jr," in *Biographical Dictionary of Evangelicals,* eds. Timothy Larsen, David Bebbington, Mark A. Knoll (Downers Grove, ILL., 2003), p., 339.

I had not felt certain that every additional trial was ordered by infinite love and mercy, I could not have survived my accumulated sufferings." [101]

And not surprisingly, he had a consistent prayer life. Having been influenced by Thomas a Kempis, Francois Fenelon, and Madame Guyon, Judson was something of a contemplative, even an ascetic.[102] If he found anything clouding his consciousness and enjoyment of the love of Christ, he would go away into the jungle and live there by himself until the sweetness of his faith had been restored to him," wrote one of his biographers.[103] Judson's joy overflowed in harsh circumstances.

His joy was contagious. The nineteenth century evangelist, H.C. Trumbull, wrote about an encounter with Judson when the missionary was home on furlough, and Trumbull was just a boy, barely 14 years-old at the time. Judson was traveling by steamboat from Boston to New York and had stopped for several hours in Trumbull's town of Stonington, Connecticut. Trumbull recognized the then famous missionary from pictures he had seen of him. Too shy to approach Judson, Trumbull ran to tell the local Baptist minister about Judson's unexpected arrival. The minister hurried to the steamboat and was soon engrossed in conversation with Judson, forgetting about young Trumbull. But Trumbull watched Judson all the same. "His face glowed," Trumbull later wrote. "The sight of

---

[101] F.W. Boreham, "Adoniram Judson's Text," in *A Temple of Topaz* (London: The Epworth Press, 1928), 130-141, cited in www.fwborehamblogspot.com/2007/02/boreham-on-adoniram-judson.html

[102] Mobley, *Biographical Dictionary of Evangelicals*, 338.

[103] Borham, "Adoniram Judson's Text," 130-141,

that countenance was an inspiration and a blessing to me. I have never forgotten it. I never can forget it." What was it about that face that had such a profound impact in Trumbull? "In his face were the signs of the many battles through which he had passed, and of the spirit in which he had been victor through all; and under all and in all there was a spiritual uplook showing that he had endured as seeing Him who is invisible." The significance of the meeting was not lost with Trumbull: "I have often prayed, as I do to-day, that the light that illumined his face may in some measure be reflected from my face..."[104]

Judson gives us a wonderful example of how joy can shine through our lives even though we are experiencing harsh circumstances. Joy is produced in us as we stay in tune with our Lord.

*101% Joy*

Whenever I shop for milk, I try to find either the 1% or 2% milk. You know what that means: It refers to the amount of milk fat present in the milk. I like the lower percentage, but I do admit, whole milk tastes better.

When it comes to joy, our Lord doesn't want us to be a 1% or 2% joy-filled Christian. He wants us to be overflowing with 101% joy.

Remember, Jesus prayed not that we would have just enough joy; he prayed that we would filled with joy. In John 15:11 he promised the disciples that if they would abide in him, their joy would "overflow." It's interesting, that word is the

---

[104] H. Clay Trumbull, *Old Time Student Volunteers, My Memories of Missionaries* (New York: Fleming H. Revell Co., 1902), pp., 22-23.

same word that the New Living Bible translators rendered with the phrase, "filled with joy," in John 17:13. It's the Greek word, *pleroma*. It means full or complete. If I am filling my glass with water and don't pay attention as I fill the glass, the water might flow over the glass. That's describes this word John used. We are not to be 1% or 2% or even 80% filled with joy, but 101%. We are filled to the point of overflowing.

We can experience 101% joy as we abide in Jesus. We can stay connected with him throughout the day as we speak with him frequently in prayer or contemplate the Scriptures. Like Brother Lawrence, we can practice the presence of God in the most mundane of situations. It can happen while waiting in the doctor's office, driving in traffic, or standing in the grocery line. Remember, it's in loving God and others that he produces fruit in our lives. Prayer is certainly one way we abide in him.

One form of prayer has helped me in focusing on God. It's called centering prayer. It's good to pray in different ways. Paul told the Christians in Ephesus to "pray in the Spirit on all occasions with all kinds of prayers (Ephesians 6:18). I think God likes variety, just notice all the different kinds of animals he created!

Centering prayer is a form of contemplative prayer that has its origins in early Christianity. The Desert Fathers and Mothers---men and women who left the cities to go into the deserts for the purpose of prayer---were for the most part simple and uneducated people. Most could not read, and written material was scarce, so their prayers were just a word or perhaps a short phrase from Scripture that had been read aloud to them. Silence and solitude became important aspects of their life.

But to practice contemplative prayer, you don't have to become a mystic or go to some remote place. Nor do you have to have some special training. This ancient form of prayer, which is being reclaimed by many in the Christian community, is really quite simple and basic. It's not complicated, which is good because I have enough things to complicate my life as it is, and I'm guessing you do as well.

You can begin contemplative prayer or centering prayer by finding a quiet place where you can sit before God and be still. This kind of prayer is more about listening and waiting than talking and informing. It's like you are an empty cup waiting to be filled with what God wants for you rather than you being a driver through the spiritual drive-through restaurant, telling God what you want. So, as you sit there quietly, you are waiting on God as you recognize you are not the one in charge, God is. It is not about you; it's about God.

I have to admit, silence is not easy. We want noise to entertain, inform, and distract us from our problems. Having noise constantly around us can mask the pain in our life and prevent God from healing damaged emotions. I've noticed this about myself: Sometimes when I'm driving, some unpleasant thought will come to mind. Maybe it's a financial problem, or an unpleasant situation at work or home, or some past sin that's already been forgiven. Often I have to catch myself because my immediate human reaction is to turn on the radio and drown out the problem rather than pausing and asking God for wisdom and guidance.

It's unlikely that you are living alone in the desert or in a monastery where silence is a way of life. But we can be intentional about seeking the silence, even if for only a few minutes a day. I start my day by getting up early, usually between 4:30 and 5 a.m. No one in my house is stirring at that hour. That's a good time to be still and rest in God's embrace.

Silence can also be an attitude of the heart. One of the ammas—the desert women and mothers—Amma Syncletica said, "It is possible to be a solitary while living in a crowd, and it is possible that a solitary is living in a crowd of his or her own thoughts."[105]

So you've found a quiet place. But don't get too still and go to sleep! Dr.Curtis Mitchell said, "To pray correctly one must be mentally alert and vigilant. Much praying is hampered by a dull, drowsy frame of mind."[106] Make sure you are wide awake. St. John of Damascus, an early church father, described waiting before God as, "the elevation of the mind to God."[107]

Then, after resting in the presence of God, take up a word, usually a single word that expresses your response to God. Maybe it's "love," or "grace" or "hope" or "Jesus" and repeat this phrase as a kind of mantra. The late Cistercian monk, M. Basil Pennington, said this word should summarize in a few letters or a single syllable, your faith-full response to God. Whenever your

---

[105] Cited by Professor William R. Cook, *The Lives of Great Christians* (Chantilly, Virginia: The Teaching Company, 2007), p., 74.
[106] Cited by Dick Eastman, *The Hour that Changes the World, A Practical Plan for Personal Prayer* (GrandRapids, Michigan: Chosen Books, 2002), p., 62.
[107] Eastman, 39.

mind wanders, as it inevitably will, simply come back to that word.[108]

I often repeat the words of an ancient prayer in the Eastern Orthodox tradition. It's called the Jesus Prayer, and has its origins in the parable of the publican and Pharisee in Luke 18:9-14. The words of this prayer are very simple: "Lord Jesus Christ, Son of God, have mercy on me a sinner." I breathe in with the first phrase, "Lord Jesus Christ, Son of God," and breathe out with the second, "Have mercy on me a sinner." I find this practice both relaxing and invigorating, and I usually feel closer to God when I leave my time of contemplation. Sometimes I pause during the day and pray the Jesus Prayer.

Pennington warns his readers about not having any having demands or expectations when practicing contemplative prayer. Our only desire is to be in the presence of God. When two people know and trust one another, words are not always necessary. Sometimes it's enough simply to be with each other. It's like that in contemplative prayer; it's enough to be with God.

Dick Eastman calls this "wordless worship." He tells the story of Professor Ole Hallesby, a diligent man of prayer. When Hallesby's children were young, they knew when their daddy was praying he was not to be disturbed. But one day his son forgot that rule, and bumped his head on the way into his dad's study. The little guy was a sensitive kind of boy, and it upset him that he had disturbed his daddy. The son looked with love in his eyes to his dad and said, "Papa...I will sit still all the time if you

---

[108] M. Basil Pennington, *Centering Prayer, Renewing an Ancient Prayer Form* (New York; Doubleday, 2001), pp., 65-66.

will only let me be here with you."[109] That's what wordless worship or contemplation is about: contentment in being in the presence of God.

We are programmed to see results. If we prayer for "A," we want to see it soon, if not immediately. And if we pray for "A" we don't want to receive "B," even if it's from God. So contemplative prayer is not easy for most of us. It's also difficult for us to understand what good it's doing, since we are making no requests. But, remember, it takes time for fruit to grow. God is working in your heart as you sit quietly before him, and the fruit will emerge at some point.

I like something Thomas Merton said shortly before his untimely death, "We were indoctrinated so much into means and ends that we don't realize that there is a different dimension in the life of prayer. In technology you have this horizontal process, where you must start at one point and move to another and then another. But that is not the way to build a life of prayer. In prayer…you start where you are and deepen what you already have…Everything has been given us in Christ."[110]

Contemplation is really nothing more than looking to God and finding your true self. As Swiss theologian and Roman Catholic priest, Hans Urs von Balthasar said, "This looking to God is contemplation. It is looking inward into the depths of the soul, and hence beyond the soul toward God. The more

---

[109] Eastman, *The Hour that Changes the World*, 38.
[110] Cited in Pennington, *Centering Prayer*, 49-50.

contemplation finds God, the more it forgets itself and discovers itself in him."[111]

We have joy; Jesus has prayed for us to be filled with it; we just have to access it. Trusting completely in God is the way. Abiding in Christ is part of expressing that trust in him.

The experience of abiding in Christ in contemplative prayer is poignantly described by Jean Vianney. He tells the story of an old peasant who used to spend hours and hours silently sitting in the chapel motionless, seemingly doing nothing. Finally the priest asked the old man, "What are you doing all these hours?" And the old peasant replied, "I look at him, he looks at me, and we are happy."[112]

This is the wonder of what Jesus prayed for us in John 17: He is praying that we will spend time in his presence, listening for him, waiting for him, abiding in him. And as we do, he fills us with joy that spills over so that others are encouraged in their difficulties. And the light he shines through us reflects him, giving him glory. It takes us through the storms. When you are desperate for him, as Elvira Smith was on that dreadful day in 1890, and all you can do is trust the Lord, then you've done enough. The joy will come, if not in the morning, someday.

---

[111] Hans Urs von Balthasar, *Prayer*, trans. Graham Harrison (San Francisco: Ignatius Press, 1986), p., 24.
[112] Pennington, p., 47.

*"Make them holy by your truth; teach them your word, which is truth."*
— John 17:17

*"I can't see a single storm cloud in the sky But I sure can smell the rain"*

— Blackhawk, From *"I Sure Can Smell the Rain"*

# Chapter Eight
# Holiness: A Faintly Familiar Fragrance

I LOVE THAT SMELL OF APPROACHING RAIN. Opening the back door just the other day, I could see storm clouds in the sky and faintly, ever so faintly, smell the rain. "It smells like it's going to rain," I predicted to my wife. It's a distinctive odor---clean and crisp, yet also musky, and it's even stronger after the rain. One reason for that is the ozone that's generated by a thunderstorm, according to Dr. Charles Wysocki of Philadelphia's Monell Chemical Senses Center. Ozone has a pleasant smell to many of us. Another reason rain has that distinctive scent is that the rain kicks up a particular bacteria---actinomycetes---from the soil, and it smells good to most people. Companies have tried unsuccessfully to bottle the smell of rain in laundry detergents and hair spray; perfumers and chemists have difficulty mimicking the minute ingredients that naturally produce those smells during a rain.[113]

It's interesting that the very thing that produces the good smell is a thunderstorm filled with energy, force, even violence.

The storms of life can, depending on how we respond to them, produce within us what the Apostle Paul called a "sweet

---

[113] http://www.npr.org/tempates/story.php?storyId+=12716163

perfume" and a "Christ-like fragrance" (II Corinthians 2:14, 15). In Ephesians 5, Paul said we are to "imitate God" in everything we do by "following the example of Christ" who "loved us and offered himself as a sacrifice for us, a pleasing aroma to God" (Ephesians 5:1, 2). Whenever we follow the example of Christ, we become more holy as we are set apart for him as pure and clean vessels for him to use. It produces a pleasing aroma. It's clean and crisp. It's attractive.

Obedience is not always easy; it can be very difficult. But it pleases God just as Christ pleased him by his obedience on the cross. And something terrible, the cross, resulted in something good, something pleasing to God, a "fragrant aroma."

Whenever we go through the storm, the trial, the trouble, the tribulation, and we respond by allowing God to use us in that storm for him and his glory, we are pleasing to God. We have been obedient even when it wasn't convenient or easy.

In John 17, Jesus prayed for God the Father to make the disciples holy by his truth. Just as the thunderstorm leaves a pleasant aroma, so do we when we remain obedient through the storm. We leave the aroma of Christ. It comes by being holy. Holiness produces an aroma, a fragrance that is pleasing to God.

Al Pacino won an Academy Award for the 1992 movie, *Scent of a Woman*. He played a character that, because of his blindness, had developed a keen sense of smell. He could smell a perfume and almost immediately name the perfume. Whenever he did he would say, "Hoo-ah!"

By his grace God has placed within each believer a desire, a "smell" for this special fragrance that comes with being holy.

Whenever we sense that smell, it's a spiritual "Hoo-ah" moment. We are never really satisfied in our spiritual lives without that fragrance. The more we smell it, the more we desire it.

When I was in grade school, I thought one way I could get the girls to like me was by wearing cologne. I had seen my older brothers put on cologne before a date, so I guessed there must be something to it. Before meeting some girls at the Plaza Theater in my home town of Altus, Oklahoma, my buddies and I would first go by Central Pharmacy, which was conveniently located only two blocks from the theater. We would "cologne up" by splashing on cologne from the samples at the perfume counter. Somehow we thought more was better. Not even the smell of popcorn could tone down what we believed was a manly smell. And to think we wondered why the girls would sniff and wince simultaneously as we sat down next to them!

When it comes to this spiritual fragrance, more is actually better. In fact, you can never get too much. That's because it comes as we express obedience to Christ as his special people.

Now, let's get down to specifics: Where does this fragrance come from? How do we get it? How are we supposed to wear it?

**Where Does This Fragrance Come From?**

Just like joy, holiness comes from a relationship with Christ. The word "holy" is used in various forms over 600 times in the Bible. So, it is an important word, an essential concept emphasized through the Bible.

The Bible says we are called to be holy in all we do: "You must be holy in everything you do, just as God who chose you is holy. For the Scriptures say, 'you must be holy because I am holy'" (I Peter 1:15-16).

Holiness is a requirement for fellowship with God: "Work at living a holy life, for those who are not will not see the Lord" (Hebrews 12:14).

The Bible also indicates that those who are not holy cannot be effectively used of God: "If you keep yourself pure, you will be a special utensil for honorable use. Your life will be clean, and you will be ready for the Master to use you for every good work" (II Timothy 2:21).

While it is an important word, we have a tendency to avoid this little word. That's partly because we have a false mental picture of it. When we mention the word "holy" we often think of something beyond us, something reserved only for the spiritually elite, the religious professional, something we mere "blue collar Christians" can never have or attain. When I say someone is a "holy" person, we might think of an old man with a white beard, an ascetic sitting on top of a mountain somewhere in India, perhaps, or maybe someone living in a monastery wearing a robe, someone who is inaccessible to the world. While those people may in fact be holy, the word "holy" as it is used in Scripture extends far beyond that.

The Greek word for it is *hagios*. It means to be "cut off" or "separated." The verb form is *hagiazo*, which simply means "to set apart for God." A kindred word or derivative of holy is "sanctified." To be sanctified is to be set apart for the Lord's special use.

A football helmet is sanctified as a piece of football equipment. A member of the band might use it at halftime for a musical instrument, but it won't work. A cheerleader might try and use it as a megaphone, but not effectively. The water boy might try to use it to hold water, but that won't work either. Only when it is used on the head of a player is it fulfilling its intended function.

Now, apply that to us. It is only when we are allowing God to set us apart for him and his service that we are fulfilling our purpose in life. So, in a very real sense, we cannot fulfill our God-intended purpose in life unless we are set apart for God, becoming the people he wants us to be and doing what he wants us to do. When we are who he wants us to be, doing what he desires, we are holy people.

When you are truly yourself, the self God wants you to be and not a cheap imitation of someone else, you are holy. Being holy then should be the most natural thing in the world for us. And this is what Jesus is praying for us to be: our true selves.

Is this who you are trying to be? Your true self is seen in the image of our Lord Jesus Christ.

As long as we are trying to be and do something outside of God's will, we find ourselves an unfilled and frustrated people. So, instead of fulfilling God's plan of what true success is, being obedient to God and using our physical, mental and material gifts to his glory, success turns into an imitation of whatever the current cultural picture of success may be, whether it's from Hollywood, Wall Street, Fifth Avenue, or the Super Bowl. And sex, instead of being a gift of God to be enjoyed within the purity of marriage, descends into something tawdry and jaded because it's primarily self-centered; and instead of living to be a "hero" for God, as the Psalmist describes it in Psalm 16, we are mainly in it for ourselves. Life becomes the fulfillment of our own little ego power-drive. And we are never quite satisfied. That's because the ego is insatiable. It is, as Augustine said, never at rest until it finds its rest in God.

From the eternal perspective of God, we are fulfilling our life purpose only when we allow ourselves to be set aside for God and his use. He created us and we are his, even when we try to ignore it or deny it.

The trouble is, we don't trust God for that. We are afraid of God. We fear that if we are obedient to God and allow him to do with us as he wills, we will be unhappy and bored, never reaching our potential. But in fact it works in the exact opposite way. It is as we let God do with us as he wills that we find joy and fulfillment in life. We fail to realize that the good life, the truly best life, is life with Jesus who himself said, "I have come that they may have life and have it more abundantly" (John 10:10, NKJ).

It is as we are holy that we emit this fragrance that can't be found in any cheap over-the-counter imitation. That's why when it's there, it smells faintly familiar: it's what we desire deep down; It's what we are longingly searching for in all the inexpensive imitations. And until we have the real deal---the kind that costs a lot (the death of Christ) and requires everything (your heart), we are never quite satisfied and instead are restless, searching for something more. Nothing can replace that holiness fragrance that brings the "Hoo-ah!" moment.

*The Seven Story Mountain* is the spiritual autobiography of Thomas Merton. Merton was a Trappist monk at the Abby of

Gesthemani in Kentucky from 1941-1968. He was one of the most influential and prolific Christian writers of the twentieth century, authoring more than sixty books, as well as scores of essays and reviews. Volumes of his journals have also been published since his death. *The Seven Story Mountain* details in 462 pages his conversion to Christianity and spiritual journey to the cloistered life of a Cistercian monk.

At one point in his life Merton's motto was "I believe in nothing." While a student at Cambridge University in England, as well as at Columbia University in New York City, Merton drank excessively, was a womanizer, and indulged in a party-boy lifestyle. While at Cambridge he fathered a child. He wrote, "I labored to enslave myself in the bonds of my own intolerable disgust."[114]

In all his efforts to find peace and happiness, Merton was searching in the wrong direction. He later reflected on how Satan deceives us into thinking we are moving in the right direction when in fact we are becoming hopelessly lost in our own confusion: "The devil is no fool," he wrote. "He can get people feeling about heaven the way they ought to feel about hell. He can make them fear the means of grace the way they do not fear sin. And he does so, not by light but by obscurity, not by realities but by shadows, not by clarity and substance but by dreams and the creatures of psychosis."[115] That's where Merton was.

---

[114] Thomas Merton, *The Seven Story Mountain* (The United States of America: Harcourt, Inc., 1998), 121.
[115] Merton, p. 30.

After a complicated struggle, Merton found peace with God. "You rest in Him," he wrote, and "He heals you with his secret wisdom."[116] Merton reminds us that the struggle is within us. God wants us simply to give up to him. "Faith transcends all... limitations," he told his younger brother when he came to visit at Gethsemani, "and does so without labor: for it is God who reveals Himself to us, and all that is required of us is the humility to accept His revelation..."[117]

And that is the only means to holiness, the only way to please him with the only fragrance he will receive.

### How Do We Get This Fragrance?

We have only one way to receive this holiness through Jesus Christ. You can't achieve it by reading self-help books; you can't earn it by living a healthy lifestyle; you can't acquire it with religious activities. Religious pilgrimages won't take you to it; church programs can't create it; spiritual gurus aren't able to pass it on to you.

It's an interesting thing about perfume and cologne bottles: Having the bottles, as attractive as they may be, won't do anything to make anyone smell good. The fragrance has to be put on. So how is this done?

We put this holy fragrance on by putting on Jesus Christ. In a passage where Paul is admonishing believers to live a pure lifestyle, he directs them to "put on the Lord Jesus Christ" (Romans 13:14). This is written to believers, so what does he mean?

---

[116] Merton, p.417
[117] Merton, p. 437.

There is a sense in which we put on Christ in the moment of conversion. We take off the old (the old self) and put on the new (Jesus Christ). We can think of this as that moment in time when we chose Christ. But in another sense, we must throw off the old and put on the new throughout the Christian life, in the same way we choose daily to take up the cross and follow Christ. Thus, although we may be holy from the viewpoint of Christ's work in us at the moment of conversion, that holiness is by no means appropriated into the Christian's life all at once. There is a daily growing in his grace as we say no to sin and yes to Christ. That's why Paul adds in the second half of this verse: "and make no provision for the flesh in the lusts thereof" (Romans 13:14, NKJV).[118]

The journey into holiness therefore begins with identifying with the person of Christ. We sometimes call this "receiving" Jesus Christ. There is a sense in which Christ declares us holy. When we choose Christ, we so to speak, change kingdoms. God now declares us citizens of the Kingdom of Heaven. Since we are in Christ, God has forgiven us and declares us righteous. That is to say, we have a right standing with God. He "credits" Christ's righteousness to our spiritual account. It is just as it was with Abraham when he "believed the Lord and the Lord counted him as righteous because of his faith" (Genesis 15:6). This is Paul's argument in Romans. We who believe on the

---

[118] As Leon Morris points to this distinction and quotes Wesley's apt observation that this is a "strong and beautiful expression for the most intimate union with Him, and being clothed with all the graces which were in Him." See Leon Morris, *The Epistle to the Romans*, (Grand Rapids, Michigan: William E. Eerdmans Publishing Co., 1988), p., 473.

Lord Jesus Christ are pronounced righteous. Yes, we are still sinners, we are still subject to temptation and we fall, but God has declared us guiltless. We are "justified freely by his grace" (Romans 3:24).

Remember this is an act of God's grace. Theologians say our position in Christ has changed. What this means is that we are in Christ. If that is true, the immediate question is, "What about that sin? If we are declared righteous, and therefore holy, why not just sin as we please?" Paul answers this question in Romans 6. He says that since we have been delivered from slavery to sin, we are now free to obey God, which "leads to righteous living" (Romans 6:16). Righteous living is very much a part of being holy. Since we died to sin, we don't have to live in bondage to it any longer, although we still struggle with it.

The reason for this struggling is that we carry into this new kingdom in which we are free to obey God, the habits of our old nature. This means we are not beyond sin or sinning. Paul admonishes us to "reckon" or "consider" or "count" ourselves dead to sin. We are not to let it "reign" or "rule" in our lives. This is of course an act of the will. We will choose to let it rule or not. But since we are now under the power of Christ, we can through him overcome the reign of sin in our lives. Our will is influenced by the power of Christ, and the closer we stay to him, the more power we have to let go of the sin "so easily trips us up" (Hebrews 12:1).

What all this means is that we are declared holy by the work of Christ but are being made into his holy vessels as we respond in obedience to his will for our life. We chose to identify with him, but it was not by our work that he declared us holy. We believed that Jesus Christ is the Son of God, our only hope of salvation and we "threw" ourselves upon his mercy, and by his grace he declared us righteous.

When, as a nine year old boy, I formally chose Christ, he had already by his grace been working in my life. When I opened my life to him, he saw me through Christ. "For God's will was for us to be made holy by the sacrifice of the body of Jesus Christ, once for all" (Hebrews 10:10). It was there on the cross that "the great exchange" took place. He took my sin; I received his holiness. "God made Christ, who never sinned, to be the offering for our sin, so that we could be make right with God through Christ" (II Corinthians 5:21).

You see, I've always had that desire for holiness, deep down in my heart. The fragrance of obedience to God has always been faintly familiar and oh so pleasing. It was planted there by the grace of our Lord. Once I chose him back, I couldn't get away from it; the perfume of obedience and its pleasant fragrance is present whenever I am living in obedience to the Father.

This is why the Cross is so essential. Apart for what Christ did there, we are hopeless and still dead in our sins. Paul determined to know nothing but Jesus Christ and him crucified.

Paul warned us about the cross being "emptied of its power" (I Corinthians 1:17). That happens when we try to think of a sweet Jesus who forgives us but doesn't call us into holiness. It happens whenever we have Christianity without the sacrifice that Christ made for us. The cross means something. Jesus died for me. The only way to holiness, which is the only way to God, is by way of the cross. I know of no other way. A cross without Jesus Christ becomes merely a quaint decoration.

Occasionally, I will see someone wearing a ball cap with a team logo on it. Sometimes I ask that person if they are a fan of the team or just wearing the cap. And more often than you might guess, people wear a team logo because they just like the colors. I sometimes want to ask people who are wearing the cross, "Are you a believer, or do you just like it as a piece of jewelry?"

The right standing we have with God is a gift. With that right standing I am holy, from God's perspective. He sees me though the Son Jesus Christ with whom I have appealed for help and identified with as my Savior. Holiness in this sense is a gift of God as I look to him for salvation.

Some years ago I went to Honduras as part of a mission effort. I had to have a passport to get into that country. A member of our team, the man who organized and led it, paid the fee for my passport. I didn't have to pay anything for it. I just had to agree that I was going to preach at this crusade, or of course there would be no point in me having a passport in the first place.

When we passed through customs, all I did was show my passport and then the customs agent let me pass through. To him, all that mattered was that I was a citizen of the U.S. He didn't ask me if I said the Pledge of Allegiance, or if I sang the National Anthem at athletic events, or if I paid my taxes, or if I voted in the last election. You see, I had been legally declared a citizen of the United states on that passport.

When we come to Christ we are legally declared citizens of the kingdom of God. And with that declaration, God sees us as holy through the blood of the cross. It covers my sins, so I may freely enter into the presence of a holy God. The cross reminds me of that. I am not declared holy and righteous because I made a donation to the church or served chicken and the church dinner or sat through a hundred and fifty-five worship services.

But the cross also reminds me that Christ suffered on the cross. My passport did cost something. It just didn't cost me anything. And no amount of money can purchase holiness for me. I need someone who is sinless, perfect in holiness to take my place on this death row that we humans call life. We are only waiting to die. Again the great exchange is that Christ on the cross suffered my death. Remember, not just anyone could do this. It had to be someone who was without sin and therefore perfect in holiness. God in his mercy sent to us the perfect Son of God. When we look to the Cross, we remember and are grateful. And it is there, at the cross that we find our direction through the storms of life.

Charring Cross refers to a district of London where Edward I erected, in about 1290, the last of a series of crosses in memory of his wife Eleanor of Castile. The original position of the cross was recognized as the geographical center of London. Locations in London were measured by their distance from Charring Cross. The spot, located at the junction of Strand, Whitehall, and Cockspur Streets, is often referred to simply as "the cross."

The story is told about a little boy getting lost in London. He is seen by a London "bobby," as they refer to their police officers, standing on a street corner crying in despair. The child is so upset that he cannot remember his own address. After repeated questions from the officer, the child says, in between sobs, "If you will take me to the cross, I can find my way home from there."[119]

We get lost here on our journey to heaven. Here on this earth, like the little lost boy, we have trials and tribulations. But the Lord reminds us that in the midst of the storms of life, the cross will guide us home. It is the centerpiece of our faith; it guides us even as it is itself the way unto holiness, which is the way into the presence of God. We sense it. The sweet aroma of the cross smells faintly familiar. It's the aroma of obedience. God has placed that honing system within us. Follow that spiritual instinct. And remember the way of the cross leads home.

### How Do We Wear this Fragrance?

Living our lives for Jesus is a holy life because we are consecrating or setting aside our lives for him. That's in essence what a holy life is. So, it's more than a declaration from God. "You are a holy nation" (I Peter 2: 9); it's also a striving on our part to be holy, as it says in I Peter, "in all your behavior" (I Peter 1:15).

"All your behavior" would include thoughts, words, and actions. That involves offering ourselves as "a living and holy sacrifice---the kind he will find acceptable" (Romans 12:1). This

---

[119] Paul Lee Tan, ed., *Encyclopedia of 15, 000 Illustrations, Signs of the Times* (Dallas, Texas: Bible Communications, 1998), p. 1390.

would mean resisting sin so that it does not "control the way we live" (Romans 6:12).

So here we are, as it were, citizens in a new kingdom with the smell or fragrance of the old kingdom about us. How do we live in the new kingdom as children of God? By simply obeying the dictates of the king. Our behavior reveals our true kingdom.

Supposedly, St. Augustine, once had a dream when he was a young man in his early thirties. Although he was a Christian, Augustine was intensely absorbed in Cicero, the Latin philosopher In the dream Augustine died and came to heaven's gates. The gatekeeper asked, "Who are you?"

"Augustine of Milan," he answered.

"No," said the gatekeeper, "You are a Ciceronian." When Augustine asked for an explanation, the angelic being replied, "All souls are estimated in this world by what dominated in that. In you, Augustine, not the Christ of the Gospel, but the Cicero of Roman jurisprudence, was the dominating force. You cannot enter here."

The dream so startled Augustine that he awoke; and once he was fully conscious, he determined that not only his actions but his thoughts would be dominated by Christ.

So how is it with you? What dominates your thoughts these days? What is the motivating factor in your life? Is it really Christ and his Kingdom?

We must choose whom we will follow and that comes down to basic decisions of each day. If we want transformation, we must seek the presence of God. Seeking his presence sounds easy, but how does it take place? Just how do we experience this transformation? If I am declared "holy" and thus a part of God's forever kingdom, a citizen in the kingdom of God, yet still a bundle of bad habits which I brought from the "other kingdom," that of the flesh, how am I to live a pleasing life for my new master? Paul the Apostle gives us the answer in Romans 12:2: "Don't copy the behavior and customs of this world, but let God transform you into a new person by changing the way you think. Then you will learn to know God's will for you, which is good and pleasing and perfect."

This is where the transformation takes place: in the mind as I change the way I think. This new way of thinking, this "mind transformation" will enable you to know God's good and pleasing will for your life. (Romans 12:2). Remember this passage is written specifically to the Christians in Rome, whom Paul described as "loved by God" and "called to be his own holy people" (Romans 1:7). If you are in Christ, that describes you as well and means your mind too is to be transformed by Christ.

But how? How does this mind transformation take place? It can only occur in one place, and that is in the presence of God as we are directed by the Holy Spirit. This can happen in times of worship, as we praise God; it can happen in our private time of prayer as we bring ourselves into the presence God in our alone times; or it can happen as we pray with others; or it can take place as we meditate on the Scriptures. It occurs as we live our lives in obedience to him.

The Scripture will be our essential guide in all of this. Apart from the nourishment of God's word, our prayers may become dry and desiccated; without the direction of the Word of God, our worship may drift into the imagination of our own "untransformed minds." We may be enticed to follow false teachers and eventually even fall into heresy.

When Jesus prayed for the disciples, he prayed that they would be "sanctified" or "made holy" by the truth. He immediately tells us what the truth is: "Thy word is truth." (John 17:17). As we encounter the Word of God, our lives are transformed.

The Scripture is described as "inspired by God," "God—breathed," and therefore "useful to teach us what is true and to make us realize what is wrong in our lives. It corrects us when we are wrong and teaches us to do what is right" (II Timothy 3:16). In another place the Word of God is described as "the sword of the Spirit" (Ephesians 6:17). And it is said to be "sharper than the sharpest two-edged sword, cutting between soul and spirit, between joint and marrow. It exposes our innermost thoughts and desires" (Hebrews 4:12).

As we get in touch with the Scripture, God uses his own Word to pierce our hearts where we have strayed and strengthen us where we are weak. The Word protects us from the foolishness of following the wrong way and bad advice.

The Scripture is then used by God to transform our minds. As we immerse ourselves in his Word we grow in holiness.

We've all known Christians who know the Bible well but live it poorly. Their knowledge is impressive; their lives are not. Indeed they live terribly hypocritical lifestyles. They profess one thing and live another.

This is because it is possible to come to the Scriptures with the intention of increasing our knowledge but not of deepening our relationship with God. We might search the Bible for trivia or for ammunition against an opponent or simply to prepare for a sermon or lesson. Knowing the Bible is a good thing. But knowledge is no assurance that our lives will be moving in the direction of holiness.

That comes only when we receive the Word of God as a message to be applied to our lives. It happens as we listen for the voice of God with a heart to obey. As we come to the Scriptures with an attitude of obedience to God, we may falter and fail from time to time, but if we are patient and consistent in our devotion to God's Word, our lives will slowly but surely be transformed by God into the likeness of his holiness. We will become saints, at least saints in the sense of being set apart as clean vessels for God's use.

I emphasize applying the Word to our lives. The richest times of spiritual growth in my life have been those times when, because of a storm that comes as a bitter disappointment, an illness, a personal pain, a tragedy, or a failure---I have been driven to the Word of God as my source of hope, strength and help. It those times as I have sat quietly with the Word of God in my hands, the Holy Spirit has applied just what was necessary at the moment: maybe a rebuke of discipline, a message of encouragement, or an affirmation of conviction. In any case, the growth in holiness has come when I've approached the Word with this spiritual attitude of meekness. That has acted as a stimulus to holiness.

At times I've been inspired by hearing the preaching of God's Word. And, I have learned valuable truths by reading and studying the Bible. But it has been in mediating on the Scriptures on a consistent day by day basis that has enriched my relationship with God the most. The move to holiness has taken place in that encounter with God's Word. I agree with Jerry Bridges that "if we are to pursue holiness with discipline, we must do more than hear, read, study, or memorize Scripture."[120] We must sit quietly before God and allow his Word to permeate our souls: We must encounter him in that Word and let him encounter us.

When I was a teenager, I traveled with my parents who were volunteering their time and resources for missions. Dad practiced dentistry, so we where he was needed in different countries. We would stay several weeks and then return. Usually on the return trip we would treat ourselves by stopping and sightseeing in various places along the way. Dad wanted to see as much as possible in the brief time we had. He would usually book a tour of whatever major city we had chosen to visit. I recall touring Rome by bus, as well as Athens, London, and Paris. We would get off the bus momentarily, view a few statues, take some pictures and move on as quickly as the tour guide said, "All aboard." Our hasty tours were just enough to whet my appetite for more, whether it was the Louvre in Paris, London's Bridge, or the Coliseum in Rome. I knew those places only superficially. The times I enjoyed the most often came after the fast-paced tour. Sometimes I would jog through the streets in the early morning or walk leisurely down an avenue after dinner. Strolling down the little byways and running through out-of- the way places, I got better acquainted with the city.

---

[120] Jerry Bridges, *The Pursuit of Holiness*, 99.

Dad was reminiscing recently about the time we visited Rome. The tour guide showed us where Paul the Apostle was imprisoned. But (and I had forgotten this) we, that is Mom, Dad, and I, went back on our own to see where they think Paul was imprisoned. It was after the conventional tour that we took our time in Paul's prison home. It was after the tour that the place had time to affect me. I wasn't just traveling through to say I had been there. I could smell the musty dankness of the stone walls; I could feel the confinement of the cramped quarters; I could see Paul dictating letters while he walked back and forth with his chains clanging.

And it happened in similar ways in other places: It was smelling the aroma of bread baking in Paris, or being amused by the accents of taxi drivers in London, flinching at the pungent smell of the open meat market in Addis Ababa. Often, it's the little side roads you take that lead to the unexpected places where you find yourself in the true heart of the city. And you become personally acquainted with it.

It is similar with the Word of God. We can go on the bus tour or get out and stay a bit. The hurried tour is better than not seeing it at all. At least you've actually seen it. But it is in getting out of the bus, in camping out with the Word of God, that you really get to know the Word.

I have gleaned information by reading through the Bible in a year. It has been a wonderful blessing to do that more than a few times. But it has been in the quiet of my alone time with the Word when I wasn't meeting a requirement to get through a certain section of Scripture by a particular date or find something for a devotional or Bible study that I've truly encountered the Word. It has been in the daily discovery of the little byways and nooks and crannies of God's word that I have been most nourished.

We meet Christ in the Word of God, and he is the one who is able to transform our lives. Remember in John chapter 12 where certain Greeks had come to worship during the Passover celebration. They spoke to Philip, one of Jesus' disciples, and said, and I've always like the way it states it in the King James, "We would see Jesus" (John 12:20-21, KJV). They had come to meet Jesus. This has to be our attitude when we come to the Scripture. This is not the only place we can meet with Jesus, but we know Jesus our Lord as we know him in the revealed Word of God. Listen to Hebrews 1:1-2: "Long ago God spoke many times and in many ways to our ancestors through the prophets. And now in these final days, he also has spoken to us though his Son." The Scripture, Old and New Testaments, point to him. As we read, we come to know him more and more. St. Jerome, an early father of the church, said, "Not to know the Scriptures is to be ignorant of Christ."[121] We open the Scriptures to find Christ.

An ancient form of prayer combines meditation with the reading of Scripture. It's called *lectio divina*. It has been rediscovered in recent years and has helped Christians know God better. Maybe it will do that for you. Perhaps you've already been doing something like this, but didn't know it had a name. *Lectio divina* simply means "divine reading." In essence,

---

[121] Michael Casey, *Sacred Reading, The Ancient Art of Lectio Divina*, (Liguori, Missouri: Liguori/Triumph,: 1995), p., 36.

it's is a slow, contemplative praying of the Scriptures and can enable us to experience God.

An ancient command of the prophets was, "Hear O Israel!" *Lectio divina* is a "hearing" of the Scriptures. It is listening to the voice of God in his Word. St. Benedict, the father of western monasticism, said in the Prologue of his rule that we must hear "with the ear of our hearts."[122] This monastic tradition, emerging to a large degree from St. Benedict and his *Rule*, developed over a period of years the art of *lectio divina*. It took on a certain form or outline with several steps or directions.

The first, referred to as *lectio*, was a slow reading of the Scriptures. It is a reverential reading of God's Word which allows for a gentle listening to hear words or phrases that speak to the reader. It's the first reading through of a given passage of Scripture.

The second reading is *meditatio*---meditation. The image of an animal ruminating, quietly chewing its cud is a symbol of this ancient form of meditating on God's Word. This involves a slow repetition of the words of Scripture, even memorizing it, but not memorizing for the sake of memorizing but a slow meditating on the Scripture. The Scriptures are sometimes burned in the memory.

The third reading of the same passage is called *oratio*- prayer. That may seem confusing, since the entire process is prayer. But at this point we might speak out loud the cry or prayer of our heart, although it doesn't have to be more than a

---

[122] Joan Chittister, *The Rule of Benedict, Insights for the Ages* (New York, NY.: The Cossroad Publishing Company, 1992.), p., 19.

whisper. Here we are praying the Scriptures themselves. We personalize it. We allow the Word which we have been pondering to touch and change our deepest selves. In fact, it reveals to us our true selves. We pray the Scriptures. We bring our most secretive, pain-filled experiences to God and allow the healing word or phrase to penetrate them. The turmoil of David is the Psalms for example may speak to similar experiences in your own life. But we don't stop at the identification. We pray through that Scripture with a consecrating prayer of the Scripture itself. It sometimes convicts us; at other times it heals wounds, and in another instance it can encourage us or all of these at one time.

The final stage is *contemplatio*—contemplation. In this stage or movement we simply rest in the presence of God and invite him in his loving way to transform our inner self, our true self. We rest in the embrace of God whom we contemplate through his Word.

Michael Casey in his book on this subject writes that *lectio divina* is an essential element in contemplation. So this last stage leads naturally to it. Contemplation is a shift in our consciousness away from an awareness of all that we feel, see, touch, and smell, and think about in regard to those things, to a God-consciousness, so that we empty ourselves of ourselves, and we are as Paul wrote, filled with all the fullness of God (Ephesians 3:19).[123]

The goal of *lectio divina* is not the mastering of another process; the goal is the same as the other forms of prayer we've

---

[123] Michael Casey, *Sacred Reading*, pp., 58-59.

discussed: knowing and experiencing God. And knowing and experiencing God means that we will follow him with a burning desire to be holy even as he is holy. We will walk in the ways of a holy God and be conformed to the image and likeness of his Son. *Lectio divina* is simply another form of prayer that can assist us in knowing and loving God more.

I love the story about the farmer who lived in the middle of Kansas. This farmer raised two sons. They both joined the navy. The farmer's brother, and therefore the uncle of these boys, was a psychologist. He came for a visit. As he was eating supper with his brother, the farmer and father of the boys said, "You know, it's an interesting thing. I raised my two boys out here in the middle of Kansas on this farm which is miles from any body of water. How is it that both of them joined the navy?

The brother said, "That's an interesting question. Let me think about it."

That night he slept in the boys' room. The next morning, when he joined his brother for breakfast, he said, "I think I may know why both of your boys joined the navy. Follow me to their room."

They walked upstairs to the boys' room. The first thing they saw when they walked in was a beautiful picture of a ship in the middle of the sea. The psychologist then told his brother to lie down on the bed. "What do you see when you get up from the bed?" he asked.

The farmer said, "I see the picture."

The psychologist said, "The first thing you see when you walk into this room is that picture. The last thing you see before you go to sleep is that picture. The first thing you see when you awake and get up is that picture." Then he asked, "Did the boys have that picture in this room for very long?"

The farmer said, "Yes, since they were about three years old."

Then the brother said, "If you think about a picture like that long enough, you might become a sailor."

And if we think about the Scriptures, if we meditate on it long enough, we will surely become the saints God wants us to become.

Yes, the Lord God wants you to become a saint because that's who you are supposed to be. Remember the definition of a saint? It is someone who has been set apart for God's use. So, when you are being sanctified, that is when you are set apart by God for his use, God is pleased because you are being and becoming who you really are: your true self and not your false self.

My Grandmother Moore (my mother's mom) lived a simple life style in a one bedroom house on the edge of a small town, Glencoe, Oklahoma. Just outside the bedroom window where I used to sleep when we would visit her was an open field, the country. The morning doves' songs awakening me early in the morning were an abrupt but natural reminder of where I was: Grandmother's house.

Grandmother tended a garden just large enough for what she needed. I looked forward to her words, "Davey, let's go pick some berries." I knew what she meant: strawberries and ooh were they good. I would stay close to her side as we picked, for I was unsure, being the city boy I was, which ones to pick and which ones to leave on the vine a bit longer. The best part was bringing those strawberries into Grandmother's kitchen. We would set them in the sink for her to wash. Then Grandmother would place the freshly picked and washed strawberries on the table. I would stare at them for a moment with a sense of accomplishment that I had something to do with them being there.

Then I would take a deep breath.

"Can you smell them?" Grandmother would ask me. Ahh, the aroma of fresh strawberries filled that little kitchen with the ambrosiastic delights I would forever after associate with Grandmother's kitchen. After relishing that fruitful fragrance, we would at last sit down and enjoy a bowlful of strawberries fresh from the vine.

The closer we get to God, the holier we become, the sweeter is the smell of our spiritual fruit. How could it be otherwise? "Our lives are a fragrance presented by Christ to God" (II Corinthians 2:14). Now, every now and then I sense the aroma of fresh strawberries. I don't mean the store bought kind, although they can be mighty good. But there is something special about the ones fresh from the vine. Whenever I do smell fresh berries, maybe from someone's garden or perhaps at a fruit stand by the side of the road, I sense something faintly familiar: It's Grandmother's kitchen. The aroma puts me back there with her as she, with a smile on her aged face, would proudly present her strawberries for me to enjoy.

And so it is with us. The aroma is faintly familiar. It's better than any cologne at Central Pharmacy or overly ripened fruit at a supermarket. It's the fruit of obedience giving rise to the fragrance of holiness that our Lord, with a satisfied smile, takes to the Father.

Do you smell it?

*"Just as you sent me into the world, I am sending them into the world."*
—John 17:18

*"I didn't know people cared about me so much."*[124]
—Larry Allen, resident of Joplin, Mo, upon returning to his home demolished by a tornado and learning that neighbors had been searching for him.

---

[124] "Joplin hunts for survivors in debris," *The Courier-Journal,* May 25, 2011, p. A4.

# Chapter Nine
# Mission-Mindedness: Set Apart to be Sent Out

AFTER THE DEVASTATING TORNADO HIT JOPLIN, Missouri on Sunday, May 23, 2011, John DeGraff and another friend searched for their neighbor, Larry Allen. Allen's home had been destroyed by the terrible twister. Allen had tried to get to his basement when the tornado hit, but he didn't make it that far. He waited out the storm in his stairwell. And it was a good thing, too. The entire upstairs of his house fell into his basement. After the storm had done its damage, Allen walked away and stayed with some friends for a couple of days. But his neighbors didn't know that and rummaged through the rubble of his home looking for him. When he returned home and learned that neighbor John DeGraff and others had been digging through what was once Allen's home, he was overwhelmed. "God bless you," he responded with gratitude to his neighbors. He had no idea others cared so much about him.[125]

When we love the Lord with all our heart, soul, mind and strength, then joy is produced in our lives. And as we love our Lord, we are set apart for his purposes. We are used as his holy vessels. Once we have been set apart, we are sent out to love

---
[125] Ibid.

others and in so doing, we are fulfilling the command of Jesus to love others as ourselves.

In Luke 10, an expert of the law came to Jesus and asked a similar question as the man in Mark 12:28 did. His question was, "What do I have to do to inherit eternal life?" (Luke 10:25). When Jesus asked him what the Law of Moses said, the man had the answer: "Love the Lord your God with all your heart, all your soul, all your strength, and all your mind.' And, 'love your neighbor as yourself'" (Luke 10:27). It was the answer Jesus had given the legal analyst in Mark 12.

But this guy, "in order to justify his actions," (and that little statement is so very telling) wanted Jesus to qualify who a "neighbor" was. In other words, the man was saying, "The Law my say that, but surely it doesn't mean that. Surely it can't mean I should love just *anybody*." And like he so often did, Jesus answered with a story. It's a familiar one: the story about the Good Samaritan. You will recall that the Good Samaritan was the only one---not the priest, not the Levite---to stoop and help the Jewish man. The despised Samaritan was the only one who bothered to love his neighbor.

Jesus left no room for his listeners. When Jesus said "love your neighbor," he meant everybody. And lest we try and interpret "love your neighbor," only in ethnic terms, Jesus also said we are to love our enemies too. (Matthew5:43). So "neighbor" in effect includes everyone.

In John 17 we hear the prayer of Jesus. And at this point in his prayer we hear him saying we are to be sent into the world. Just as the Father sent Jesus into the world, so we are to be sent. Being sent is our mission.

Our English word for mission comes from a Latin word which means "to send." What does our mission include? Jesus said we are sent into the world. We are to befriend the world, and keep in mind the world is made up of actual people. We are to love them because these people are our neighbors. Jesus is praying for the disciples. He is telling the Father that he, the Son, is sending them. In so doing, Jesus is praying that his followers will be mission-minded. Loving our neighbor, whoever that happens to be, will ever be on our mind.

But, it's easy to forget our mission.

Years ago I read a story about a group of people who lived in a small community located on a dangerous area of sea coast. Shipwrecks were not unusual in this area and lives were too often lost. So the people decided to build a rescue station. They didn't have the resources for much, but they managed to operate a small rescue station. Some were trained in CPR to help those who were brought to the station; others were skilled at spotting those in danger on the sea; still others would go out in boats to rescue the ones stranded in the water. They even tried to warn boats and ships of the potential dangers of the sea. They were vigilant in their efforts to save lives. And they had some stunning successes. People were saved because of the workers at the rescue mission. A newspaper reporter did a story on the little mission, and soon others wanted to help. It became quite chic to be involved in the rescue mission.

The mission grew; more people joined the cause; donations were made; soon they were able to build a bigger and much nicer rescue station. The new building was beautifully decorated and nicely furnished. In fact, someone made the comment that it resembled a country club. Not long after that, another ship wrecked, and the victims muddied the plush new carpet, and a few even got blood on it. Some of the newer members of the rescue mission didn't like what had happened to their new building. They wanted to keep the new building for recreational purposes only and use the older, smaller structure for the actual victims. Others didn't like that idea; they argued that the new building was built for the victims of the sea. But the ones lobbying for a social club won, so the other group went a little further down the coast and built another small mission. The ones who stayed behind weren't really interested in the mission of saving lives anyway.

After a number of years, the new rescue mission had grown, and a new building was erected. It looked more like a country club as well. By now, you've guessed what happens, haven't you? This rescue mission split just like the first one as a majority wanted more of a social club than a rescue mission. The story was repeated time and again as the coast line became dotted with rescue missions that turned into social clubs, and fewer and fewer people were interested in the original mission of saving lives.

The story illustrates what often happens to churches: It's not that they deliberately deny their mission; it's a matter of the distractions that lead to competing interests. Once having elevated another interest to that of the original cause of the mission, that original purpose is submerged until it is only a memory, if it is even that.

Jesus had a mission; through his life, death, and resurrection he would glorify the Father. Now he prays that we too will be sent on a mission. As Rick Warren reminds us, "The mission Jesus had while on earth is *now* our mission because we are the Body of Christ." In answering his own rhetorical question, "What is that mission?" Warren succinctly answers, "Introducing people to God!" [126]

If anyone, including enemies, can be our neighbor, we are to do what we can to introduce them to Christ. Our task or mission is "reconciling people to him" (II Corinthians 5:18). So each of us, are instruments God has set aside to point people to Christ. We find our spiritual gifts and use them in helping others. As we do, we glorify God.

Our mission began in the heart of God and was expressed to us in Jesus Christ. We continue what Jesus began through the power of the Holy Spirit.

## The Source of our Mission

Jesus prayed to God the Father, "Just as you sent me into the world, I am sending them into the world" (John 17:18). How did the Father send the Son into the world? It was an act of love within the Godhead resulting in the Son taking on flesh and coming to us as a baby born in a manger. What in inauspicious beginning of the mission on earth.

John explicitly stated it in that passage that we love to quote as much perhaps as any verse in the Bible: "God so loved the world that He gave his only begotten Son that whoever believes on Him should not perish but have everlasting life" (John 3:16). The motive was love, the love of God. This is what

---

[126] Rick Warren, *The Purpose Driven Life* (Grand Rapids, Michigan: Zondervan, 2002), p.282.

we call agape love, or love that expects nothing in return, love that loves simply because it is the nature of the lover to love. It is God's nature to love us. God does not love us because we are good people or because he needs the likes of us on his team. God loves us simply because God loves us. It is therefore an unconditional love. Paul makes this clear in his letter to the Romans. "Now, most people would not be willing to die for an upright person, though someone might perhaps be willing to die for a person who is especially good," Paul tells us in Romans 5:7. He then drives home his central point in the next verse: "But God showed his great love for us by sending Christ to die for us while we were still sinners." How did Christ come to us? In an act of love he humbled himself, taking the form of a servant, dying our death for us. In so doing, he addressed our deepest need as people.

Somebody said it like this:

> *If our greatest need had been knowledge,*
> *God would have sent us an educator.*
> *If our greatest need had been technology,*
> *God would have sent us a scientist.*
> *If our greatest need had been money,*
> *God would have sent us an economist.*
> *If our greatest need had been pleasure,*
> *God would have sent us an entertainer.*
> *BUT, our greatest need was forgiveness, so God sent us a Savior.*

The picture we should have of God the Father should not be that of a holy tyrant but of a Father who loves; a God who wants the best for us. Salvation comes in our recognition that we do not always know what is best, that left to ourselves we would be hopelessly flawed, and that God is the only one who can bring that to us what we really do need: forgiveness and the peace with God.

Peter Mackenzie was an English Methodist preacher of another generation. When he announced that he was preaching on the text John 3:16, he said, "There are two striking things in my text: When God loves, He loves a world. When He gives, He gives his Son."[127] Such is the length, width, depth, and height of God's love (Ephesians 3:18). It is impossible for us fully to comprehend it.

Because God has given his love, we share what we have been given. If Jesus came to us from the Father's love, we must share that same love with others. An evangelist is one who shares the Good News out of a spirit of love. Our motivation is to share God's love. Because we cannot control how people respond to that love or know who will receive it and who will not, we randomly distribute God's love. This naturally involves a sacrifice. Like our Lord, we may be rejected, mocked, ignored, and abused. Therefore, it is not always easy to share this unconditional love. But when we have experienced his transforming power, we cannot help but share it.

---

[127] Paul Lee Tan, ed., *Encyclopedia of 15,000 illustrations*, *Signs of the Times* (Dallas, TX.: Bible Communications, 1998) p, 1009.

As Jesus reclined at the very table where he would that very evening voice this prayer to his Father, he said, "Love one another. As I have loved you, so you must love one another" (John 14:34-35.) Just as he set us apart to receive this love, we are sent to share it.

**The Scope of our Mission**

Jesus prayed that we would be sent into the world. The world tells us the extent of our mission. In Matthew 10:5, Jesus "sent out the twelve apostles with these instructions..." This was a specific mission he gave to his disciples. Jesus gave them detailed directions on how they were to carry it out. They were not to go the Gentiles, for example. They were not to take money with them, or a change of clothes, or even a walking stick. After the resurrection the mission was expanded. The Jewish people preached the Good News of the risen Christ. The church decided, based on the revelation of Christ to Peter and Paul, that this Good News was for everyone (Acts 9:15, 10:34-35, 15:1-31).

Before he ascended into heaven, Jesus clearly and repeatedly gave the command to all believers. In Matthew 28:19 he said, "Go..." and again in Mark 16:15 those words appear again, "Go..." and again in Luke 24:48, "You are witnesses..." and in John 20:21: "As the Father has sent me, so I am sending you." The command requires some sort of action on our part. The scope of the mission is limitless; it is worldwide; it is to "all nations" or "peoples."

The challenging part is in the going. Going may for one person involve sharing the gospel to a family member at home;

to another it could mean sharing Christ with a next door neighbor; for still another, it could mean traveling across the world, sharing Christ with people of another culture in a far-away country. It always requires a decision to share in some way this Good News. In today's world, one can witness around the world via the internet. The gospel is proclaimed through books and recordings. The possibilities are limited only by us.

Thus, both before and after the resurrection Jesus gave the command for his followers to go and share this Good News. The only change was the extent of the mission. Since it is a command, it is not optional for the follower of Christ. If it's a command, we find a way to do it.

When I was in high school I played football. I was not the best player by any means, but I doubt anyone enjoyed the game any more than I did. In those days we ran an option offense that was popular called the "wish-bone." I played halfback. On 282 Sweep the quarterback had the option of giving the football to the fullback, keeping it, or pitching it to the left halfback. The right halfback (in this instance me) had the responsibility of blocking the defensive end.

We had a rugged defensive end at the time named John Trest. John would later earn a full scholarship in football to the University of Oklahoma. He was every bit of 6ft.5 in. tall and weighed a solid 240 pounds. That was a great thing for our team when we played an opponent. It wasn't so pleasant when in practice I had to block John Trest. As much as I loved football and wanted to give it my best, my scrawny 5 ft. 5in. 140 pound frame was no match for Trest.

Our offensive coordinator at that time was a man named Butch Brown. Coach Brown was a stout, solid former lineman himself. A Native American Cherokee Indian, he was built like a large fire plug. All it took for him to look like a Chief on the warpath was for him to pull his ball cap down over his forehead while squinting his eyes. Just thinking about that "Coach Brown look" still makes me wince in fear even today! Yet, Coach would be there whenever one of "his boys" was in need. We loved and respected him.

So there I was, tiny David Whitlock, with the unenviable assignment of blocking John Trest. Trest was in front of me, Coach Brown behind me! We ran the option, and Trest casually stepped on me, and easily made the tackle. We trotted back to the huddle, and Coach Brown gave the command: "Run it again and see if Whitlock can make the block." We did. This time Trest swatted me aside like I was a pesky fly. As I and the poor halfback whom Trest tackled, limped back to the huddle, Coach was livid. He grabbed me by the shoulder pads, lifted me an inch off the ground and through clenched teeth commanded, "Whitlock, I don't care if you have to bite him, kick him, or pull his hair, just get the defensive end out of the way!"

I'm not sure which approach I took; maybe I all tried all three. I do recall Trest falling on top of me and threatening me, "Whitlock, if you ever do that again, I'll kill you!" And I told him I had rather him try to kill me than have Coach Brown do it for sure!

But my motive was not totally based on fear. I truly loved Coach Brown as an athlete loves a coach who cares and demands respect. I feared disappointing him more than I feared

*Surviving the Storms of Life*

blocking John Trest. So, in a very real sense, love for my coach was the motivating factor.

Most of us have a fear of being on mission for Christ. We fear rejection; we fear embarrassment; we fear humiliation. These are common apprehensions. Most Christians rarely if ever share the Good News, and much of the reason is because of our fears. Perhaps if we had more of a healthy fear of God---not the kind of fear a child has who cringes when a capricious parent walks in the room, the child never knowing if the parent is going to randomly punish and reject—a fear that yearns not to disappoint, then maybe we would be more likely to find a way, some way, to share the Good News. And if we had a lack of knowledge or training, then we would do what is necessary to acquire the skills to accomplish the mission.

We are much too complacent. Over ninety percent of Christians never lead another person to Christ.[128]

This doesn't mean we must be smooth talkers. Neither are we professional salespersons. Remember the words attributed to Francis of Assisi: "Preach the Gospel; use words if necessary." We will find a way to display the Good News.

So, we preach the gospel wherever we are because we live it. Benjamin Franklin once said, "A good example is the best sermon." We preach wherever we are with whomever we happen to be: the supervisor down the hall at work; the student seated across the aisle at school; the parent at the P.T.O. meeting; the family across the street. Again, we don't have to manipulate; we simply share the Good News about our Lord.

---

[128] Tim Beougher, "Personal Evangelism for the 21st Century," *Southern Seminary Magazine*, Summer 2004, p. 11.

We have been set aside through the loving choice of our Father to tell the world about his love.

**The Strength for Our Mission**

How can we possibly accomplish such a challenging mission as bringing the world to Christ? It is only through the power of the Holy Spirit. As Jesus was preparing the disciples for his death, he promised the Holy Spirit would come. The Holy Spirit would enable the church to do even greater works than Jesus had done. (John 14:12) And as they went on mission, the Holy Spirit would convict people of sin and point them to righteousness. Furthermore, he would guide the disciples into all truth. (John 16:5-15)

In his prayer to the Father, Jesus used the word "sent" to describe how we would go. It is the Holy Spirit who strengthens us to go. And he comforts us and empowers us along to way.

The word John used for "send" in John 17:18 is the word "apostello." We get the word "apostle" from that word. An apostle is one who is sent. In II Corinthians 5:20-21, Paul wrote, "So we are Christ's ambassadors; God is making his appeal through us."

We are sent as ambassadors by the power of the Holy Spirit who not only provides the motivation for our going but the direction and strength for it as well. An ambassador is an official representative of one government or country to another government or country. The host country usually allows the ambassador and his or her staff control of a specific territory called an embassy. Now think about this: Ambassadors represent their country on foreign soil, in a different culture, where a different language is spoken, where different traditions are observed, and different lifestyles are the norm. How the ambassador represents his or her country in that different place is how the people there view his country. Ambassadors can be poor representatives or good ones.

In representing their country, ambassadors have to have their own country's interest above their own. They are there at the behest of their country. Ambassadors must unflinchingly abide by the command of their government, even if it means being unpopular in the eyes of the people in the foreign country.

William Barclay points out that in Paul's day the word "ambassador" was used primarily in two ways.[129] In a Roman province that was not peaceful but prone to violating Rome's authority, the Emperor himself appointed the ambassador who would take orders directly from the emperor. In this instance, the ambassador's authority was from the emperor himself. Seen from this perspective, Paul was saying that we as Christians serve in a hostile world where the Kingdom of God is rejected, sometimes violently. We are in a sense under attack from the world. But, the Lord Jesus Christ himself has appointed each one of us as his ambassadors in this foreign land where we represent him. As Christ's ambassadors we represent him and his kingdom to the world, which, from a spiritual standpoint, is governed not by Christ but by Satan. It is "Satan's country." As ambassadors for Christ we bring Good News to a world governed by Satan. Christ has reconciled the world to God through his sacrificial

---

[129] William Barclay, *The Daily Study Bible Series, The Letters to the Corinthians*, Revised ed., (Philadelphia: Westminster Press, 1975), pp. 209-210.

death on the cross. As a result people are "made right with God through Christ" (II Corinthians 5:21).

## Standing strong in hostile territory

As a young child Raymond Kolbe, born in 1894 in Russian occupied Poland, caused his parents grief. He was the child who always seemed to get in trouble, requiring more disciplinary action than his two brothers combined. Kolbe's parents were devout Roman Catholics, and they taught young Raymond the truths of their faith. On one occasion, at the age of twelve, after another parental reprimand, Raymond asked the Virgin Mary what would become of him. He later told of having a vision of Mary holding two crowns, one white and the other red. When she asked him if he would accept either of the crowns---the white representing purity, the red, martyrdom, Raymond said he would accept both.

That vision would shape him for the rest of his life. He would become a Franciscan priest, earn a doctorate in theology, teach church history at Krakow Seminary, and start a religious newspaper that would reach a circulation of 750,000 copies a month. He also started a monastery in Nagasaki, Japan that would survive the atomic bomb and remain a center for Franciscan work to this day.

Raymond took the name Maximilian in 1911 when he professed vows as a Conventual Franciscan. As a missionary, he was sent to India but his health forced him to return to Poland in 1936, the same time the Third Reich was building its ascendancy to power just three short years before it would invade Poland, igniting World War II. Kolbe used his radio program and newspaper to criticize the Third Reich. When the Nazis invaded Poland in 1939, they arrested Kolbe, but released him a few months later. He and his Franciscans brothers continued their work, even aiding 3,000 refugees, including 2,000 Jews.

In 1941 Kolbe was again arrested and eventually placed in Auschwitz where he was branded as prisoner number 16670. In July, 1941 a man from Kolbe's barracks escaped, prompting the Deputy Commander to enforce the prison's policy of randomly picking ten men from the barracks and starving them in Block 13, notorious as a place of torture. (The escaped prisoner was later found dead in the camp latrine.) One of the men chosen to die was Franciszek Gajowniczek. As they were leading Gajownicizek away, he begged for mercy. "My wife and children!" he sobbed. It was then that Kolbe did a most extraordinary thing: He stepped forward, spoke with the Deputy Commander, identified himself as a Catholic priest, and asked to die in place of Gajowniczek. The Commander agreed, and Kolbe was led away with the others.

There in Block 13 Kolbe led his fellow prisoners in daily prayers, the rosary, and singing. Bruno Borgowiec, an assistant to the janitor and an interpreter in the underground bunkers, later testified to what happened. He had the impression he was in church, so faithful was Kolbe in leading the others in prayers and singing. But gradually their strength failed as one by one they starved to death until after two weeks only Kolbe remained alive. It was only when authorities decided the cell was needed for new victims that one of the guards was ordered to inject

Kolbe with carbolic acid. As he died, Kolbe prayed for his executioner.

I think Kolbe was a "sent one," able to fulfill his mission as an ambassador for Christ in one of the most hostile places imaginable because Kolbe was empowered by the Holy Spirit. He brought a piece of the Kingdom of God into a living hell. In so doing he fulfilled the prayer of Jesus that the disciples would be sent just as he was sent. Sometimes serving as an ambassador for Christ is not prestigious, from the earthly view. Sometimes it's a mean, nasty, distasteful work.

But that's not the only way the word "ambassador" was sent. Provinces that were peaceful and did not require the occupation or Roman troops to maintain peace were senatorial provinces. In this case the Roman senate appointed the ambassador to this newly conquered province to set up the terms of agreement by which it would become a part of the Roman Empire.

**Making a difference at home**

Sometimes we serve as ambassadors in more peaceful settings. We are not under Satan's direct assault. We can be thankful that the Lord has delivered us from our enemies, that we are not persecuted, and are free "to serve him without fear in holiness and righteousness before him all our days" (Luke 1:74-75, NIV). A man named Joseph Cafasso was a man who did just that.

Joseph Cafasso lived a spectacularly unspectacular life, but nonetheless changed the world around him for Jesus Christ. Cafasso came from a simple background: What his uneducated parents did not have financially, they had spiritually. And their son, Joseph, caught their religion. As a young man, Joseph took an interest in spiritual matters; He loved to attend Mass and spend time in private prayer. His parents sacrificed so he could attend seminary in Turin, Italy. Joseph was ordained at the age of 22. As a priest he was known for his kindness, gentleness, and sincerity in loving others. He would later say, "We are born to love; we live to love; and we will die to love still more." Taking note of his sharp mind, Church leaders appointed the twenty-five year old priest as an instructor in theology at the seminary in Turin. Ten years later, he became the Rector at the Seminary and remained there until his death at the age of 49. He would live and die within thirteen miles of his birthplace.

Cafasso ministered daily. He taught young people in his parish and developed conferences---we would say "retreats," to instruct priests. He took a keen interest in the deplorable conditions of prisons of his day. Something of a social activist, he denounced the practice of public hangings. As he sought reform in the prison system, he ministered to the prisoners themselves, accompanying over 60 to the gallows, listening to their confessions, offering them hope, comforting them in death. "Heaven is filled with converted sinners of all kinds, and there is room for more," he would often tell them.

And so Father Joseph-- known as "the Priest of the Gallows"-- humbly served, loving others, seeking the best for priest and prisoner alike. His work was nothing spectacular from the world's view, but it was something quite profound from the spiritual side, so much so that Pope Pius XII proclaimed Joseph Cafasso a saint in 1947. Cafasso's seemingly inconspicuous efforts had a profound effect. Two of the people he mentored were themselves declared saints: St. John Bosco and St. Joseph Cottonlego. And then, there were the many prisoners Cafasso brought to Christ. Of course, his work with priests would multiply the impact for the kingdom of God.

Joseph Cafasso is an example of a Christian ambassador serving in a more friendly "country." He did not face a Nazi concentration camp; he was not under intense pressure to compromise Christ; nor did his work flower into a popular movement for Christ. But he reminds us that we can still make a tremendous difference close to home. You see, there is always work to be done for Christ, whether it's having the courage to take another's place in death, as Maximillian Kolbe did, or preaching, teaching, and caring for all kinds of people, as was the case with Cafasso. In whatever territory we are in, our mission is the same: Proclaim the Good News as we seek to equip more people who will win more for the cause of Christ. Cafasso's message was the same as Kolbe: Come back to Christ; be reconciled to him; Christ has provided the way to receive God's grace. As Paul said, II Corinthians 5:21: "God made him who knew no sin to be sin for us, so that in him we might become the righteousness of God" (NIV). Because of the cross, we receive God's gift of grace, Jesus Christ.

An ambassador has the privilege of representing his government. Do you recognize the privilege and responsibility of being an ambassador for Christ? An ambassador is the highest ranking diplomat representing one country to another. It is an honor, a privilege that comes with huge responsibilities. As believers we too are honored to be ambassadors. Paul said in I

Corinthians 4:1 "Since through God's mercy we have this ministry, we do not lose heart."(NIV). As official representatives for Christ in another country, we do not lose heart because God in his mercy has privileged us with this work. Like Christ, whom we represent, we do not force our message on others, but we are there for our Lord in whatever capacity he would have us represent him.

Like our Lord, we are humble as we go on our mission. "Though he was God," Paul wrote probably reciting a hymn of the early church, "he (Jesus) did not think of equality with God as something to cling to. Instead, he gave up his divine privileges; he took the humble position of a slave and was born as a human being. When he appeared in human form, he humbled himself in obedience to God and died a criminal's death on a cross" (Philippians 2:6-8). If our Lord came in humility, so must we.

If ambassadors have a proud, arrogant approach to the people in the foreign land, they will likely cause a degree of resentment or even hostility toward the country they represent. If they are humble, the ambassadors likely receive a more favorable response. It's similar for us as Christian ambassadors. If we are prideful, if people get the impression that we look down upon them because of they are not Christians, if we convey a "holier than thou" attitude, then we create a negative reaction to the gospel.

Pride causes us to speak more than we are willing to listen. We are not interested in hearing what another has to say, because of course what we have to say is so much more profound, more enlightening, more interesting. And it may very well be...to you. But if all we do is talk and not listen, we cannot discern the hurts, needs, and concerns in another's heart.

We are ambassadors. But we do not appoint ourselves; ours is a derived power: it is not of ourselves; it is not our own; it is not our possession: it is from Christ. When we are humble, we allow the Spirit to work through us. We recognize our utter dependence on him. And we look for that divine image in that person to whom we are sharing the Good News. Actually, this increases our confidence, since we are convinced the other person is of worth and value to God. In humility we sense in them God's creative work. Opportunities open up when we have a humble attitude.

**Changing the world from George Street**

That was the situation in the life of a humble servant simply known as Mr. Genter. Francis Dixon told his story. Dixon, an evangelist, was leading a revival in Sydney, Australia, when a young man named Nowell shared his testimony. Nowell was in the military and was stationed in Sydney. He told of walking down George Street in Sydney one day when a white-haired man stopped Nowell and asked him a question.

"Excuse me, sir, I wonder if you might let me ask you a question? I don't want to offend you, but if you were to die today, where would you spend your eternity? The Bible says it's either heaven or hell. Think about it. That's all. Have a good day."

Nowell thought about it, found a church, heard the gospel, and made a decision to become a Christian.

As Nowell shared this story that night in the church service, another man named Peter listened. As he listened to Nowell, Peter thought to himself, "Nowell's story is just like mine." After the service, Peter sought out Dixon and Nowell and said, "I, too, was walking down George Street not long ago and was stopped by that white-haired man. He asked me the same question, and I too became a Christian because of the question he asked me."

Dixon continued his preaching tour in Australia. His next stop was Adelaide, and there Dixon told the story of Nowell, Peter, and the white-haired man on George Street in Sydney. After telling the story, a man in the audience couldn't contain himself. He raised his hand, "That's my story, too," he said. "I was walking down George Street in Sydney when a white-haired man stopped me, asked that same question, and as a result I too became a Christian."

Dixon went on to Perth, Australia. He told the story of the three men who came to Christ because the white-haired man on George Street, in Sydney had asked them that question, "If you were to die today, do you know where you would spend eternity?" After the service a deacon in the church approached Dixon. "Do you have a minute?" he asked.

"Of course," Dixon replied.

"You may find this difficult to believe," he said, "but one day I, too, was walking down George Street in Sydney when that white-haired man stopped me and asked me the same question. I had to get it settled, so I found a pastor who told me how I could become a Christian. I accepted Jesus Christ as my Savior and Lord and have followed him since."

Dixon continued to share this amazing story as he traveled from city to city on his way back to England. Once back in England, Dixon was leading services in a church, and he told the story of the white-haired man on George Street in Sydney, Australia, and of the four men who had come to know Christ because the man asked a simple question. After the service, a woman spoke to him and said that she too had made her decision for Christ because she had once walked down George Street and the same gentleman asked her the same thought-provoking question.

Not long after that Dixon was speaking at a conference in England and told the story of the many people who had come to Christ as a result of the haunting question of the white-haired man on George Street in Sydney, Australia. And once again, after the service, a man told how he too had been walking down George Street when a white-haired man asked that same piercing question. And as a result this man had also accepted Christ.

After the conference, Dixon went on a world tour, preaching the gospel. In each city he would tell the story of the white-haired man on George Street in Sydney, Australia. When Dixon was in Jamaica he met another man who had come to Christ because of the white-haired man on George Street.

Then when he was in India, he spoke at a mission conference. An older missionary heard Dixon tell the story, and told how he too, years ago, had been approached by the white-haired man who said, "I don't mean to offend you, but if you were to die today, where would you spend eternity? Would it be heaven or hell?"

Amazed by all the people who had come to Christ as a result of the white-haired man, Dixon decided to find him. On his way back to England, he stopped in Australia, looked up one of his friends in Sydney and asked if he knew of the white-haired man in George Street who asked the question to anyone passing by, "If you were to die today, do you know where you would spend eternity?"

"After asking the question," Dixon said, "the man walks away."

Dixon's friend said, "I know of him. That would be Mr. Genter. He can't get around very well now, and his eyesight is poor." The friend gladly took Dixon to visit the man. When Dixon told Mr. Genter the story of Dixon's travels and of the many people who had come to Christ because of the question he asked, Genter broke down and began to cry. He told them that was the first time he had heard of anyone accepting Christ because of his witness.

Later, Dixon told this story with Gene Warr in Oklahoma. Warr later shared it in a church in the United States, and a woman raised her hand and said, "I, too, was in Sydney, Australia, walking down George Street, and I invited Jesus into my life because of the question that same white-haired man asked me."

God invites us to join him on this mission of introducing people to God. We look for people, we search for them, just as diligently as a good neighbor digs through the rubble of a destroyed house in hopes of finding someone alive. God uses us when we agree to go on mission. Sometimes, like Francis Dixon or Maximillian Kolbe, the mission may take us to far away and even to hostile places. And for others, like Joseph Cafasso and Mr. Genter, we stay in one place. But always he sends us into the world on mission.

How about you? Are you on a mission?

*"I pray that they will all be one, just as you and I are one---as you are in me, Father, and I am in you. And may they be in us so that the world will believe you sent me."*

—John 17:21

*"During the recent heavy weather, I've had the opportunity to watch all of you at work on deck and aloft. You don't know wood from canvas! And it seems you don't want to learn! Well, I'll have to give you a lesson."*

— Captain William Bligh, from the 1935 film, *Mutiny on the Bounty*

## Chapter Ten
## Unity: the Power of Many in One

THE 1935 MOVIE *MUTINY ON THE BOUNTY*, starring Clark Gable, was a huge success, racking up several Academy Award nominations and winning the movie of the year. Although the movie has numerous historical inaccuracies, it was based on the real life story of the H.M.S. Bounty, which left England in 1787 to find breadfruit plants and take them to the West Indies as a source of inexpensive food for slaves. The captain of the ship, William Bligh, is portrayed as a sadistic and tyrannical villain whose cruelty incites resentment, then division, and finally mutiny. The mission is not accomplished; it died in the rebellion. Bligh's animosity toward his own fellow sailors is revealed early in the movie when they encounter a fierce storm. Despite the dangers, he insists they sail on. His lack of concern for human life compromised his leadership, eventually jeopardizing his position as the ship's captain.

For various reasons, the church is not accomplishing its mission. Chief among those reasons is division within the body of Christ, the church. Too often, disunity is caused by a lack of respect for fellow travelers on the journey toward the kingdom of God. Unfortunately, Christians too often look down on those who do not hold their formulation for spiritual success on the voyage for Christ

In John 17:21 we read the words of Jesus. He is praying that all future believers will be one. This begins the third part of Jesus prayer when he specifically includes everyone who would ever believe. Think of the millions and millions of people this encompasses. And the first thing he prayed for was unity. Jesus knew a threat to unity was a threat to the accomplishment of the mission.

The roots for division were found within the disciples themselves. Earlier in Jesus ministry they had argued about who would be greatest among them. Jesus used the occasion to teach them a lesson on leadership: "Whoever wants to be first must take last place and be the servant of everyone else" (Mark 9:35). Apparently they didn't get it because not long after that, James and John came to Jesus and asked if they could have seats of honor next to Jesus' right and left whenever he took his place on his throne. The other disciples were indignant at the audacity of James and John's request. As Jesus taught them once again about being a true servant, he mentioned the persecution his followers would encounter. [130]

Jesus knew if the disciples did not stay together, they would easily be torn apart during persecution. The mission would fail before it ever got started. Their situation then was a bit like that of the founding fathers of the United States.

---

[130] Mark 10:35-45

When fifty-six members of the Continental Congress signed the Declaration of Independence, they were not just signing a document, they were risking their very lives, for they accused the King of England, still technically their king, of being a tyrant, and that was considered treason, a penalty punishable by death, death by hanging. The men who signed that document were a diverse group: eight were born in Europe, not America, two were clergyman, four were physicians, twenty-four were lawyers, and the signers ranged in age from the twenty-six year old Edward Rutledge to the seventy year old Benjamin Franklin. They did not all sign the document for the same reasons; neither did they all hold the same political views. John Hancock was perhaps the boldest. When he signed the document, he wrote his name in big letters. "There," he said, "King George should be able to read that without his spectacles." And everyone was curious about what the wittiest of the group would say. Benjamin Franklin was known for his pithy aphorisms. And, Franklin did not disappoint. "We must all hang together," he said, "or most assuredly, we shall all hang separately."

The disciples, a smaller but no less diverse group than those fifty-six who signed the Declaration of Independence, had to overcome their differences and find unity around a common mission. Although six were fishermen, two of the six were apparently better off than the other four, the two ---James and John—having a father who owned a fleet of boats; another apostle was a tax collector for the Roman government, while another probably had ties to the Zealots, a radical anti-Roman sect.

Like the signers of the Declaration of Independence, they would have to hang together if they were to find success in proclaiming the Good News about Jesus. When Jesus sent out his disciples, he was not sending them on a casual field trip. "I am sending you out as sheep among wolves," he warned. And speaking prophetically he said, "You will be handed over to the courts and will be flogged with whips in the synagogues. You will stand trial before governors and kings because you are my followers"(Matthew 10:17-18). Jesus continued to tell the disciples that they would experience stormy times not only from without but from within, from their own families, "A brother will betray his brother to death, a father will betray his own child, and children will rebel against their parents and cause them to be killed" (Matthew 10:21) No, he wasn't sending them on a leisurely stroll in the park.

Jesus had just prayed that the disciples would be mission-minded, that just as they were called apart, they would be sent out. We do well to remember that Jesus sends us on the same mission of proclaiming the Good News. As Jesus shifted his prayer from the disciples to future believers, he prays for us, we who share the same mission with the disciples. We should therefore at least expect the potential for opposition when we truly proclaim the gospel. "Students are not greater than their teacher," Jesus said in the Matthew 10 episode, "and slaves are not greater than their master...and since I, the master of the household, have been called the prince of demons, the members of my household will be called even worse names" ( Matthew 10:24-25).

## Stand Together or Fall Separately

Since we go as sheep among wolves, proclaiming the gospel in potentially hazardous situations, it is imperative that we ourselves hang together. Yes, indeed, for if we don't, Satan will pick us off separately.

Martin Niemoeller was a German Lutheran pastor when Hitler's Third Reich took control of Germany. Niemoeller was a national conservative, and at first he was a supporter of Hitler, but later Niemoeller came to vehemently oppose Hitler. Niemoeller helped found the Confessing Church, which stood up against Hilter's nazification of the Protestant churches. Niemoeller was imprisoned at Sachsenhausen and Dachau, narrowly escaping execution. Although he did all he could to oppose Hitler, Niemoeller regretted not fighting sooner. He wrote,

> *"First they came for the socialists, and I did not speak out—because I was not a socialist;*
> *Then they came for the trade unionists, and I did not speak out—because I was not a trade unionist;*
> *Then they came for the Jews, and I did not speak out because I was not a Jew;*
> *Then they came for me—and there was no one left to speak for me."*[131]

We should pray for a spirit of discernment to see Satan for what he is: A thief who is determined to steal from the

---

[131] www.history.ucsb.edu/faculty/marcuse/niem.htm#discourses.

church the courage, tenacity, and perseverance necessary to stand united in the mission of our leader, the Lord Jesus Christ. There is a real battle going on, invisible as it is, a battle for the souls of men, women, boys and girls. And if Satan can simply divide us, get us to focus on our differences, he can disrupt the church, and the battle will be lost before we have an opportunity to utter one word on behalf of our Master, Jesus Christ.

Unfortunately, the church has been marred by divisions, by infighting, by inner turmoil, that has left us weak, emaciated, paralyzed, unable to sound the trumpet of freedom, the trumpet announcing to captives their eternal salvation, a salvation that frees them from the tyrant that rules them, destroying what life they have.

And Jesus is praying from the right hand of the throne of the Father that his church will be unified.

I love the story about the pastor who was speaking to the children during the children's sermon one Sunday morning. Trying to impress upon them the importance of church unity, he emphasized, "God wants us to be one!"

One of the children who had turned four almost a year ago, his birthday now only a few short months away, protested: "I've already been one; I want to be five."[132]

It reminds me of the church: we should be one; we want to be one; but we aren't. We are many, indeed, many more than five. And often, more often than we would like to believe, we are many, even within one congregation, a congregation of

---

[132] Michael Hodgin, ed., *1001 More Humorous Illustrations*, (Grand Rapids, Michigan: Zondervan Publishing House, 1998), p. 332.

congregations, subdivided into so many enclaves, each vying for attention, each clamoring for special treatment, each jockeying for positions of influence and power, dividing again and again, proliferating like so many cancer cells, sucking life from the body, draining it of energy and vitality---forgetting along the way the virtues of humility, cooperation, service and most of all, love---surviving just above death, languishing just below life, shuffling zombie-like, tramping as a sleep-walker, mindlessly following the other decaying corpses, following with one jaundiced hand upon the shoulders of the other, emitting the stench of staleness, decay, death, and finally collapsing into the velvety smoothness of the comfortable casket they call church.

      The result: the Christian movement is hamstrung by its own disagreements and divisions. How often has the church been stymied by its own multiple personality schizophrenia?

      That wasn't Jesus' desire for us. His prayer for unity was not only for the twelve disciples but for us as well. Jesus prayed that we would be one. Despite its potential for ugliness, Christ has chosen to love the church. He gave himself up for the church, going to the cross for it. After his resurrection, Jesus ascended into heaven where today he is "seated in the place of honor next to God..." (I Peter 3:22), and where he "lives forever to intercede with God" (Hebrews 7:25) on behalf of believers.

      If you are a believer, he is praying for you, praying that you will be one with the body of believers. Through all the cross words—back stabbings, fault-findings, and nay-sayings—through all the geographical divisions, north and south, east and west, through the doctrinal debates---theotokos vs. christotokos, pre vs. post millennial, predestined vs. free choice, and on and on

---through it all, Jesus has been praying, praying for our unity. He loves his church.

Certainly, then, his prayer for the church encompasses all that he prayed for earlier in his High Priestly Prayer. It is a prayer for his disciples then and now, disciples multiplying from a tiny twelve into untold millions, a vast array of believers, red and yellow, black and white, each one precious in his sight, believers reaching, preaching, teaching all things that he commanded, until the farthest regions are touched by his grace, until he comes again, in power and authority, he, the one who prayed then and now for these very believers, including you and me, marching together as one, brimming over with joy, drinking from his fountain of life-giving fresh water, drawing life from it, spilling over from believer to unbeliever, changing the world with one eternal, endless, ageless, breathless, Jesus-prayer at a time.

**What kind of Unity?**

But, just what kind of unity was Jesus praying for anyway? Was it an organizational unity? I don't think so, for Jesus prayed that we would be one, just as he and God the Father are one, just as he is in the Father and the Father in him. That doesn't sound like an organizational kind of unity. Besides, as we look at the history of the early Christian church, we find a loosely organized outfit. Their lack of organizational sophistication didn't stop them from reaching people for Christ. As the church grew, it became more efficiently organized, but that organization didn't always bring God's blessing. After all, not everyone in a union, either a labor union or a religious one, is actually unified as one. You can tie the tails of two cats together, throw them over a clothesline and say they are in a union of sorts, but they will by no means be in unity!

Nor was it a unity based on uniformity. Conformity in outward behavior and various expressions of likeness, from the foods we eat and the drinks we imbibe, to the clothes we wear to the expressions of worship we display---do not always mean we are as one. These outer expressions of conformity can all be enforced upon people from the outside. Within, people can be as divided as ever.

So what did Jesus mean? The key to the answer is in words of Jesus prayer, "I pray that they will all be one, just as you and I are one---as you are in me, Father, and I am in you" (John 17:21). Our oneness as believers is in some way a reflection of the oneness between Jesus the Son and God the Father. Gregory of Nyssa, writing in the fourth century, identified the bond of unity between the Father and the Son, and with us as well as the Holy Spirit. When we have the Holy Spirit within us, we too have the bond of divine unity. The source of our unity is the third person of the Trinity. According to Gregory, "Now that his human nature has been glorified by the Spirit, this participation in the glory of the Spirit is communicated to all who are united with him beginning with his disciples."[133] The Baptist preacher, Charles Spurgeon, proclaimed essentially the same truth centuries later: "Above all," he emphasized, "*the Holy Spirit*, who dwells in every believer, is the true fount of

---

[133] Thomas C. Oden, gen. ed., *Ancient Christian Commentary on Scripture*, *New Testament, 12 vols.* (DownersGrove, Ill.: InterVarsity Press, 2007), vol. IVb, *John 11-21*, Joel C. Elowsky, ed., pp. 258-259.

oneness."[134] Unity is a condition created in us by the Holy Spirit as we express obedience to our Lord Jesus Christ and glorify God the Father.

Unity, then, is **not** the same as uniformity, because uniformity connotes a sameness in appearance and thought; it is not the same as union because that can simply mean we are organizationally connected; nor is it the same as unanimity, for that can denote a sameness of opinion, which we do not always have, even when we are in unity. Unity, the oneness for which Jesus prayed, is based on obedience to Jesus Christ whose mission and message is ours as we minister to the world around us. As we are obedient to our Lord, as we acquire the mind of Christ, the Holy Spirit grants unity to the body of Christ, the church.

**One Mind**

Our unity, if it is true unity must begin with the mind, for if we don't begin there, with the mind, then we are doomed only to struggle for outward uniformity, conforming to an image without being transformed from within. This produces tension and friction within the body. We don't usually set out to go the wrong way in our physical bodies or in the body of Christ, the church. We get distracted, side-tracked. We are like the blue tick hound that was on the trail of a trophy buck. He is chasing this beautiful deer when a fox crosses in front of the dog. The hound dog then begins to chase the fox. The hound is in hot pursuit of

---

[134] Charles Haddon Spurgeon, *The Treasury of the Bible*, vol. VI: *Luke 15:8-Romans 3:25* (Grand Rapids, Mi., Baker Book House, reprint ed., 1988), p. 612.

the fox when a rabbit runs in front of the dog. Once again he changes course and runs after the rabbit. Then a mouse runs in front of the dog, and the dog takes out after the mouse. The mouse runs down a hole in the field. So, the hound that was once on a noble hunt, chasing a trophy buck, ends up looking down a hole in a field, pursuing a rodent.

We are too often like the dog. We have this noble calling: Love the Lord our God with our heart, mind, soul, and strength and love others as God loves them. We are reaching up with all we have as we wrap our arms around the world, seeking to draw them into the body of Christ, helping them grow in Christ, encouraging them as they allow Christ to shape their lives. And as we do, Christ is being formed in us.

But then, in the process we get sidetracked, chasing the insignificant, pursuing the trivial, worrying about the same things that plague the world, showing our lack of faith and vagueness of vision. And the body of Christ, the church, instead of pursuing the kingdom of God, divides over the color of the carpet in the sanctuary, or the placement of the organ (or whether to have one at all), the times we meet (or whether or not we do), which rooms we meet in, what kind music we will use in worship, or what translation of the Bible we use. The list goes on and on.

What are we to do? We have to be of one mind. The unity of the Father, Son, and Holy Spirit must be reflected in us. It is inconceivable for God the Father, God the Son, God the Holy Spirit to be divided. God is three in one, one mind. And so we find our unity in God.

And how is that to happen? Only by the grace of God. For the people of God to be of one mind is nothing short of a miracle. For us to open ourselves to such a work of God is a work of God's grace in us.

We are to acquire his attitude, his perspective, his way of thinking.

But how exactly does it happen? How do we acquire the mind of Christ? Do we do like the young Dr. Frankenstein did in the *Young Frankenstein* simply send Igor to the brain lab for a brain? If only it were that easy (or dangerous!). Change takes place in the brain as we think. What we think about determines the kind and extent of our transformation. Paul wrote to the Romans, "Let God transform you into a new person by changing the way you think" (Romans 12:2).

Having decided to be a follower of Christ, we give the Holy Spirit free reign to renew us, and redirect our thoughts---our mind---to Christ. Then we learn what his will is, and we in humility, do it. So, what we must do is take on the attitude that our Lord had. We acquire his mind as we follow him and his way. And the result will be a spirit of unity.

Philippians 2: 1-11 is one of the most beautiful passages in the New Testament. It's also one of the greatest Christological passages in the Bible. For centuries pastors, theologians, and teachers have analyzed, examined, and re-examined it. Countless Bible studies and books have emerged from those studies. Here Paul talks about the mind of Christ. In verse 5, he wrote, "Let this mind be in you which was also in Christ Jesus." (KJV). The word mind means "frame of mind," or "attitude." Eugene Peterson translates the verse, "Think of yourselves the way

Christ Jesus thought of himself." [135] If we can think of ourselves as Christ did, we will be of "one mind," and unity will be the result. How did Christ Jesus think of himself?

Jesus had an attitude of humility that was expressed in loving acts of service and sacrifice.

Being humble before God means we understand he is the one in charge. We humble ourselves or put ourselves beneath him. As we humble ourselves before the Lord, we have a humble attitude toward others, particularly those in the body of Christ. We look to the interests and needs of others, loving them as we love ourselves. This is the key to our unity in the body of Christ. We respect others and don't engage in behavior that bulldozes our opinions and preferences over theirs.

Let's face it: We will not all see eye to eye on all issues. We come from differing backgrounds, cultures, and we have varying perspectives. But with humility, this essential aspect of the mind of Christ, we can still walk together in harmony on the journey.

The word translated "form" in verse 7 means, "an outward expression of an inward nature." That means from eternity Christ was and is God. He had all the glory and praise of heaven; he ruled the universe with the Father and the Holy Spirit. Moreover, this passage tells us he did not consider equality with God something to grasp or hold onto. He thought of others, so that he was willing as the Son, to come to us. To do that, to enter our world, he had temporarily to give up some of

---

[135] Eugene H. Peterson, *The Message, The Bible in Contemporary Language* (Colorado Springs, Colorado: NAV Press, 2002), p. 2138.

these divine privileges, taking the form of a servant. He retained his divine nature, but he set aside the fullness of that outward glory that he possesses. He showed it for a brief moment in what is called "The Transfiguration." But his glory was hidden. He set aside the glory he enjoyed in heaven, coming to us as one of us, a human.

He was born in a manger, not into privilege, his home town rejected him when he first preached in Nazareth; his own family questioned his sanity, and his own disciples would abandon him. And, at any moment he could have called it off, ordered ten thousand angels to come to his rescue. The people who challenged his thinking, mainly the Pharisees, were by comparison, like an ant challenging Einstein, if it were possible. And the Lord put up with it. But not only does he endure their ignorance, he serves them, he loves them, he dies for them.

Have you ever noticed as you read the Gospels how often you find Jesus serving others? He serves all kinds of people: tax collectors, fisherman, wealthy religious people, prostitutes---whomever he encountered he was willing to serve. He was not too good for that. This is humility. 'Even the Son of Man came not to be served, but to serve and to give his life a ransom for many" (Mark 10:45).

Our unity begins with humility and manifests itself acts of service and sacrifice. It's an attitude that says, "I am not too good to set aside my likes and privileges and do what is necessary to minister to all kinds of people." We are a society that clings to privilege. We have it coming to us and we want what we deserve, and once we get our place in line we are not about to move.

But if we want to pattern our lives after Christ rather than the world, we have no other choice but to accept this adventure of acquiring the mind of Christ.

Years ago the Salvation Army in the United States wanted to have William Booth, the founder of that organization, come and speak at one of their national meetings. But Booth was by then retired, living in London, and virtually blind. He would not be able to attend. Then they asked, since he could no longer travel, if he would dictate a letter that they could read at the meeting. Arrangements were made and a request was sent to Booth. But as the time of the meeting approached, no letter came. It was the day of the meeting, and still there was no letter from Booth. During one of the general sessions of the conference, a messenger came with a telegram from Booth. The moderator announced this to those gathered in the meeting hall. A hush fell over the crowd as the moderator of the meeting opened the envelope. What would Booth say to them? What words of wisdom would he have? The moderator read it; "My friends," the moderator said, "the message from General Booth contains only one word: 'Others.'" That was the message. That was what Booth had lived for and that was what he would impress on those who followed him in the ministry of the Salvation Army.

If we are to have the mind of Christ, we must in humility serve others. Our Lord came not in the pomp and elegance of an earthly king, but as a servant, born in a cattle stall, despised, rejected, spit upon, cast out, crucified. But that didn't stop him from serving others---people like you and me.

If we are going to have the mind of Christ we have to understand that this attitude of humility will extend beyond serving to embrace sacrifice. You can't truly have one without the other. At some point, serving others will cost you something. Too many people have the idea that they can serve from a distance. What they really mean is that they want to get credit for doing what they got someone else to do. It's a bit like the two little boys who went to the dentist. The first boy said to the dentist, "I need a tooth pulled. And I don't want any deadening cause we're in a hurry. We don't have any time to waste."

The dentist was taken aback. "Let me get this straight," he said, "You want a tooth pulled, but you don't want any anesthetic because you are in too much of a hurry to wait on the anesthetic to deaden the mouth."

"That's right," answered the first boy.

"Well," says the dentist, "let me take a look at the tooth."

At that point the little guy who has been doing the talking turns to his buddy and says, "Show him your tooth, Albert."

So, we say, "Sure we should minister to those (whoever "those" may be) people. I wonder who we can get to do that?"

"Sure, I think we ought to have this ministry. Let's do it. But don't expect me to be there or give of my money to support it."

We're big on talking it up. Yes, let's sacrifice...as long as it's someone else that's on the altar.

I'm reminded of the story of Mother Theresa who was being visited by some folks from the United States. They had come to observe her work. Mother Theresa was at one point changing the wound of a one of the poorest of poor. And it was a nasty wound, made worse because the patient had not been able to change the dressing. The bandages should have been changed long before; infection had set in; it smelled putrid. As Mother Theresa was gently binding the wounds, one of the tourists without thinking, blurted out, "I wouldn't do that for a million dollars."

And Mother Theresa said, "Neither would I."

At some point, if we are humble, and stay with it, at some point our service will lead us to sacrifice. It will be different for each of us, but the sacrifice will nonetheless be there at some point.

Giving our time and resources is a sacrifice. When we are unfaithful in giving, whether it's with or finances or time or both, and we call on a reduction of the ministries in the body of Christ to shrink so they will fit our own unfaithfulness, we are leading the body into disobedience. And that is dangerous.

At a religious festival in Brazil, a missionary was going from booth to booth, looking at the displays. He saw a sign above one of the booths that said, "Cheap Crosses." He thought to himself, "Cheap crosses. That's exactly what many Christians are looking for."

Are you looking for a cheap cross?

Because Christ was willing to go the distance for us, we don't have to. But, we must follow him wherever he leads. How do you know where he is leading you? You spend time with him, you read his word, allowing it to master you, so you begin to love the things he loves, and hate the things he hates. And that love you acquire from his mind leads you to embrace a hurting world that's right outside your door.

There's a story about a boy who was found alone after one of the bombings in London during World War II. His entire family had been killed and his home destroyed. His life had been turned upside down, and he didn't know which way was up. A minister was futilely trying to find someone that knew the boy. In great despair, the little boy cried to the minister, "You don't understand, I ain't nobody's nobody!"

We live in a dehumanized, devil directed world where millions believe they are nobody's nobody. In humility we unite and go to them with the message of the Cross of Christ, the Cross that saves, the cross that cost Christ everything, the cross he offers us, the cross that says to people everywhere, regardless of where they live or what they look like, "You are no longer nobody's nobody. You are God's somebody."

Being of one mind unifies our mission.

**One Mission**

The mission, sharing the Good News, introducing people to Christ, includes everybody, people of all kinds, not just the religious folk. Jesus was willing to dine with a religious Pharisee (Luke 7:36) as well as the "sinners," whether the sinner was a tax collector (Matthew 9:9-13), or a prostitute (Luke 7:37). Whether it was Nicodemus or Mary Magdalene, Jesus saw people as full of potential.

The book, *Same Kind of Different as Me*, is the story of two men who are extremely different. One, Denver Moore, is a black man from rural Louisiana, raised as something of a modern day slave, and the other man, Ron Hall is a white man from Ft. Worth, Texas, graduate of Texas Christian University, and well-to-do art dealer. The two are brought together by the common mission of Ron's wife, Deborah, a mission to reach the homeless with the Good News of Jesus Christ. It's an amazing story of faith, hope, and love, and another example of how Jesus Christ can bring different people together for a common mission. By entering into the world of Christians who are different than we are, our eyes are opened to the potential of others we would otherwise fail to see. In one of the last chapters of the book, Denver and Ron travel back to rural Louisiana to the place Denver had left so many years ago when he hopped a freight to Ft. Worth, Texas. Ron is shocked by what he saw: "I could hardly believe places like that still existed in America. I thanked Denver for taking me there, for taking my blinders off."

Denver responded, "Mr. Ron, they're livin better than I ever did when I was livin here. Now you know it was the truth when I told you that bein homeless in Fort Worth was a step up in life for me."[136]

And Denver had his eyes opened as well. "I've learned not to pass judgment on anybody," he confessed, "'cause I don't know the things they been though that made them who they are today...Mr. Ron and his friends, they changed my attitude about rich folks." [137] In a penetrating statement from which the name of the book was taken, Denver says "I found out everybody's

---

[136] Ron Hall, *Same Kind of Different as Me*, with Lynn Vincent (Nashville, Tn.: Thomas Nelson, 2006), p. 228.
[137] Ibid, p. 243.

different---the same kind of different as me. We're all just regular folks walkin down the road God done set in front of us."[138]

These two very different men learned to see others in different ways, thanks to Ron's wife, who gave them a common mission: minister to the homeless.

Without a common mission which binds differentness into oneness, we tend to see only our "own kind." As we enter into the lives of believers who are sometimes very different, we learn how Christ has worked in their lives, and we begin to see how others are the "same kind of different as us."

Evangelist Martin Higginbottom told of coming home and finding his mother feeding a tramp at her kitchen table. She had observed that he was not only in desperate physical need but also in spiritual need as well. Martin listened in on the conversation between his mother and the transient. "I wish there were more people in the world like you," he said. His mother replied, "Oh there are, you just have to look for them."

Then the homeless man said, "But lady, I didn't look for you---you looked for me!"

We want the sheep that have are already fed, cleaned, sheared, and ready for show, the ones that will improve the status of our flock, the blue-ribbon, prize-winning sheep. We conveniently overlook the dirty, smelly, wayward sheep, the ones way out in the pasture, lost to all because no one cares to search.

---

[138] Ibid, p. 235

There's a story about a little child in an African tribe. The child wandered off into the tall grass of the jungle. When the child could not be found, mom and dad went looking. When they couldn't find their child, they called to the leaders of the tribe. They joined with others and walked through the tall grass.

Still they couldn't find the child. They doubled their forces and searched all night, and still they couldn't find the child. Finally, at daybreak, having scoured the field all night, the leaders called on all the men of the tribe to join hands and walk through the field. And it was then, after they had joined hands that they found the child. But it was too late. It was in the mountain region of Kenya, and the cold of the winter night was too much for the child. He died of exposure. With her small child in her arms, the mother dropped to her knees in the middle of the field and cried in anguish, "If only we had joined hands sooner, if only we had joined hands sooner..."

The sheep are all around us, they need someone to find them, and tell them they no longer need to fear, now they can come and find their freedom, their joy, their life, in Jesus Christ, the Shepherd who cares.

In the Middle East it can take time to find a lost sheep, sometimes up to two or three days. And, when a sheep becomes lost, it tends to panic. All it does is cry or bleat. Even when it hears the voice of the shepherd, it remains immobilized, frightened and frozen, unable to move. The shepherd must physically pick up the sheep if it is to be brought back to the fold. In the rugged terrain of the Middle East, this can be a challenging task. Sometimes a hired hand is given the responsibility of finding the lost sheep. Because it is a difficult, even dangerous task, he would sometimes just as soon not find the sheep and bring back some evidence that the sheep was dead. But, if the shepherd is good, he is faithful in going after his sheep, even in the midst of danger, even when the sheep don't have enough sense to recognize they are being rescued from imminent danger.

Jesus, in contrast to the hired hand who doesn't care, is the good shepherd who "sacrifices his life for the sheep" (John 10:11). Jesus isn't just mildly interested in us; he is crazy about us. He loves us with a sacrificial, unconditional, love that won't let go. Furthermore, Jesus said he had "other sheep" who were "not of this sheepfold" and that he had "to bring them also" (John 10:16). These "other" sheep are the Gentiles. Jesus first came to the Jews, but he would include Gentiles in his plan, a plan that included all peoples of the world. No fence on the face of the earth can be built to keep Jesus from going after his lost sheep. Jesus in giving us the scope of our mission, the world, also gave us the object of our mission: lost sheep.

How do we go after them, these lost sheep? By exercising the spiritual gifts he has given us in the body of Christ. Each of us has been given at least one spiritual gift. The body is strong and able to seek out the sheep, bringing them back and restoring them so that they too can exercise their gifts. It takes a church to raise a sheep! As diverse as we may be with our many gifts, we are united in Christ. "There are different kinds of spiritual gifts, but the same Spirit is the source of them all" (I Corinthians 12:4). We reach different people in different ways, but we must remember it is "the same God who does the work in all of us" (I Corinthians 12:6).

Sometimes sheep get in low places and have to be rescued. God knows their condition and is creating within them a hunger and thirst for him. It's our responsibility to exercise our gifts in the body of Christ. God uses our giftedness like a rope in his hands, to draw them in where he can use another's gift to clean them and another's gift to feed them, and another's gift to lead them and another's gifts to... well, I think you get the point.

## One Message

If going after the lost sheep is our overarching, common mission, what is our message? Just what is it we are saying? What we say has everything to do with who we are. Are we expressing words of hope, love, and encouragement? Do we proclaim judgment on a godless world? Or do we pronounce the potential for good in people? Do we cry, "Repent"? Or do we proclaim, "Be healed!"? Just what is our message? Is it all of these and more? Or is it only one message? What is the message we are to live and proclaim?

Most believers, I am convinced, simply don't know. We don't know what our message is. We get immersed in our church routine and forget what we are saying with all our actions. We are like the cartoon about the marathon runner. The first marathon was supposedly run by a Greek soldier named Pheidippides. After the Greeks defeated the Persians at the Battle of Marathon, Pheidippides ran 26 miles, bringing the news to the people of Athens. As he finished the run, Pheidippides collapsed from exhaustion. As he lay dying, he managed to whisper, "Niki," that is, victory. It's a touching story. But the cartoon version I mentioned is slightly different. It has the fatigued runner carrying the torch, exhausted, and gasping for breath as he finishes the race, but unlike the original version, he looks at the crowd and says, "I forgot the *message!*" [139]

That seems hauntingly familiar for us who are involved in religious work. We toil; we labor; we strain. We contribute; we give; we sacrifice. We stick; we stay; we endure. And having done all that, we look at those sheep to whom we have ministered, and with a blank stare, we say, "I forgot the *message!*"

Just what is the message we must live, proclaim, and never forget? In his inaugural sermon, Jesus gives us the essence of what his message would be. His message is ours. We may not say it in exactly the same way he did that eventful day in the synagogue of his hometown in Nazareth. But, it is the measuring rod, the standard that should loom over all our church slogans, billboards, and creative ministry titles. It's the theme we must consistently return to as we examine what we are saying. After all, since Jesus is our role model, our message should reflect his.

In this initial sermon in Luke 4, Jesus proclaimed that he was anointed to bring Good News to the poor, the prisoners, the blind, and the oppressed. The word "anointed" comes from the Greek root, *crio*, "to anoint." We get the word, "christ," from it, Christ being the "anointed one." Christ was always anointed, but at his baptism we see the visible evidence of his anointment. That event happened for our benefit, not his. So, when we share this Good News, it is a specific kind of Good News. It's not just good news---be it good news about who won the ball game, or

---

[139] James F. Colaianni, Sr. *The Book of Pulpit Book of Humor*, volume II, (Ventnor, New Jersey: Voicings Publications, 1988), p. 97.

who got an A on the exam, or who got the promotion. Those bits of good news, like so many others, are also pieces of bad news for some: for the team that lost, or for the one who didn't get the expected A or the promotion. The Good News we share is grounded on the anointed one, the Christ. It goes back to that statement of Jesus: "The Spirit of the Lord is upon me" (Luke 4:18). This Good News doesn't have to be bad news for some and good news for others. It can be the Good News for all who will receive it, for all who are "poor" enough to recognize their need of it.

Who are these "poor" Jesus is referring to? Because there is no article "the" preceding the word "poor" in this particular passage, it is likely that the poor that Jesus spoke of referred more to a condition than to specific individuals.[140] The Hebrew word for the poor and humble or what we might think of as "pious poor" is *anawim*. After the return of the Hebrew people from their exile in Babylon, a social class emerged who "were known for their commitment to the *Torah* and the temple as for their economic poverty."[141] Their poverty is closely associated with their piety, their humility. These *anawim* seemed to have lived near the temple, worshipping God and awaiting the Messiah. Simeon is an example. Luke describes him as a "righteous and devout" man who was "eagerly waiting for the Messiah to come and rescue Israel" (Luke 2:25). We may assume that he had been waiting for some time since the Holy Spirit had

---

[140] Max Zerwick and Mary Grosvenor, *A Grammatical Analysis of the Greek New Testament* (Rome: Biblical Institute Press, 1981), p. 186.
[141] Scot McKnight, *The Jesus Creed* (Brewster, Massachusetts: Paraclete Press, 2004), p. 296.

revealed to him that he would not die until he had seen the Messiah. Likewise, Anna, "a prophet was also there in the Temple" (Luke 2:36). Luke tells us "she never left the Temple but stayed there day and night, worshipping God with fasting and prayer" (Luke 2:37). With Simeon, "she talked about the child to everyone who had been waiting expectantly for God to rescue Jerusalem" (Luke 2:28).

The Good News is for everyone, but the poor, as understood here, seem to be those willing to hear and receive the Good News. This poverty is not a necessarily a condition of having less monetary resources than others, although more often than not, they don't have many possessions. It seems to be a description of those who recognize their need for the Good News.

These are the people the Lord specifically identified as special recipients of his message. Thomas Merton said, "We must never overlook the fact that the message of the Bible is above all a message preached to the poor, the burdened, the oppressed, the underprivileged."[142]

What Jesus had for them was the Good News. But what was the Good News they were to receive, the news they had longed for, yearned for, waited for? It was not just news but the *euangelion*, the Gospel, the Good News. In this sense, Jesus *was* the news, the Good News. The centrality of our message is not about religion, it's about a person, Jesus Christ. Just as he

---

[142] Thomas Merton, *Opening the Bible*, with an Introduction by Rob Stone (Collegeville, Minnesota: The Liturgical Press, copyright, The Thomas Merton Legacy Trust, 1970; "Introduction" copyright, 1986), p. 51

brought the Kingdom of God in himself, he brought the Good News. He was the living Good News, for he was to inaugurate the Kingdom that the pious, the humble, the religious had longed for.

This means that our Good News is not good news about itself, but Good News about Jesus. Only in Jesus does it truly become the Gospel. We bring the Good News about Jesus to the ones who are longing for hope, whose spirit is broken and bankrupt; who recognize their only hope is in one greater than any government program for assistance, longer lasting than any jackpot won at a lottery, richer than any financier has means to provide. I believe it was Martin Luther who said sharing this Good News is simply one hungry beggar telling another hungry where he can find food.

And this message, when it is truly the message of Christ, will not simply proclaim words: These words result in feeding the hungry, clothing the naked, and resisting evil in every area of life.

These poor, the *anawim*, may be closer to you than you think. Look around. Do you see them? One may sit next to you on Sunday mornings. Another may serve in your church's soup kitchen or clothes closet. Another may simply "hang around" church, loving God and others as best they can.

I think of a homebound member of the church I pastor. Ruby lived just a block away from the church. Although her age and physical condition prohibited her from being present on Sunday morning, she was still a devout lover of God's people. I would make a visit to her small home from time to time, and the deacons' would take the Lord's Supper to her whenever we offered it. As soon as she would open the door, she would greet me with a warm smile and welcoming heart, and I would see her opened, worn Bible there next to her chair. Mrs. Ruby didn't seem to have much, only that little house, nicely and simply decorated. Ruby became more and more feeble but her spirit remained always strong. I visited her in the hospital in her last days. I commented on her positive attitude, for she did remain optimistic even at the end. She spoke of the assurance she had in Lord and how she looked forward to seeing him.

I said, "Mrs. Ruby, even though you are weak physically, you are strong in your spirit." She looked up at me and said, "Oh preacher, you've got a strong constitution." That was her word, "constitution." "You've got a strong constitution; I watched how you remained strong and faithful during your wife's illness and death." Even in death she was humble, thought of others, and encouraged me, her pastor.

These people, these *anawim* are rare individuals. I was surprised, really shocked, but I shouldn't have been, when after Ruby's death, I learned that she had left a substantial amount of money to the church. She could have lived in a nicer home, enjoyed a higher standard of living; she chose a different way. The *anawim* are like that. Her name will be forgotten, but her gift will live on, in God's time, forever. Her way may not be your way, or mine, but I do know this: the blessing is hers; hers is the joy. Jesus' message, and ours, is Good News for people like that.

The *anawim* wait expectantly for the Lord, even while they fellowship with him now. They want more of Him. Do you?

Such it is with the *anawim*: always looking and waiting and longing, and always finding, receiving, and enjoying.

When Jesus spoke that day at the synagogue in Nazareth, he was speaking to his own people, the people he had grown up with, the people he had done work for as a carpenter, the people he had been to the synagogue with, the people he had laughed with, worshipped with, and the people he had heard crying out, yearning for the Messiah to redeem them and release them from their captors.

When the Lord said he had been sent to "proclaim that captives would be released" his audience would have resonated with him, for they knew what it was like to be captive: it was their history and their reality. The Jewish people---Jesus' neighbors, had been subjected to foreign rule for thousands of years. The Egyptians, Syrians, Babylonians, Persians, Greeks, and during Jesus day, the Romans, had all ruled the people in Palestine. This was their history.

Jesus brought them the hope of release. And the message we proclaim declares freedom and justice to those in politically repressive situations. We are bold in proclaiming the Word wherever we are. With Peter and John we say, "Judge for yourselves whether it is right in God's sight to obey you rather than God. For we cannot help speaking about what we have seen and heard" (Acts 4:19-20, NIV). And we must realize that when we fail to stand with those who are beaten down by oppressive governments, we lose, bit by bit, our own freedom.

So when Jesus spoke of release to captives, he spoke to an audience in a cultural context in which captivity, in the form of either politically oppression or slavery, or prejudice of gender, was a living reality. To proclaim release to these captives did not simply provide an element of hope, but set the agenda for the radicalness of Jesus message. His was not an innocuous, bland, tepid message. It was charged with the announcement of a coming change: the inauguration of a new kingdom and with it the implication of a new social and political agenda. Jesus was to be the embodiment of the kingdom many of the Jews had longed for. This was His message; It must be ours.

Father Jerzy Popieluszko was a Roman Catholic priest who lived in Poland. He died in 1984 at the age of 37. Popieluszko is best remembered for his ardent support of the Polish Solidarity Movement. During the Soviet occupation of Poland, which lasted from the end of World War II until 1989, the Solidarity Movement fought for the personal rights of the Polish people and for Polish independence.

From the pulpit of his small church in North Warsaw, Father Popieluszko vehemently spoke out against the Soviet-controlled government. Large numbers of people filled his church to hear his sermons, which were even broadcast over Polish radio. Popieluszko became an extremely popular Polish nationalist. The government arrested him several times and demanded that he speak only on religious matters. He bravely and boldly ignored their threats, and continued to apply the Gospel to the political situation in Poland. At one point during the Solidarity Movement, Polish factories went on strike. Popieluszko crossed the police lines, entered a factory and gave communion to the workers in the courtyard.

Finally, on October 19, 1984, Polish Security Police kidnapped Popieluszko. He was later found beaten and murdered, his body dumped into the Vistula Water Reservoir where it was recovered on October 30, 1984. A rock had been tied around his neck and his hands bound. The public was so outraged by his murder that they took to the streets and rioted. In order to appease the public's outrage, the murderers, three agents of the Polish communist internal intelligence agency, were found, tried and convicted.

Popieluszko's death was not in vain. Pope John Paul II nurtured and guided the movement for Polish independence. And Solidarity rose again. Lech Walesa led the movement, and factory walls once again reverberated with the cry, "There is no freedom without Solidarity." But the church had first voiced the message that echoed in those factories. By 1989 Solidarity was legal again, and Poland was on the way to freedom.

The message we proclaim is one of freedom. It is the Gospel Jesus preached. It's for anyone willing to hear and for all who will follow. It is our cry for unity, for solidarity. Instead of proclaiming, "There is no freedom without Solidarity," we shout, "There is no freedom without Christ," and his message of Good News is our solidarity.

As we find our way through the rough seas this side of eternity, we proclaim with a united voice the Good News of hope in Jesus Christ, in whom we stand as one, or sink separately.

"Father, I want these whom you have given me to be with me where I am. Then they can see all the glory you gave me because you loved me before the world began!"
—John 17:24

*"A pilot's business is with the wind, and with the stars, with night, with sand, with the sea. He strives to outwit the forces of nature. He stares with expectancy for the coming of the dawn the way a gardener awaits the coming of spring. He looks forward to port as a promised land, and truth for him is what lives in the stars."*

— Antoine de Saint Exupéry, <u>Wind, Sand, and Stars</u>, 1939[143]

---

[143] Antoine de Saint-Exupery, *Wind, Sand and Stars* (Boston: Houghton Mifflin Harcourt., reprint ed., 1992), p.166

## Chapter Eleven
## Security: A Place with Him Forever

Captain Shane Devlin is a flight commander with the 53$^{rd}$ Weather Reconnaissance Squadron located in Biloxi, Mississippi. Devlin and other members of that squadron were interviewed in a segment on the Today Show shortly before Hurricane Irene slammed into the East Coast of the United States on August 26, 2011. "Everything you learn as a pilot, an aviator," Devlin said in response to reporter Peter Alexander's question about the squadron's work, "is to leave bad weather, and we do just the opposite." That's because the 53$^{rd}$ Reconnaissance Squadron's mission is to provide aerial weather surveillance for tropical storms and hurricanes, primarily in the Atlantic Ocean, the Caribbean Sea, and the Gulf of Mexico. Their work is crucial in tracking the path of these storms. Lt. Col. Jon Talbot, the squadron's chief meteorologist, says the most critical element in their task is finding the geographical center of the storm. Alexander added his own commentary to Talbot's statement, "If you don't know where it's starting, you don't know where it's gonna finish." [144]

---

[144] Peter Alexander, "Hurricane hunters fly into eye of storm, "August 26, 2011, www.today.msnbc.msn.com/id/26184891/vp/44285408#442854408, and www.403wg.afrc.af.mil/library/factsheets/factsheet.asp?id=7483.

Like the 53rd Squadron, Christians also have a mission, only ours is introducing people to Jesus Christ. And rather than focusing on a few geographical regions, our mission is worldwide. Like the 53rd Squadron, we encounter danger. Sometime it's because Christians swim against the stream; we are part of a counter-culture movement. Standing for the truth and resisting evil is challenging and sometimes risky business; we sometimes fly into the eye of the storm to help people prepare for or avoid it.

Sometimes we encounter trouble because it's the nature of the world we live in; Christians are not spared the pain of sickness, tragedy, and death. The difference for the Christian is that we are not alone as we travel the journey. The Holy Spirit guides us as we listen to him. And all the while Jesus Christ is praying for us from the right hand of the throne of God. As we encounter the storms of life, Jesus is praying for us.

In John 17:24, Jesus expressed his strong desire that we be with him and see him in his glory. The fact that the verb *thelein* can mean both to "wish" or to "will' led Professor Raymond Brown to quip that we might speak of this verse as "the Last Will of Jesus, provided that we recognize that it is not the will of a dead man but the continuing will of the living Jesus who is with the Father."[145] Jesus wants us to be with him in heaven. It's his will.

The storms we encounter along our journey of faith can confuse us. We may not know exactly where we are in all the turbulence. But like a good pilot, we try our best to find the way

---

[145] Raymond E. Brown, *The Gospel According to John (xiii-xxi)* (Doubleday, Inc.: Garden City, New York, 1970), p.779.

home. As Antoine de Saint Exupéry observed, good pilots use every means possible in finding their direction home, looking forward to port as, "a promised land."[146]

For the Christian, the Promised Land is heaven. We keep our eyes on it; it gives us direction: we may not know the source of our trouble, our trials, and tribulations, or even our exact location, but we are confident of where we will finish when we finally land.

When we learned my first wife, Katri, had cancer, it was first diagnosed as "fourth stage cancer of unknown primary." That meant it was in the bones, fourth stage, but that its source or origin was unknown. The doctors' educated guess was that it was breast cancer. Months later they did find the source, and it was breast cancer. They then knew for certain, and that knowledge helped doctors in their treatment.

But I wanted to go back further. I wanted answers to questions that couldn't be answered. I wanted to know what caused the cancer. Where and how did it first enter her body? Was it in the water back in Miami, Oklahoma? Was it a result of some cancer causing agent some believed was in the oil refineries of Lake Charles, Louisiana? Was it something in the air? I wanted to know.

But there was no answer. Finally, after I'd asked that question for the umpteenth time, Katri's oncologist responded, "If you knew, would it really make any difference now?" And I had to admit, it wouldn't. Dwelling on what may have caused the cancer and finding out where that came from wouldn't help at that stage in our battle with our storm.

---

[146] Antoine de Saint-Exupery, ibid.

But knowing where she would finish was of tremendous comfort. Heaven awaited her, even though we tried to keep her here as long as possible. Heaven provides hope for the future and confidence in the midst of today's and tomorrow's storms. Jesus wants us to have the security of knowing where we will be when we finish the race.

When Jesus prayed in John 17, he knew that he would be crucified and that his disciples would lose heart. He knows our weaknesses, too. Like his disciples then, we too are made of dust and are likely to be scattered when the storm's winds blow in our direction. But he wants us to have a sense of security now, here in the storm. Knowing we have a place with him in heaven can give us that security.

Can we experience some of heaven now? Is it a real place in time and space? What will we do in heaven? Who awaits us there? Having a better understanding of heaven can help us as we guide our ship through the storms of life toward our heavenly port.

**Heaven Here and Now**

It's interesting that Jesus prayed using the present tense when he said, "I want those whom you have given me to be with me *where I am*" (John 17:4, emphasis mine). John didn't use the future tense to write what Jesus said in Aramaic. You would anticipate Jesus saying, "Where I will be." Neither did he use the past tense, "Where I was." Jesus is so certain of where he is going that he uses the present tense as though he is already there. Jesus is experiencing as much of heaven as any person on earth can humanly experience. He had that kind of assurance and confidence in where he would be when he finished his earthly journey.

This is not heaven. We are still on the journey: We still have storms, some of them severe; we still have sorrows, some intensely painful; and we still have disappointments, some devastating.

And yet because we are believers, we can experience a little bit of heaven this side of eternity. Along the way we have heaven, or at least a taste of it. Heaven is not only something "out there" that we will experience after death; it's something we can enjoy today, here and now.

A saint of the Middle Ages, Catherine of Siena, experienced little bits of heaven along her journey, even though her circumstances were less than ideal. From an early age, she received visions of Christ. At the age of 7, she vowed not to marry but to give herself completely to God. When she was 15, her parents tried to force her to marry, and Catherine refused. When she was 16, she joined the Dominicans, and for a period of about three years she lived in silence and solitude. She had more visions, and she wrote about them.

Catherine combined a mysticism with an activism most often expressed in ordinary disciplines of spiritual life: "When the soul is lifted by a great, yearning desire for the honor of God and the salvation of souls, it practices the ordinary virtues...so that it may know better God's goodness toward it. It does this because knowledge must come before love, and only when it has attained love can it strive to follow and to clothe itself with the truth."[147]

By no means did she spend all her time in other-worldly trances. She ministered to the poor, nursed those dying with the plague, and dutifully went about her duties as a Dominican. She was also involved in the politics of church and state in 14th century Italy, and even urged the pope to reform the clergy.[148] She also experienced trials: She was betrayed by jealous nuns who lied about her, and she suffered physical illness much of her life. Catherine led an austere life, praying much, sleeping little, and fasting often. For her, heaven was something to be received in the here and now. In fact, she penned these words, "All the way to heaven is heaven."[149] Heaven was not only something to anticipate but also something to appropriate.

Jesus was certain that he was on his way to glory, and it was as if he were already experiencing it as he prayed before the disciples. It's true that the more we think about something the more real it becomes to us. The less we think of something the more distant it is in our world. Which raises the question, "What world do you live in most of the time?" Is it the one ruled by the forces of Satan and under his control? Or is it the one where Jesus is, where he is praying for you? Do you think about that world very much? Paul admonished that since we have been raised to a new life in Christ we are to set our sights "on the

---

[147] Catherine of Siena, *Little Talks with God,* Henry L. Carrigan, Jr., ed., (Brewster, Massachusetts: Paraclete Press, 2001), p. 1.

[148] Ibid., p. vii-ix.

[149] Cited in Regis Martin, *The Last Things: Death, Judgment, Heaven, Hell* (San Francisco: Ignatius Press, 1998), p. 39.

realities of heaven, where Christ sits in the place of honor at God's right hand. Think about the things of heaven, not the things of earth" (Colossians 3:1-2).

English Puritan pastor and writer Richard Baxter was another one who experienced heaven on earth in difficult circumstances. He was of the most prominent Christian leaders in England during the 1600s. Baxter's heart was for the pastorate, and he did his best to avoid the disputes between the Anglicans, Presbyterians, Congregationalists, and other denominations of his day. He was fond of saying, "In necessary things, unity; in doubtful things, liberty; in all things, charity." He was a peacemaker who stood firmly for what he believed. For example, he was the first minister to decline the terms of ministry set forth by the national church in the 1662 Act of Uniformity. He wrote tirelessly on behalf of other ministers like himself who refused to accept the national church's dictates.[150]

As a result of his refusal, Baxter was barred from ecclesiastical office and not permitted to preach to his church flock in Kidderminster. And from 1662-1688 he was persecuted. One time he was imprisoned for 18 months, and he forced to sell his extensive libraries. Many of his belongings were confiscated. But instead of becoming bitter he became better. His days as a pastor may have been over but not his impact for Christ. He wrote furiously (he penned 135 books) and preached periodically, even though doing so was dangerous. Baxter

---

[150] Timothy Larsen, ed., D.W. Bebbington and Mark Noll, consulting eds., *Biographical Dictionary of Evangelicals* (Leicester, England: InterVarsity Press and Downers Grove, Illinois: InterVarsity Press, 2003), p.39.

became even more powerful in the pulpit: "I preached as never sure to preach again, and as a dying man to dying men," he said.[151]

How did he maintain the Spirit of Christ during those circumstances? Baxter thought a lot about heaven and its impact on life. In fact, he wrote a book which has become a devotional classic, *The Saints Everlasting Rest*. In that book, which he wrote while struggling with his own personal storm of physical illness (Baxter struggled with illness much of his life), he asked the question, "Why are not our hearts continually set on heaven? Why dwell we not there in constant contemplation?"[152]

Good question, don't you think? If we really believe it, truly have strong convictions that we will spend eternity in that place, and that our life on earth is just a mist, a vapor, why don't we think about heaven more? Listen to Baxter's challenge:"Bend thy soul to study eternity, busy thyself about the life to come, habituate thyself to such contemplations, and let not those thoughts be seldom and cursory, but bathe thyself in heaven's delights."[153]

Baxter offered several suggestions on how to lead a heavenly life on earth. For one, he said we can't expect heaven on earth while we are knowingly living in sin: "Every wilful sin will be to thy comforts, as water to the fire; it will utterly indispose and disable thee, that thou canst no more ascend in

---

[151] http://www.christianitytoday.com/ch/131christians/pastorsandpreachers/baster.html.
[152] Richard Baxter, *The Saints' Everlasting Rest* (London: Fisher, Son, and Jackson, 1829), p. 140.
[153] Ibid., p. 142.

divine meditation, than a bird can fly when its wings are clipped. SIN CUTS THE VERY SINEWS OF THE HEAVENLY LIFE."[154]

He also warned against an earthly or materialistic mindset: ""O the folly of many that seem to be religious. They thrust themselves into a multitude of employments, till they are so loaded with labours, and clogged with cares, that their souls are as unfit to converse with God, as a man is to walk with a mountain on his back."[155]

Baxter included among other hindrances to living a heavenly life on earth: the danger of maintaining ungodly companions, being prideful, arguing about insignificant religious matters, assuming that merely studying religious truth is the same as living it, and laziness. When he writes about laziness, Baxter seems to have in mind what spiritual writers of an earlier age referred to as acedia, a spiritual listlessness or boredom in which a once spiritual soul has lost the drive to try and seek God.[156] For Baxter, leading a heavenly life is more than going through the motions---bending the knee, moving the lips, saying the words---it's "to separate our thoughts and affections from the world, to draw forth all our graces, and increase each in its proper object, and hold them to the work till it prospers in our hands, this, this is the difficulty."[157]

---

[154] Ibid., p. 162.
[155] Ibid., p.163.
[156] Kathleen Norris has an excellent study of the subject in her memoir, *Acedia and Me, Marriage, Monks, and a Writer's Life* (New York: New York: Penguin Books, 2008).
[157] Baxter, *The Saints' Everlasting Rest,* p. 170.

But Baxter doesn't only tell us what to avoid. He holds out the positive. If you want to have heaven on earth, he said, you have to be convinced that heaven is the greatest treasure you can have. That's because God is there, and we should prefer nothing more than being with God. Baxter not only recommended thinking about heaven, but he also encouraged talking about it as well. Meditation, the chief end of which is "to have acquaintance and fellowship with God,"[158] is a simple digesting of God's Word, which nourishes the soul. "Are we not lost, and have nothing to fix our thoughts upon, when we attempt to think of God and glory, without the Scripture manner of representing them?"[159] Contemplating the truths of Scripture results in a godly, heavenly life, wherein we "make friends of enemies" and allow our feelings, which "so often are the means of drawing us from God..." to "be made instruments for raising us to Him."[160]

As you read Baxter, it becomes clear that the key for heavenly thinking and therefore holy living is meditating on the Scriptures and allowing them to direct our thoughts and actions heavenward. In the regular contemplation of Scripture, immersing ourselves in it, our lives are changed, we gain strength and courage for the storms, and we live in a heavenly way on our way to heaven. It certainly seemed to work for Baxter: From his affliction he produced much good. Like Catherine of Sienna before him, Richard Baxter---and thousands of other godly men

---

[158] Ibid., p.184.
[159] Ibid., p. 202.
[160] Ibid., p. 201.

and women across the years--embraced heaven before arriving there.

And so can you. But it takes time; it takes discipline. You don't live a holy life by surfing channels on television for hours and letting whatever attracts your eye direct your mind. Spending time digesting the Word means not spending time doing something else. It's as simple as that. But it can be done. Think of the spiritual benefits: We are more joyful, less likely to get snared by sin, and we are more likely to make a positive difference in the lives of others. When we keep the positive results before us, we are more motivated to discipline ourselves.

I really would rather stay in bed than get up early and work out. But I think of the positive benefits: I feel better, I have more energy, and I'm healthier. Reminding ourselves of a good habit's benefits motivates us to persevere and avoid the negative effects of bad habits. Think of the positive things that happen in your life as you meditate on eternal truth.

Besides, if we truly believe we are going there, don't you think we spend some time preparing for it?

I'm reminded of the story about the nobleman who died quite suddenly. His personal servant ran to tell the other household servants that their master had just died. The personal servant, being a simple man, asked the others where his master had gone. "He went to heaven," one servant told him.

The nobleman's servant paused and appeared to be pondering what he had been told. "No," he responded, "I don't think he has gone there. Heaven is a long way off, and I never knew my master to take a long trip without preparing for it and talking about it beforehand. And I've never heard him say anything about heaven; I never noticed him planning to go there. No, I don't think he's gone there."

As we've seen in the lives of Catherine of Siena and Richard Baxter, thinking about heaven isn't an escape from the present. It motivates us to make a heavenly difference in the here and now. In his classic book, *Mere Christianity*, C.S. Lewis wrote, "If you read history you will find that the Christians who did the most for the present world were just those who thought most of the next. The apostles themselves,...the great men who built up the Middle Ages, the English evangelicals who abolished the slave trade, all left their mark on earth, precisely because their minds were occupied with heaven." [161]

When you are doing the right things, when you are doing your best to love God with all your heart, mind, soul, and strength, and your are trying your to love others as yourself, then heaven breaks in at the most surprising times. In the church I pastor, a retired couple, Curtis and Barbara Tindall, have made it their mission to visit regularly in the retirement homes. They spend time sitting and talking with the residents, some of whom have few friends and relatives left to care for them.

On one occasion, Curtis and Barbara were visiting with several of the elderly in the lobby of the retirement center. Curtis is one of these guys who loves to share the gospel. He passes out gospel tracts and will frequently ask, "Have you received Jesus as your Savior?" His style of evangelism may not be mine, but Curtis has a heart for others, and he reaches people

---

[161] C.S. Lewis, *Mere Christianity* (New York, NY: HarperCollins, 2001), p. 134.

with the gospel. And that day in the lobby of that retirement home, he did just that. As they were all sitting there, he handed a gospel tract to each person, summarized it, and then said, "Read the tract because I want all of you to go to heaven." And as soon as he said the word, "heaven," a dear lady in the retirement home who once faithfully attended the church I pastor but now suffers from Alzheimer's disease, began singing "The Old Rugged Cross," and almost simultaneously the rest joined her in singing it too. My friend who suffers from Alzheimer's may not have known where she was, but she still knew where she was going. Then, as Curtis was telling me the story, he momentarily lost his words as his eyes misted with tears. "Preacher," he said, "it was like heaven came down in that place." Indeed it is so.

As we cast our thoughts heavenward, heaven on occasion breaks in and glory fills our souls.

## Heaven Then and There

I can appreciate what the preacher said after what seemed like hours of interrogation by a Pastor Search Committee. They had grilled him about every aspect of his theology, peppered him with inquiries about his administrative style, and probed aspects of his family life. Finally, the chairman paused, and looking down over his reading glasses at the preacher, posed a hypothetical question for him. "Would you be willing to go to hell for the glory of God?"

And, you've got to love the exasperated preacher's answer: "No, but I would be willing for this committee to!"

One thing is for sure: Believers will go to heaven for the glory of God. But, where is heaven anyway? If we can experience a little bit of heaven here on earth, is there a real heaven "out there" somewhere? According to the Scriptures, heaven is in a real place. After all, Jesus told the disciples, "I go to prepare a place for you" (John 14:2). In his very thorough book on heaven, Randy Alcorn writes, "Because Heaven is a place where angels live, where finite beings come and go, it appears to be a finite environment, a specific location."[162]

Alcorn is careful to distinguish between what he calls "the present Heaven or intermediate Heaven," and "the eternal Heaven or the New Earth." He eschews using the one word---*Heaven*---as an all-inclusive term for both. Here's the distinction he makes: The present heaven is where the saved go at death. It's a temporary place where we wait until Christ returns and our bodies are resurrected. "The eternal Heaven, and the New Earth, is our true home, the place where we will live forever with our Lord and each other."[163]

The present heaven is located in the angelic realm, "out there," but the eternal heaven will be on the new earth. Heaven, God's dwelling place, will be on this new earth. Alcorn cites Revelation 21:1-3 where John says, "Then I saw a new heaven and a new earth, for the old heaven and the old earth had disappeared...And I saw the holy city, the new Jerusalem, coming down from God out of heaven...I heard a shout from the throne, saying, 'Look, God's home is now among his people!'"

Some people actually believe that what Alcorn describes as the present heaven is located somewhere in the northern skies.

---

[162] Randy Alcorn, *Heaven*, (Carol Steam, Illinois: Tyndale House Publishers, 2004), p.44.
[163] Ibid.

They quote, usually from the King James Translation, Psalm 75:6, where it says, "For promotion cometh neither from the east, nor from the west, nor from the south." Promotion or exaltation is interpreted to mean salvation or being taken up into heaven. Since it doesn't mention the north in that passage, they reason heaven must be somewhere in the north. Many other translations use the word "desert" for "south," which complicates matters a bit for those who hold to this idea of heaven being located in the north.

Another verse those holding to this interpretation use is Job 26:7 where it says, "God stretches the northern sky over empty space and hangs the earth on nothing." They maintain there is an empty space in the north of the universe and that heaven is now located there. They point out that astronomers have found only one empty place in space and that appears to be near the North Star.[164] This interpretation seems to be a stretch primarily because, in an effort to prove a point, passages are taken from their context.

But, wherever heaven is located, we know God is there, and that is enough. When we die we will spend eternity in heaven with God. Knowing that much surely affects not only how we live but how we approach death.

In the 1999 film, *The Green Mile*, John Coffey (Michael Clarke Duncan) is an enormous black man falsely convicted of raping and killing two young white girls. He is a gentle giant with a power to heal. The guards love and respect him

---

[164] Richard W. De Haan, *Our Eternal Home* (Grand Rapids, Michigan: Radio Bible Class, 1991), p.11.

tremendously. Knowing John's innocence, Paul (Tom Hanks) asks John if he wants to be freed, to walk out of prison. When John asks Paul why he would do such a foolish thing, Paul asks John,"

On the day of my judgment, when I stand before God, and He asks me why did I kill one of his true miracles, what am I gonna say? That it was my job? My job?"

And John tells Paul: "You tell God the Father it was a kindness you done. I know you hurtin' and worryin', I can feel it on you, but you oughta quit on it now. Because I want it over and done. I do. I'm tired, boss. Tired of bein' on the road, lonely as a sparrow in the rain. Tired of not ever having me a buddy to be with, or tell me where we's coming from or going to, or why. Mostly I'm tired of people being ugly to each other. I'm tired of all the pain I feel and hear in the world everyday. There's too much of it. It's like pieces of glass in my head all the time. Can you understand?"[165]

And Paul understands.

Life can be nasty. The world can be a mean and awful place filled with hateful, murderous people who commit unspeakable atrocities. We can experience untold misery this side of eternity. Certain unusually spiritually-gifted people, like the character John Coffey, seem to feel the ugliness of the world more than others. Maybe that's because they are more like Christ. To such, heaven is a gift they long to enjoy.

Prior to John's execution, the guards ask him if there is anything he would like. He's never seen a movie, so he asks for

---

[165] http://sfy.ru/?script=green_mile

that. They arrange for a special showing of a Fred Astaire movie. In it Astaire dances and sings the song, "Heaven." John can't stop smiling as he watches the movie, and he carries visions of it to his execution, repeating the word "heaven," over and over again.[166]

We look forward to heaven, and it will be far more wondrous than any movie we've seen, book we've read or experience we've had on earth. The Bible tells us God will wipe away every tear (Revelation 21:4). Think of that. No suffering, pain, or loss will be there to cause us to cry. And no one will say or do anything to bring a tear to the eye. Death will be no more, so there will be no more funerals, no more vigils by the side of a loved one who is near death, and no more murders, or accidents or natural disasters. Neither will there be darkness, for the glory of God will illuminate heaven (Revelation 21:23-25). And of course, there will be no sin or anything to cause sin. "No longer will there be a curse upon anything" (Revelation 22:3), so the curse of a sinful nature and all its implications will be removed. Wherever it is, heaven will indeed be a glorious place.

In the United States in the early 1900s, before the adoption of the Social Security program in the 1930s, "poorhouses" were places where indigent and homeless elderly people were placed. The story is told about a doctor visiting one such facility. An elderly woman was near death, and the doctor heard her whispering something. He couldn't make out what she was saying, so he bent over to hear. "Praise the Lord," she whispered over and over.

---

[166] Ibid.

He quietly asked her, "What could you possibly praise the Lord about in this place?"

And I love what she said, "Oh, that's easy. I just keep thinking about the move I'm getting ready to make to my heavenly mansion."

A complete understanding of heaven and a certainty about its exact location is beyond us now, but we know it's a real place, a home we long for, a wonderful place that will more than surprise us in all its glory.

## "We Shall Behold Him"

The prolific composer, Dottie Rambo, penned the words to one of my favorite gospel songs, "We Shall Behold Him." The words envision what it will be like when the trumpet sounds, the dead rise, and we meet our Lord and Savior. "We shall behold him, oh yes we shall behold Him/Face to face in all His glory."

Oh yes, I almost forgot the line, "And those remaining shall be changed in an instant."

Being transformed the moment we see Jesus our Savior and Lord literally changes everything. John wrote, "We are already God's children, but he has not yet shown us what we will be like when Christ appears. But we do know that we will be like him, for we will see him as he really is" (I John 3:2). It doesn't say we will be Jesus the Lord but that we will be "like" him. We are in the process of becoming more and more like Jesus Christ. The transformation will be complete when we see him face to face. We will have become who we are supposed to be in that moment.

In John 17:24 Jesus prayed that we would be with him where he was. He was speaking of heaven. Think of it: Jesus wants us to be with him in all his glory. He wants us to enjoy his presence.

Imagine coming to the completion of a huge project in your life. You strained, you've striven, you've struggled. And now you're almost there. The word around the office is, you've in for a big promotion. In fact, your boss has hinted that a ceremony is in the works to acknowledge your superb performance. You've been told, although you're not supposed to know, that a select group of people of your choice can join in the honorary ceremony. Who do you want to be there? Maybe someone who's been with you through the project? A close friend? Your wife? Children? Parents?

Jesus is thinking of heaven, and he knows once he has suffered, been crucified, placed in the grave, he will rise again and be seated at the right hand of the throne of God. And when that happens, when he puts back on the glory robes he left behind in heaven, he wants you to be there to see him, to enjoy him, and to experience the fullness of his glory. That's how important you are to him.

How can we possibly take it in, this glory of his? After all, we are mere humans. The answer lies in the fact that we will be transformed, changed. As we see him as he really is, we become like him. Only as we see him are we transformed. In seeing him we become who we really are. Apart from that instantaneous final transformation, we would not be fit for heaven.

That's why some things are difficult for us to believe about heaven. For instance, in heaven we will be worshipping God, we will be singing praises and dancing as we glorify him for eternity. For eternity? In the natural, we immediately struggle with how that would be possible.

I'm reminded of a story I heard about Calvin Miller when he was a pastor in Omaha, Nebraska. He had been talking with a young Christian about the glory of heaven. When the young man asked what we will be doing all day in heaven, Dr. Miller said, "We'll be praising the Lord." The young man hesitated a moment before asking, "Forever and forever? We're going to be standing before God praising him forever?" When Miller assured the new Christian that we would, the young convert hesitatingly asked, "But won't we be able to stop every now and then and just mess around?"

We tend to equate the worship of God with what we know about our worship times, and while there are some similarities, heaven will be incomparably greater. Our finite minds have difficulty with the concept of doing anything forever. But remember our transformation will be complete, we will have heavenly bodies, and our minds will be capable of completely comprehending eternal realities. We won't be distracted, either. In every moment, what pleases Jesus will be pleasing to us, as it should be now.

To enjoy our Lord in all his glory will be to enjoy his creation, heaven itself. All that we do in heaven will be to God's glory, since we will be without sin. Nothing we do will be beyond God's will, so all that we do will be worship. Worshipping God will encompass far more than three hymns, a prayer, and a sermon. I suppose we will fall on our faces before God. We will actually see God face to face, and that in itself is amazing.

No one has seen the face of God and lived. Moses caught a glimpse of God but not God's face. (Exodus 33:12-23). Yet, Revelation 22:4 says, "They will see his face." The only way that's possible is for our transformation to be completed as we see the Lord face to face. It will happen in a millionth of a nanosecond. Suddenly we are who we are supposed to be in eternity. Only then can we gaze into the face of God.

We will be mesmerized by his glory---the revelation of who he is in his character and nature, his essence. We will enjoy basking in his glory, and a thousand years will be like a passing moment. Apparently, time will exist in heaven ("there was silence in heaven for about half an hour," Revelation 8:1),[167] but we will no longer by under its curse; all that we do will be a joy, and when we do something we enjoy, time is a blessing not a burden.

Rather than being a boring place, heaven will be the most exciting adrenalin rush we can possibly imagine. We will reign with Christ. Imagine what that will entail, the planning, the thinking, the working, work that will no longer be a curse but a blessing. Perhaps there will be planets to explore, books to write, music to sing, art to create. The possibilities are limited only by our finite brains. As theologian Anthony Hoekema notes, "The possibilities that now rise before us boggle the mind.

---

[167] For a further explanation of the concept of time in heaven, see Alcorn, pp. 261-265.

Will there be 'better Beethovens on the new earth?. . . better Rembrandts, better Raphaels? Shall we read better poetry, better drama, and better prose? Will scientists continue to advance in technological achievement, will geologists continue to dig out the treasures of the earth, and will architects continue to build imposing and attractive structures? Will there be exciting new adventures in space travel?. . . Our culture will glorify God in ways that surpass our most fantastic dreams."[168]

Indeed, when we behold him, it will last more than lifetime; it will endure forever.

## "Welcome Home"

As I mentioned earlier, when I was in junior high and high school, my father volunteered his time as a dentist to serve as a short term missionary. Mom was his dental assistant, and I traveled along with them. Over a period of years, we traveled to Zimbabwe, Yemen, India, and the Dominican Republic. I received untold blessings on every trip, but I was always overjoyed to come home. Home was where the rest of my family was, my brothers and their families, my friends, and when I was in high school, my girl friend. Home was where we had clean water and modern conveniences. It was where Mom could prepare a real home-cooked meal. I enjoyed those different places, but I also longed for home.

---

[168] Anthony A. Hoekema, "Heaven: Not Just an Eternal Day Off," *Christianity Today* (June 6, 2003), http:www.christianitytoday.com/ct/2003/122/54.0html, cited in Alcorn, *Heaven*, p.416.

Although we've not literally been to heaven, as citizens of that heavenly kingdom, we long for it. I think when we trusted Jesus, he placed within us a desire that only heaven can fill. It's a desire to be home, home with our heavenly Father.

The trouble is, we get comfortable along the way and think what we see here is as good as it gets. Partially because of misunderstanding what heaven will be like and not recognizing just how glorious it will be, we prefer what we know on earth to what we don't know or understand about heaven. Sadly, instead of longing for heaven, we almost dread it. C.S. Lewis said something about that in his book, *The Problem of Pain*, "Our Father," Lewis said, "refreshes us on the journey with some pleasant inns, but will not encourage us to mistake them for home."[169]

We forget we are just passing through. I recall a story about a man visiting a well-known Jewish rabbi. When the visitor arrived, he noticed the meager surroundings in the simply decorated room where the rabbi lived. The visitor asked, "Where are all your belongings?

The rabbi said, "This is all I have. Where are all your belongings?"

The guest said, "I don't have any here. I'm just a guest passing through."

"So am I," said the rabbi, "so am I."

Jesus indicated that he was going to prepare a place for us. (John 14:3) Our Lord is preparing a room for us. When I travel, I like to know that there is a room that awaits me at the end of the

---

[169] C.S. Lewis, *The Problem of Pain* (New York: Macmillan, 1962), p.115.

day. It's frustrating to travel and not know if a room is available, then find out it's not and have to keep traveling. That's happened to me before; that's why I like to call ahead, estimate my time of arrival, and make sure I have a room.

I'm amazed at the number of people who plan their vacation to the last detail and give little or no thought to where they will spend eternity. My true home is in heaven, and based on what Jesus said, I know I have a reservation for it.

Eddie Fisher's Baseball Camp was the first time I was ever really away from home for any length of time—all of one week. And it was less than 30 miles from my home! I was in the third grade, and I had my first bout with what is called "homesickness." I longed for the familiarity of home.

Years later, southern Gospel singer Squire Parsons sang at my church in Livingston, Alabama. He was known for singing that song, "Beulah Land." I recall being amazed with the richness of his deep, bass, voice. "I'm kind of homesick for that country to which I've never been before..." he began. And when he did, I couldn't help but think back to my homesick time as a child at ball camp. And I wondered, "Am I that homesick for heaven, or am I pretty much satisfied with the way things are?" And I had to admit, I wasn't longing for heaven very much at all. But, you see, that was because I hadn't thought much about heaven. The more we set our eyes on the realities of heaven, as Paul told us we should in Colossians 3:1-2, the more we will long for that place.

Are you feeling just a bit homesick for heaven? If we only had just a taste of how wonderful it will be, we would long for it constantly. We would be ready for a "Welcome Home Party."

Dr. James Montgomery Boice told how he would take his family on an annual winter vacation in the Pocono Mountains. With the busyness of the Christmas and New Year's season at the church he pastored, Tenth Presbyterian Church in Philadelphia, escaping to the mountains immediately after Christmas and New Year's was something their family anxiously anticipated. They stayed in the same hotel each year. And each year they would look forward to getting away. The very thought sustained them during the pressures of the holiday season. They would usually arrive at dusk, as the sun is settling behind the mountains. And as they arrived at the entrance of the hotel, the doormen would be there to grab their bags, and they would say, "Welcome home. Welcome home!" Boice knew of course that it wasn't actually home but a gimmick to make them feel welcome. But he loved it nonetheless.

When we arrive in heaven it will be genuine. Our Lord will be there to welcome us home after we've piloted our ship through the stormy seas to port. It will really be home, and in that joyful, glorious moment he will say, "Welcome home." And we will indeed be home at last.

*"O righteous Father, the world doesn't know you, but I do; and these disciples know you sent me. I have revealed you to them, and I will continue to do so. Then your love for me will be in them, and I will be in them."*

—John 17:25-26

*"Like all of us in this storm between birth and death, I can wreak no great changes on the world, only small changes for the better, I hope, in the lives of those I love."*

—Dean Koontz

# Chapter Twelve
# Love: Passing it On

JESUS CONCLUDES HIS PRAYER BY acknowledging the intimacy he has with the Father. He is at one with the Father in a relationship of love. The world doesn't know it, but the disciples do because Jesus revealed the Father to them. Certainly the miracles attested to Jesus as the Messiah. But Jesus doesn't refer to them in the last words of his prayer. He does talk about love. Jesus revealed God's love to the disciples. Now they are to pass it on.

Of all the virtues, love is the greatest. I Corinthians 13 is sometimes known as the "love chapter," because Paul so eloquently speaks of love in that section of God's Word. He writes that faith, hope, and love are all great virtues; they will last forever. But he concludes that "the greatest of these is love."

Think about it: Love gives rise to and undergirds all that Jesus has requested for the church in this prayer. Without love, all the other petitions---faith, joy, holiness, mission-mindedness, unity, and security---would soon wither and die. Christianity would falter and fail. Indeed, it would difficult if not impossible to appropriate any of them into our lives. So Jesus ends this prayer with love. It is what holds together everything Jesus has prayed for the church thus far. And, it's what the church is most about. When all else fails, the church will survive the storms because love prevails.

The members of the Church of God in Lady Lake, Florida, came to this realization during a most trying circumstance. Their church building was destroyed by an early morning tornado one Friday morning. But the church---the people---gathered that Sunday morning for worship, even though they had no building in which to meet. The joined their Pastor, Larry Lynn, to celebrate being the church bound together in an enduring and unbreakable bond of love. Florida's Governor, Charlie Crist, attended the service. Pastor Larry Lynn had told him, "The building may be down, but the church lives on."[170]

The church lives on because of love. And for the church to survive from one generation to the next, from country to country, from to family, from person to person, it must pass on the gift of love.

**Where Love Comes From**

A love that is eternal, real, and true is the kind of love we want to pass on to others. That's because it's an unconditional love with no strings attached. This is the biblical concept of God's love for us. And it is how we are to love one another.

I read about the owner of a photographic studio who had a college student come in with a framed picture of his girlfriend. He wanted the picture duplicated. It had to be removed from the frame. When he removed the picture, the studio owner noticed

---

[170] www.CNN.com 6/13/2007, cited by Brian Harbour, "Is it the Building or is it the People?" *Brian's Lines* 13 (September/October, 2007), p. 23.

an inscription on the back of the photograph, written by the girlfriend. "My dearest Tommy: I love you with all my heart. I love you more and more each day. I will love you forever and forever. I am yours for all eternity." It was signed "Diane" and contained a P.S. "If we ever break up, I want this picture back."[171]

We can laugh at that, but that is the way love is too often expressed in our culture. An African husband had several wives. An American missionary confronted him about the Scriptural mandate for monogamy. The African noted there was little difference between his marital status and that of Americans. He said, "In America you just marry one wife at a time. Here, we just keep our old wives while marrying new ones." Some have called us "Serial Polygamists." We're still polygamists; we just don't keep all our wives at one time. It's been said that a successful marriage requires falling in love with the same person over and over again.

This love Jesus is praying about is more than a feeling. He prayed to the Father about this love. The Father loved Jesus before the world began, since the Father and the Son are eternal. As we know God, we know him as a God of love. We love others as God loved us. John later penned these words, "Let us continue to love one another, for love comes from God. Anyone who loves is a child of God and knows God" (I John 4:7).

The Greeks had several words for love. They used *Eros* to describe love in the sense of sexual passion. *Philia* is the love

---

[171] Michael Hodgin, ed., *1001 Humorous Illustrations* (Plattville, Co.: Saratoga Press), p.64.

expressed between friends. *Storge* is the love in a family, family love. *Agape* is love of the highest kind, love with no strings attached, and as you might guess, this is the kind of love Jesus prays for us. This doesn't mean that the other loves are wrong, only that the highest, most supreme love is unconditional love.

Jesus refers to how he knows the Father: "The world doesn't know you, but I do..." (John 17:25). If God's very nature is love, then God was love before the creation of human beings. And since it is impossible to love when one is alone, in order for love to be possible, God's being must have a structure that permitted that. The theological word for that is the Trinity. God is three: Father, Son, and Holy Spirit, and yet God is one. We speak of a plurality of persons within the one Godhead. This one God---known to us as God the Father, God the Son, and God the Holy Spirit---is a God of love. God is love, and he invites us into a loving family fellowship. The Gospel declares God to be a fellowship of the Father, Son and Spirit in the unity of one essence, essentially a fellowship of loving mutual relationships. In the strictest sense, God doesn't need the world he created. He is not dependent on the world. But we know he loves this world, because God is love. God wants to relate to us in love; he invites us into a relationship of love. Now, Jesus is praying that as others see our unity in him, they will want to be a part of this loving relationship.

The love that Jesus is praying about to the Father is not based on what we've done or even who we are, but rather on who God is: a loving God who accepts us just as we are, but loves us enough not to leave us just as we are. We are gradually being transformed into his likeness.

It is important to keep in mind that God defines love. Love doesn't define God, God defines what love is. If you want to know love, true love, then look to the ways of God.

Our problem is we don't realize how much God loves us. I heard about a little boy was acting up in church. He did that quite frequently. In fact, he had a reputation for being a disruptive child. The preacher dreaded to see the little guy in the worship service, because the pastor knew the boy would distract from the message. It was the same way in Sunday School, where he gave the teacher fits. One Sunday the teacher had enough. He threatened the boy with these words: "I may not see you every time you act ugly, but God does, and He will never take his eyes off you!" It really shook the boy up.

On the way home from church, the boy was silent. He was still disturbed by that statement. "God's out to get me," he was thinking to himself. The boy's father asked him what was bothering him. At first he said nothing, but after repeated questioning, the boy blurted out what the teacher had told him.

The wise and sensitive father sensed a teachable moment. "Son, what the teacher meant," the dad said, "was that God loves you so much that He just can't take his eyes off you."

God loves us, period. He can't take his eyes off us. As we are courageous enough to receive that love, we can, by his transforming grace, become the authentic persons he intends us to be.

Two missionaries, the story goes, held a meeting late into the night in the African village where they had been sent to serve. Everyone in the village came, and no one wanted to go home. Finally, around 2 a.m., one missionary asked the people:

"Why don't you go home and go to sleep? It is very late, and we are tired."

The tribal chief answered, "You have told us about a God who is not an evil spirit trying to harm us, but a loving God who gave His only begotten Son for our salvation and that if we turn away from our sins and trust him, we may have deliverance from sin, guidance in our confusion, and comfort in our grief. How can we sleep after a message like this?" The missionaries were suddenly energized and shared with the people until the break of day.

"Jesus loves me this I know, for the Bible tells me so." How can we sleep after a message like that? Let's stay awake as we love again and again and again with the true love of Jesus our Savior.

**Could this be Love?**

A little girl was sitting on her grandfather's lap as he read her a bedtime story. From time to time, she would take her eyes off the book and reach up to touch his wrinkled cheek. She was alternately stroking her own cheek, then his again. Finally she spoke up, "Grandpa, did God make you?"

"Yes, sweetheart," he answered, "God made me a long time ago."

"Oh," she responded as she continued thinking. Then she asked, "Grandpa, did God make me too?"

"Yes, indeed, honey," he said, "God made you just a little while ago."

Feeling her grandpa's face while at the same time stroking her own, she concluded, "God's getting better at it, isn't he?"

For eons God had been trying to show humankind how much he loved them. Then he sent his one and only, his only begotten Son, to show the Father's love. And here in John 17:26, he said "I have revealed you to them, and I will continue to do so. Then your love for me will be in them, and I will be in them."

Where was that love most revealed? Where is this love most dramatically displayed? We could point to many events in the life of Jesus: the time he healed the blind man on the Sabbath Day. The Pharisees challenged him. "Is it lawful to heal on the Sabbath?" The love of Jesus for people is obvious in his answer: "If you had a sheep that fell into a well on the Sabbath, wouldn't you work to pull it out? Of course you would. And how much more valuable is a person than a sheep! Yes, the law permits a person to do good on the Sabbath" (Matthew 12:11-12).

Then there was the time Jesus stepped in and rescued the adulterous woman. I know the most ancient manuscripts don't have this story, but it is so in keeping with Jesus actions of love that it rings true to his life. "Let the one who has never sinned throw the first stone!" Jesus declared in John 8:7. I suppose that woman was forever grateful for Jesus' act of love.

And then there was the time when Jesus came to console Martha and Mary in the death of their brother Lazarus. Jesus wept at the news, the Scripture tells us, and "the people who were standing by said, 'See how much he loved him!'"(John 11:37). And I suppose Lazarus was forever grateful that Jesus not only wept but gave Lazarus new physical life when he raised him from the dead.

And then there was the time Jesus displayed his love for his disciples by washing their feet. "I have given you an example to follow. Do as I have done to you" (John 14:15).

We could share stories from the Bible all day that show how much Jesus loves us.

But where is the love of Jesus *most* dramatically displayed?

I think you would agree with me that the love of Jesus is most dramatically and emphatically displayed on the cross. There Jesus made the greatest sacrifice of love; there his love had the most far reaching effect; there he openly showed his love for us.

Could this be love? How could something so ugly---a symbol of torture---be at the same time a display of love? Henri Nouwen tells the story of a family he knew in Paraguay. The father was a physician who spoke against the injustices in the government, particularly human rights abuses. The local police retaliated against this man by arresting his teenage son. They tortured him until he died. It was a brutal and senseless murder. The father responded with most a most emphatic statement. He did it without speaking a single word. Instead of having the funeral home embalm and restore his son to his pre-death physical likeness, the father had his son's body displayed at the funeral just as the father found it in jail---naked, scarred, twisted from the electrical shocks, burned by cigarettes, bloodied from the beatings. And he wasn't placed in a coffin but on the blood-stained mattress from the prison.

That's a horrid story, but the father would not cover up the ugly reality. When we talk about the cross, we have to remember there was no cover up; it was a horrible reality that our heavenly father allowed. And the miracle is that the father turned this despicable act of people into something amazingly good.[172]

How could this detestable, awful thing show God's love? What kind of God would allow this? The answer is, the kind of God that loves us more than any of us truly realize.

Jesus prayed in John 17:26 "I have revealed you to them." Those episodes from Jesus life I mentioned a moment ago are examples of Jesus revealing God to the disciples. But notice Jesus is not finished. He adds, "and I will continue to do so," in John 17:26. He must be referring to the cross and resurrection. So the cross reveals to us the very love of God. Some people pit an angry, wrathful Father who accuses us of sin, against a loving, forgiving Jesus who forgives. That's a false picture of God. God does hate sin; God does judge sin; God is so utterly holy that he cannot look upon sin. But God loves the sinner; God wants to forgive the sinner; God loves us so much that he can't take his eyes off us.

So here's the problem: God hates sin, judges sin, and can't look upon sin. And, God loves us, wants to forgive us, and can't take his eyes off us. BUT, we are sinners. Here's why the cross was necessary: it was the only way the problem of sin could be addressed and forgiveness offered. On the cross God says, "I love you. You have sinned. You have offended me. You deserve hell, eternal separation for me. But, because of my love for you, I provide you a way. It's through the sacrifice of my only Son.

---

[172] Lois Holk, Manfred Holk, Jr., Eds. *The Minister's Annual Manual*, (Nashville: Church Management, Inc., 1991/1992), p., 86.

Because of who he is, and what he did on the cross, I offer you my forgiveness."

After Jesus prayed to the prayer in John 17, he crossed the Kidron Valley into the Garden of Gethsemane. There he prayed, "Father, if you are willing, please take this cup of suffering away from me. Yet I want your will to be done, not mine" (Luke 22:42). Jesus wasn't trying to avoid his mission. He was not looking forward to the suffering that was ahead of him. There was no other way. The only way to salvation is through the cross. God in his love provides the way of hope and forgiveness and peace for us, the way to salvation---it's the way of the cross. There the love of God is displayed. The cross is the way of salvation. From the cross God is saying: "I love you." Roman 5:8 says, "God demonstrated his love toward us in that while we were yet sinners, Christ died for us." We have difficulty comprehending how much God loves us. It's an unconditional, everlasting, limitless love.

But again, the question, "How does the cross show or display that love?

It addresses our central problem: sin. We are sinners; God is holy, perfectly holy. How then can we be made right with a perfect God? David said in Psalm 51:5, "I was born a sinner—yes, from the moment my mother conceived me." This sin has affected the way we think. I Corinthians 2:14 says, "People who aren't spiritual (or as the NIV puts it, "without the Spirit") can't receive these truths from God's Spirit. It all sounds foolish to them and they can't understand it, for only those who are spiritual can understand what the Spirit means." In other words, we can't think our way into a right relationship with

God because sin has affected our mind. The only thing that can remove the sin problem for us is Jesus' work on the cross.

That's because at the cross Jesus took our sin. Every wrong thing any one of us ever did, Jesus took on the cross. Remember the penalty for Adam and Eve's sin? If you eat the fruit of the tree you shall surely die. Why didn't they die? Before they sinned they were naked and unashamed. Suddenly after they sinned they experienced shame.

That's what sin does. God gave them clothes, animal skins, to wear. Some maintain that an innocent animal died in place of Adam and Eve and that was the beginning of the sacrificial system, which in time became much more complex. Those sacrifices had to be repeated, and they only covered their sin; they didn't remove them. Only Christ could do that. So, Christ took our sins, all of them, and as we identify with him as a follower, we are not only forgiven but placed in a state or righteousness. Only Jesus on the cross could do that. That's why it displays God's love and why Jesus prayed in John 17 to the Father, "I have revealed them to you, and I will continue to do so." The cross was a huge part of that "continue to do so."

Samuel D. Proctor said it like this: "But this raw nature of ours, this Adamic trace that enters the world with every new infant, is dealt with most particularly in the holy history of the Bible when the Son of God, who was without sin, became for all of us the Lamb slain on the altar to pay the ultimate price that we might know the transforming, renewing, restoring, integrative, sin-forgiving, guilt-removing, mind-changing, soul-warming, heart-healing, spirit-filling, power-availing, heaven-binding love of God."[173]

"But wait a minute," you say, "I wasn't there that day Jesus died. I had nothing to do with that." I know some people accuse preachers of trying to induce a sense of false guilt in people by saying, "You were there. You put Christ to death." But that's to misunderstand the point. We are already guilty. Jesus died for my sin; he took my sin on the cross. Our sin is sin against God, first and most primarily. David prayed, "Against you, and you alone, have I sinned" (Psalm 51:4).

In Rembrandt's painting of the crucifixion your attention is first drawn to the crucified Jesus. Then you see the crowd gathered around the cross. The master artist showed various attitudes on the part of the people. Most are downcast, one appears to be scoffing, and another is shocked, not in a shameful way but as if to say, "How did you get yourself in this predicament?" But what's fascinating is the lone figure, almost hidden in the shadows. It's Rembrandt himself. The artist painted himself into the scene because he realized his own sins helped nail Jesus to the cross.

When we realize that it was not God's wrath but God's love that allowed the cross to happen, we begin to realize, at least to a degree, just how much he loves us. God gave his Son, his beloved Son, his only begotten Son, because he loves you and me. Will you take his Son, who loved you so much that he was willing to endure the suffering of the cross for you?

---

[173] Samuel D. Proctor, *How Then Shall They Hear?* (Valley Forge: Judson Press, 1992), p. 53

The author of the story is unknown. It's the tale of a wealthy man and his son who loved to collect rare works of art. They had an impressive variety in their collection. Often father and son would sit together and admire the great works of art.

When the Vietnam conflict broke out, the son went to war. He was very courageous and died in battle while rescuing another soldier. The father was notified and grieved deeply for his only son.

About a month later, just before Christmas, there was a knock on the door. A young man stood at the door with a large package in his hands.

He said, "Sir, you don't know me, but I am the soldier your son died to save. As he was carrying me to safety, a bullet struck him in the heart and he died instantly. I just wanted you to know he often talked about you and the love of art both of you shared. The young man held out his package. "I know this isn't much. I'm not really a great artist, but I think your son would he wanted you to have this."

The father opened the package. It was a portrait of his son, painted by the young soldier. The father stared in awe at the way the young man had captured the personality of his son in the painting. The father's eyes welled up with tears, and he thanked the young man and offered to pay him for the picture. "Oh, no sir, I could never repay what your son did for me. This portrait is a gift."

The father hung the portrait in a prominent place, over the mantle of the fireplace. Every time guests would come to his home, the father would almost immediately take them to see the painting of his son.

The father died a few months later. He had made stipulations for his art collection to be auctioned. Many influential people came to his home the day of the auction. Naturally, they were excited about seeing the great paintings and having an opportunity to purchase one for their own collections.

The painting of the son was set on the platform in front of the people. The auctioneer pounded his gavel. "The auction will begin with the bidding for this picture of the son. Who will bid for this picture?" There was silence.

Then a voice in the back of the room shouted, "We would like to see the other works of art. Would you leave this one till later?"

"No," the auctioneer firmly persisted, "Who will bid for this painting? Who will start the bidding? $200, $300?"

Someone else shouted with more frustration: "We didn't come to see this painting. We came to see the other fine pieces of art. Can't you start with the better works of art"?

The auctioneer ignored the complaint and continued. "The son! The son! Who'll take the son?"

Finally, a voice came from the very back of the room. It was the longtime gardener of the man and his son. "I'll give $25 for the painting." It was all he could afford.

"We have $25, who will bid $50?"

"Give it to him for $25. Now, let's see the real works of art." The crowd was becoming angry. They didn't want to see the picture of the son any longer. They wanted to see the more worthy investments for their collections.

The auctioneer then pounded the gavel. "Going once, twice, SOLD for $50." A man sitting on the second row shouted, "Now let's see the collection!"

But the auctioneer laid down his gavel. "I'm sorry, the auction is over."

"What about the paintings?" someone in the crowd protested.

"'I am sorry. When I was called to conduct this auction, I was given a stipulation in the owner's will that stated only the painting of the son would be auctioned. Whoever bought the portrait of the son would receive the entire estate, including the paintings. The man who took the son gets everything!"

God gave His son 2,000 years ago to die on the cross for us. Much like the auctioneer, God's message is: "The Son, the Son, who'll take the Son?" You see, whoever is willing to take the Son gets everything.

Could this be love? You better believe it. Because if you don't, you'll miss the greatest love you could ever possibly have.

## Will You Pass it On?

In commenting on John 17:26 the early church preacher and theologian, John Chrysostom, called love, "the mother of all blessings." He then challenged his readers: "Let us then believe and love God, that it may not be said of us, 'They profess that they know God, but in their works they deny him.'"[174] Chrysostom rightly associated the importance of love in action. Our love for God is expressed in actions to others as we pass it on.

---

[174] Thomas C. Oden, gen. ed., *Ancient Christian Commentary on Scripture,* New Testament, 12 vols. (Downers Grove, Illinois: InterVarsity Press, 2007), vol. IVb: *John 11-21,* by Joel C. Elowsky, p. 263.

I love the story about the professor of theology who had spent years studying the New Testament concept of love. He had written several books on the different Greek words for love. He became known internationally for his word studies on love. One weekend this man was working on a project at home. He was putting in a new driveway. He had been to the hardware store, bought concrete, along with a video telling him how to successfully pour the concrete. Finally he did it. He poured the concrete. He sat back, exhausted but proud of his accomplishment. As he admired his work, some children riding their bikes took a shortcut right through the wet concrete. Well, our professor of love snapped. He instantly snatched up a rake and ran after these boys. He was at the point of scraping these kids with the rake when a neighbor intervened. "Get a grip, Professor. Remember who you are. You are the guy who wrote all those word studies on the subject of love."

And the professor, still chasing the boys, who had tromped in his cement hollered back to the neighbor, "That was love in the abstract, not love in the concrete!"

How do we love in the concrete? How do we pass it on? There are many ways, but I would like to suggest seven. In 1975 Paul Simon had a hit song entitled, "50 Ways to Leave Your Lover." I would like to suggest 7 ways we can love our neighbor.

When I say, "neighbor," I mean that word in the most comprehensive sense possible. Our neighbor not only includes the person next door, but anyone we encounter on any given day.

An encounter can include a starving child on the other side of the globe that you see as you watch the evening news, or it could be a prayer request you receive by email, or it could be the request of a friend. Get the picture? So how do we do it? How can we pass it on?

**Tell them.**

That's one way to let others know of God's love. Proverbs 15:23 says "It is wonderful to say the right thing at the right time." What could be more fitting than to tell others you love them? I tell my wife I love her several times a day. I tell my children I love them every day as well. I tell my family I love them. But I'm not going to say to my neighbor as he or she is pulling out of their driveway, "Hey, just wanted you to know, I love you." That would be borderline inappropriate.

I was on the subway in New York City. We were there visiting my daughter, Mary-Elizabeth. I can assure you I didn't turn to whoever was closest to me and say, "I love you."

But at times, I have been gotten to know people enough to share the Good News with them. I've said something like, "The reason I'm sharing this with you is because I'm a Christian, and Christians love others, and that includes you."

But there are other ways too. We can let people know we love them with positive words of affirmation and encouragement. We don't have to literally say, "I love you," to let people know we love them. A fellow worker who is having a bad day or week, a friend who just got laid off work, an acquaintance who has lost a loved, all of these can be helped by saying the right thing at the right time. And remember, sometimes, as in the case of deep tragedy, saying nothing and only being there speaks the loudest.

**Write them.**

Paul wrote letters to churches in part because he wanted to remind them of his love for them. To the church in Corinth he wrote, "I will gladly spend myself and all I have for you, even though it seems that the more I love you, the less you love me" (II Corinthians 12:15). To the Philippians he wrote, "God knows how much I love you and long for you." (Philippians 1:8). In explaining why he wrote to them as he did, Paul said to the Corinthians, "I wanted you to know how very much I loved you" (II Corinthians 2:4). To the church in Thessalonica, in referring to his previous visit, he said, "We loved you so much that we shared with you not only God's Good News but our own lives as well" (I Thessalonians 2:8).

Since Dave and Mary-Liz could read, I've written them little notes each morning. I'd always sign it "Love Dad." They picked up the practice themselves and would write me notes too. I have a whole file folder filled with their notes. I think one of my favorites from Dave was written when he was seven, "Dad?! I hope you get all of the rest of your work done and I love you. By: Davey, to: My greatest Dad. But I never had a nother(sic) Dad."

Just before she left for the summer, Mary left me a note on my desk: "Daddy, I love you so much! Thanks for being an amazing dad! Love you forever, Smiles."

When Harrison and Madi moved here I did the same thing to them. I would leave them little notes too. And in time, they picked up the habit. On one of my birthdays, Madi wrote, "I hope you have a great birthday! Thank you for all you do. I'm glad I can be here to celebrate with you! Love, Madi."

I think my favorite from Harrison is this one: "I drove very carefully from Bardstown! Took me almost an hour...I love you so much, thx for being there for me., love, your son, Harrison."

We can extend this practice to others outside our family, even beyond our church family. Look in your local newspaper for something good about someone. Send them a short note of congratulations or gratitude for what they've done. When a person is in need, you can write a note telling them you are praying. This is one of the blessings of having a prayer room. As people intercede in our church's prayer room, they write notes to people in some kind of hurt. It helps.

This is a very small thing that can make a huge difference in someone's life. Remember, you needn't write a lengthy letter, just a short note. A young minister received a note from one of his church members. It simply said, "Your sermon met me where I was on Sunday---the crossroads of confusion and hurt. Thanks for preaching it!" Just 20 words. But those words met the pastor where he was---at the intersection of confusion and pain. The words encouraged the pastor to keep going and not give up.

**Listen to them.**

I said one of the loudest ways we can speak to those in deep pain is to say nothing. Just being there is enough. We are paying attention to their needs by not offering advice or trying to explain why something terrible happened.

We need to "stop, look, and listen." That's what Jesus did in his ministry. I don't think any of us has more to do than Jesus did. Yet, he so frequently stopped. One day Jesus was walking down the road to Jericho and two blind men starting yelling at him. The Bible says this in Matthew 20:30-32: "Two blind men shouted, 'Lord, have mercy on us!' Jesus stopped and called,

'What do you want me to do?'" And Jesus listened to what they said.

It's difficult to love people if we are too busy to listen to them. Here's our problem: we listen faster than people can talk. Do you find your mind wandering while someone is talking to you? Do you know what that means? It means you are quite normal. You don't necessarily have attention deficit disorder. Most people speak at an average rate of about 120 words a minute. But most people can *listen* about four times faster. So our mind fills in the gaps by thinking of other things. That means we have to intentionally slow down our listening, forcing ourselves to stay focused and comprehend what the other person is saying. Look at the other person in the eye. Pay attention to what they are saying.

Newscaster Diane Sawyer talked about writer Michael Arden. He told her the greatest act is to pay attention. Sawyer agrees, "I think the one lesson I've learned," she said, "it that there is no substitute for paying attention."[175]

## Touch Them.

Early in his ministry people were coming to Jesus *en masse*, and from every direction. The Scripture says "the touch of his hand healed everyone." (Luke 4:40). You may not have the gift of healing, but a touch, a hug, a pat on the back can be an expression of love and affirmation.

Family therapist, Virginia Satir says we need 4 hugs a day for survival, 8 hugs a day for maintenance, and 12 hugs a day for growth. And Vikas Malkani said it's the attitude that's most

---

[175] Jack and Garry Kinder, *21st Century Positioning, Proven Selling Precepts* (Dallas, Tx.: Taylor Publishing Co., 1996), p. 95.

important, so it doesn't have to be a full frontal hug. A sideways hug is good too.[176]

When Katri was ill, in her last stages of cancer, she couldn't give a good strong hug. Her bones were brittle. She couldn't hug as she once did, not because she didn't want to but because she couldn't. We had to be careful with Dave. Like Katri, he loved to hug, and he would unintentionally hug too hard and possibly break a bone. So Davey couldn't hug his mom like he once did. After Katri's death, when Lori came into the picture, one of the first things Dave said to her was, "Can you give me a hug? I've been needing a hug for a long time." And Lori reached down and gave him a great, big hug. That was the start of a warm and loving relationship.

You can't hug everyone in a solid embrace, but you can touch with affirmation. And that lets people know you love them.

**Help them.**

Another way we can love our neighbors is to help them. People need help, all kinds of help.

One day a Roman military officer heard that Jesus had come to his town of Capernaum. The slave of this officer was deathly ill. So he sent some Jewish elders to ask Jesus to help and heal the slave. They begged Jesus, "'If anyone deserves your help, he does,' they said. He loved the Jewish people and even built a synagogue. Jesus started to come and on his way, he met some more friends of the officer. He had sent them to tell Jesus he

---

[176] http://www.lifepositive.com/mind/personal-growth/hug/c_719_hug-therapy.asp

didn't need to come all the way to his home; he could heal the man where Jesus was. Jesus was amazed at the man's faith. And Jesus healed the slave" (Luke 7:1-10)

Now, this officer had to have some friends who would help him get the word to Jesus. The man had great faith. But even when we have great faith, we need friends to help. And, we need to be the kind of people who are willing to help. Those Jewish elders didn't heal, but they did get their friend to someone who could.

Maybe you can help someone who needs a ride to the doctor or who needs a friend to get a message to someone. It doesn't have to be complicated. A simple act of ministry can get someone to the place where healing can occur.

Our community has an annual "Ham Days Festival." People come in from the surrounding communities for the festivities. Our church is located downtown, and we let people use our parking lot. It's always in early September, so it's usually still rather hot. I recall walking back to church and finding an elderly lady sitting in the shade of a tree near our church's parking lot. I asked her if she was okay, and she told me she had gotten confused and couldn't remember where she had parked her car. I helped her into my car, and drove her a few blocks down the street where she thought she had parked. Sure enough, she had. I really thought nothing of it, but for months that lady really "talked me up," to people everywhere. I heard about it from several people. Evidently something small meant a lot to her. It often does when we truly care for people.

**Understand them.**

When the two blind beggars cried out to Jesus, he heard them, and the Scripture says, "Jesus was moved with compassion. (Matthew 20:34). The word is *splachna*. The word refers to the intestines, which they thought was the "seat of the emotions." Have you ever heard the expression, "I could feel it down in my gut?" That's what it means. Jesus felt for those in need. He cares deeply about you. And we are to have compassion for others. We have to understand people to do that. That means we have to be willing at least to try and see things from their perspective.

Poet Shel Silverstein wrote a touching piece entitled, "The Little Boy and the Old Man." In it Silverstein portrays a young boy talking to an elderly man.

"The boy says, 'Sometimes I drop my spoon.'

'I do that too,' replies the old man.

'I often cry,' continues the boy.

As the old man nods, he responds, 'So do I.'

Then the boy says, 'But worst of all, it seems grownups don't pay any attention to me.'

And at that moment the boy feels the warmth of a wrinkled old hand.

'I know what you mean,' says the old man."[177]

Jesus wants us to at least try and know what they mean. He asks those of us who have accepted Jesus as Savior to love others as he loved us. That's impossible on our own, but by his grace, it is possible.

---

[177] http://famouspoetsandpoems.com/poets/shel silverstein/poems/14823

**Remember them.**

Hebrews 13:16, says "Don't forget to do good and to share with those in need. These are the sacrifices that please God." We need to remember people. We need to do the six things I've talked about here, but we have to remember to do them. It's easy to get busy and forget others. Do you know what kind of business the church is in? The people business.

Every Wednesday evening she waits, looking out her door window. Ms. Christine Gribbins anticipates my wife and my visit, I'm convinced, more than for the meal we bring her.

People have needs, and one of those needs is to be remembered. Sure it takes a little time. Sometimes it's a bit inconvenient. But these are the sacrifices the Lord loves.

An 11 year old boy from the poor side town had been to a revival meeting. He had made a commitment to Christ. Back in the projects, some of his old friends were giving him a hard time. Why did he go there, anyway? Who did he think he was? And if people at the church are so kind, why was he still wearing a pair of shoes with holes all through them? Finally, they said, "If God really loves you, why doesn't he tell somebody to send you a new pair of shoes?"

The boy thought for a moment as tears filled his eyes, "I guess He does tell somebody, but somebody forgets."

We have to remember. Remember to love. This is what Jesus finally prays for us. This is the last word he has: love one another. You see, it's not just your storm; it's everybody's storm. We're in this journey together. And along the way, Jesus want us to pass on the love we've received from him.

The question is, will you do it?

After saying these things, Jesus crossed the Kidron Valley with his disciples..."
— John 18:1


"No one would have crossed the ocean if he could have gotten off the ship in the storm."
— Charles Kettering

# Chapter Thirteen
## Crossing Your Own Kidron Valley

As I write this conclusion, the United States' East Coast is still painfully recovering from Hurricane Irene. Although Irene didn't pack a punch with ferocious high velocity winds like some other hurricanes have done, it was distinctive for its width and breadth. Hundreds of miles from the center of Irene's rotation, communities were deluged with torrential rains.

It reminds us that each storm we face in life has its own unique features with special challenges. Each is in some way different. While we learn from each storm, we have to understand that each one brings us a different set of problems: Some storms pounce on us with an intense viciousness; others would slowly but surely drown us; still others stall over us and never seem to move on.

An article in the *Wall Street Journal* documented the spectrum of lives hurt by Hurricane Irene.[178] Celena Sylvestri, a 20 year-old music-education student in New Jersey, decided to visit her boyfriend before Hurricane Irene hit. But a dam at one of the lakes upstream failed, creating a flashflood at the location where Celena attempted to cross over what was normally an unnoticeable stream. Not knowing the water had overtaken the

---

[178] "Irene Leaves Behind Tales of Death," *The Wall Street Journal*, Saturday/Sunday, September 3-4, 2011, A3.

bridge, she drove into danger. Although she called 911, rescuers were unable to find her. She drowned.

Sometimes it's like that for us in the storms of life. Perhaps somebody should have warned us and didn't. Or maybe they couldn't. In either case, we are the one who suffers the tragedy.

Then there were those who lost their lives trying to help. Such was the case with Michael Garofano. He worked for the Rutland, Vt., public works department. With Irene overhead, he checked on a valve that would keep floodwaters from contaminating the town's drinking water. Michael took his 24-year-old son with him. Apparently the brook near the valve rose suddenly, and both were swept downstream and drowned.

That happens in the storms of life, too. We try to do the right thing by helping others, and we get caught in the storm ourselves, sometimes with devastating results.

Then there were those who simply made poor choices. A surfer in Florida and a windsurfer in near Long Island, New York ignored warning signs. Others had to risk their lives for those who made reckless decisions. We've known people who have made foolish decisions that have adversely affected others. Maybe you've done that. Perhaps you yourself have been the cause of pain in others' lives.

Through this book, we've seen people caught in the storms of life: sometimes people were innocent victims; sometimes they made choices, not necessarily bad and at times even good choices, which nonetheless allowed them to be hurt by others; and sometimes they made very poor decisions that brought the storm into their life even as they harmed others.

*Surviving the Storms of Life*

  This book has been about the storms that affect all of us at some point in life and how we respond to those storms. Storms are a part of the warp and woof of life. You've probably found yourself or someone you love reflected in those stories. You've been there, to lesser or greater degrees. You are in the story; you are the story.

  What's the "take away" from this book? I'm reminded of one of Charles Schulz's Peanut cartoons. Charlie Brown was at the beach carefully building a sand castle. After completing his work, he stepped back to admire it. At that moment a storm leveled the castle. Staring at the smooth place where his work of art had moments before stood, Charlie said, "There must be a lesson here, but I don't know what it is."[179]

  I hope you've gleaned many lessons as you've read this book. Primarily, I've tried to convey the truth that as we face the storms of life, we can do so with courage, confidence, and an attitude of triumph because Jesus is praying for us from the right hand of God the Father. He literally prays us through the storm.

  We will encounter storms as long as we are this side of eternity. Sometimes we are the victim, even though we've tried to help; at other times we've been the villain, who for whatever reasons made terrible choices; and sometimes we are simply innocent bystanders. But the storms are a part of life and always will be. Get used to it. On the same page as the story about the aftermath of Hurricane Irene there is a piece about the imminent approach of another hurricane, Lee. And the news tonight updates us on another storm forming in the Atlantic, Hurricane Katia. One storm seems to follow in the wake of another.

---

[179] *Humor Connection*, vol.1005, July/August/September 1994.

Regardless of how relentless the storms may be, Jesus has never abandoned us and never will, even though it may seem to us that he is sometimes absent from our sight. Yet he is still there with us in the storm. He is the Perfect Pilot, the Courageous Captain, the Greatest Guide. I hope that's been clear in this book.

And that brings us to the Kidron Valley. Jesus could have prayed the High Priestly Prayer of John 17, and then at the Kidron Valley, said, "Enough is enough." The easy thing would have been to slip away into the night. But he didn't. He crossed the Kidron Valley where the Garden of Gethsemane awaited him, and in a short time, the Temple Guard would accost him, and then the Roman soldiers would do worse, then the mock trial, and Pilate's equivocation, the scourging, the carrying of the cross, and finally the crucifixion.

But there at the edge of the Kidron Valley, looking down at his sandals, glancing sideways at his bewildered disciples, peering into the moonlight sky above, there was still time---time to leave to it all, time to learn from this, time to live a new and different life. Settle in. Disappear in Galilee. Yes, he still had time to turn the other way and avoid a torturous murder. Save them from their crime. Just walk away from it all.

But he didn't. He crossed the valley for you and me, so we won't have to face the storms alone. He endured the fiercest of storms for us, so he could be with us, guiding us through our storm.

*Snow Storm: Steamboat off a Harbour's Mouth* is the title of an oil on canvas painting by artist J.M.W. Turner. The painting depicts a ship off the English coast struggling to stay afloat in a storm. Supposedly, Turner had himself lashed to the mast so he could better depict what the storm was truly like. He wrote, "I wished to show what such a scene was like, I got the sailors to lash me to the mast to observe it, I was lashed for four hours, and I did not expect to escape, but I felt bound to record it." Critics said he grasped the nature of the storm better than any other artist.[180]

Jesus knows the nature of the storm you are going through better than anyone because he endured it for you. He lashed himself to the cross, even though at any moment he could have called all the angels of heaven to come to his aide and destroy his attackers. He crossed the Kidron Valley knowing the cross awaited him.

Your Kidron Valley is the distance between where you are and what it takes to obtain victory over your storm. Sometimes just having the courage to face the storm is victory in itself. As you walk through that valley, you will emerge on the other side a victor. The moment you have the courage to pass through the valley, Jesus shows up, even though you may not recognize his presence. But you will notice, on the victory side of the valley, the arms, his arms, the arms that carried you through it. As you look closer, you see his hands, the nail scarred hands. Trust them. They will guide you to safety.

As you cross your Kidron Valley, remember:

**It's okay to look back but not for long.**

I wonder if Jesus glanced back before he led his disciples with him across the valley. Jesus knew where he had come from.

---

[180] http://www.artble.com/artists/joseph mallord william turner/paintings/snow storm-steam-boat off a harbour's mouth.

He was the very Son of God. He knew the Father intimately. He loved his disciples. Did he think about the good times he had enjoyed with them as he stepped into the valley? We don't know. He knew who he was, where he had come from, and where he was going. He could look back without being captivated by what had been or might have been.

A rear view mirror is good. We can glance to see what's behind us. But if we try to navigate by our review mirror, we will crash. As you face your storm, as you cross your Kidron Valley, know where you've been, but don't constantly look back while trying to go forward.

**Look forward, but not too intently.**

Looking forward helps us keep our composure in the midst of the storm. Hebrews 12:1 tells us that because of the "joy awaiting him," Jesus endured the cross. He looked forward to his return home. We too anticipate the glorious welcome in heaven. But we still must keep our wits about us as we face the storm now. Living in the future robs us of being effective in the present.

**Stay in the present moment.**

Jesus knew what was happening to him as he suffered on the cross. He forgave his tormentors, he promised the thief paradise, he committed his mother to the care of John. "We must confine ourselves to the present moment," wrote Jean-Pierre De Caussade, "without taking thought for the one before or the one to come."[181] It's in the present moment that we gain the victory.

---

[181] Jean-Pierre De Caussade, *The Sacrament of the Present Moment*, trans. Kitty Muggeridge (New York, New York: HarperCollins, 1982),

*Surviving the Storms of Life*

It's in the present moment, and only in that moment, that we truly live...one breath at a time.

But while we are in the present moment, we are aware of Jesus before us, around us, and within us in the comfort and power of the Holy Spirit. We look to Jesus, knowing he is praying us through the storm.

And ultimately, that is where the battle with the storm is won: looking to Jesus as we experience his presence in each moment.

There's a wonderful story about the theologian, Nels Ferre. Ferre grew up in a poor family in Norway. By the time Nels was 13, his parents knew they could no longer provide him the education he so desperately needed. A childless aunt and uncle in the United States offered to provide for him and pay for his education. So Nels parents made the heart wrenching decision to send their 13 year-old son to the United States. Nels was particularly close to his mother, and leaving her was especially difficult for him. His mother struggled even more. Her son was leaving home for another country far away, across an ocean. This was 1921, and with travel and expenses as they were then, his mother had no idea when her son would be able to travel home again.

The day before he was to take a cart to the train station that would take him to the ship, his mother was too emotional to utter a word to Nels. That night at dinner, Nels hoped for a word from his mother. She could say nothing and barely held back her tears. After supper, it was the same. She was silent. Nels went to bed that night and cried himself to sleep.

---

p.15.

The next morning at breakfast, Nels waited for a word from his mother. Nothing. His mother couldn't' speak. All the way to the train station there was only silence. His mother was overwhelmed and couldn't speak. Finally he boarded the train, and as it was steaming away, his mother ran to him. Nels last glimpse of his mother was one he would never forget. With tears streaming down her checks, she handed him a note on which she had scrawled the words for him to read: "Remember Jesus, most of all."

Whatever storm you face, no matter how intense and fierce it may be, regardless of its rumblings and lightning strikes, when in the violence of that storm you think you cannot possibly take another moment, remember Jesus most of all.

And he will guide you safely to shore.

www.ingramcontent.com/pod-product-compliance
Lightning Source LLC
Chambersburg PA
CBHW050548160426
43199CB00015B/2574